ARNOLD

LONDON • NEW YORK • SYDNEY • AUCKLAND

First published in Great Britain 1997 by
Arnold, a member of The Hodder Headline Group,
338 Euston Road, London NW1 3BH
175 Fifth Avenue, New York, NY 10010

Distributed exclusively in the USA by
St Martin's Press, Inc.
175 Fifth Avenue, New York, NY 10010

British Library Cataloguing in Publication Data
A catalogue record for this book is available from the British Library

Library of Congress Cataloging-in-Publication Data
A catalog record for this book is available from the Library of Congress

ISBN 0 340 66224 7 (hb)
ISBN 0 340 66225 5 (pb)

Typeset in 10/12pt Sabon by Phoenix Photosetting, Chatham, Kent
Printed and bound in Great Britain by J W Arrowsmith Ltd, Bristol

For Lindy,
Morag and Calum

Contents

Acknowledgements   v

Introduction   1

1 More news, less understanding?   23

2 Theories of news production, from 'Mr Gates' to market-driven journalism   44

3 Rhetoric and reality in 24-hour news   85

4 The history of television news and its institutions   110

5 International television coverage of the bombing of the Baghdad 'bunker'   147

6 The technology of newsgathering and production   174

7 Multiskilling or deskilling? Visions of the future and realities of today   202

References and further reading   217

Sources   227

Index   229

Acknowledgements

The research for this book started with a casual conversation while queuing for coffee in 'the Spur' at BBC Television Centre in 1979. The BBC had just started using ENG (electronic newsgathering) and a news correspondent spoke of how the new portable videotape technology had changed his job. 'How interesting', I thought, and left it at that. What I didn't know was that this source was the first of many who were to inform me about the way television news has changed both for the better and for the worse. To all such sources, I must say thank you. Thanks are due also to my academic colleagues. Nicholas Pronay put dishes on the roof and expanded my horizons. Phil Taylor set a hardworking example, showing that first-class academic work could be produced to journalistic deadlines, combining two kinds of admirable professional thoroughness, while David Morrison introduced me to a research culture which I might otherwise have never discovered. Christine Bailey supported us all much beyond the call of duty and contributed to my work in a myriad of ways. Tricia Ritchie and Sally Ellam lightened my administrative load and are good friends. Richard Howells, Steve Lax and Stephen Hay listened to my cafeteria lectures with patience and understanding. Simeon Yates helped me to see the familiar with fresh eyes, while Robin Brown and David Gauntlett brought invaluable disciplinary perspectives from which I have profited enormously. I also owe an enormous debt to my Leeds colleagues whose own extensive broadcasting experience makes my own seem the brief interlude it was. Howard Smith, Judith Stamper and Helen Sissons have all squared the circle, working with the highest degree of professionalism both as broadcasters and academics. Andrew Thorpe and Justin Charlesworth must be thanked for their good-humoured, ever smiling, toleration of my halting moves toward technical competence.

One of the great joys of teaching is seeing students develop from nervous interviewees to confident professionals. Every time I visit production centres friendly faces appear from my past, and the process came full circle when, for this research, I interviewed a multiskilled young professional I had taught years before. Of my Leeds students, Tim Gallagher deserves special thanks both for the invaluable help he gave me as research assistant and for his clear headed understanding of the nature of television journalism. Alison Preston worked alongside me for part of this research and since has developed her own excellent work on television news. Thanks are due to all those who have published my earlier work, some of which has grown to become part of this book. I owe a particular debt to Dave Culbert at the *Historical Journal of Film, Radio and Television*, and Alexis Weedon and Julia Knight at *Convergence*, three wise editors who gave me the chance to begin the process which now comes to some kind of fruition. Thanks are also due to all my friends and family for understanding the cause of my absences, both physical and mental. Thanks finally to Lesley Riddle at Arnold for her encouragement and admirable professionalism.

Introduction

Live, direct and biased?

Like any good headline writer or television sub-editor, I have got your attention with three words, one of them loaded, itself an example of a kind of bias towards overstatement. Urgent, up to date, direct, above all live and perhaps biased, is this the state of television news as the form enters its second half century? Certainly much of it is live, a significant proportion is direct and some of it is biased in one way or another, but there is a case to be made for banishing the 'b' word as it has become so overused as to be almost meaningless. 'What about bias?' asked the hurried young radio reporter sitting in my office clutching a newspaper cutting she had been given only minutes before by her equally harassed news editor. 'Let me explain', I replied, trying to square the contradictory demands of academic subtlety and even integrity with those of fluent sound bite in order to answer the question most often asked about television news.

Bias is defined as 'a one-sided inclination of the mind: a prejudice: any special influence that sways the mind' (Chambers, 1992) or, more fully: 'someone who shows bias is unfair in their judgements or decisions, because they are only influenced by their own opinions, rather than considering the facts' (BBC, 1992). It comes commonly to mean the opposite of neutral or impartial and inevitably carries a negative connotation. Most often, what is referred to is perceived political bias of one sort or another, either supposed left wing tendencies on the part of journalists or the inclination of the media consciously or unconsciously to transmit a dominant ideology, a world-view in support of the ruling classes and the *status quo*. Other kinds of bias have been identified. One subtle variant is the 'bias against understanding' articulated by John Birt and Peter Jay over 20 years ago (Birt and Jay, 1975b) to refer to what they perceived as a fundamental flaw in the television news of the time. Generally, the word comes to stand for a general accusation that news is not what it should be. What is perhaps more important, however, is to examine television news for what it has become, for much has changed since the notion of bias in television news first entered the public domain.

New technologies, new channels: a new world?

This book is a study of the changing face of television news, examining both the transmitted screen product and the newsgathering and reporting process which lies behind the broadcast bulletins viewers see every day. It is an analysis of how television reporting has changed in the age of the 24-hour news service, outlining the circumstances of the new world of television journalism. It will examine the world of rolling news, received globally: a world where the 'flyaway' portable satellite dish, the 'sat phone', the fax, the laptop computer, the digital palmcorder, non-linear editing, the edit suite in a suitcase, and the multiskilled working practices they are bringing with them have changed the way in which news stories are reported, even the way in which international relations are conducted. The changes in progress are apparent to news professionals:

> We are in the middle of a seismic shift, which will change the broad-casting landscape forever: the way we gather it, the way we receive it, the way we watch it, the way we use it (Feingold, 1996, p. 10).

It is a world where a certain new bias has developed, one which turns around technology.

At the same time that technology has radically changed the way in which news is reported, there have been enormous parallel institutional changes in the structure of broadcasting around the world. The development of dedi-cated news services such as CNN, Sky News, *Euronews*, CBC *Newsworld* and BBC *World* which are available around the clock, broadcasting across continents, indeed in some cases around the globe, has changed the infor-mation map radically. Television news is now a $3–4 billion business with institutional alliances shifting daily (Culf, 1995a, G2, p. 14). These new technological and institutional developments will be set in the context of traditional news practice, for only by examining the process of growth from the first television news to the diverse news ecology of today can one properly understand the present state to which electronic journalism has evolved. The dynamic changing nature of the phenomena under study can-not be overestimated. News is by definition a volatile, time-critical medium where the constant changes in content which constitute its very essence are very often paralleled by changes in form. In a competitive, technologically intensive industry where great value is placed on being one step ahead of the competition there is a constant search for the new and the different. Paradoxically, however, the news professional is in many ways a conserva-tive creature, one to whom the term experimental could rarely be applied. These issues, from the global to the technological, to the institutional and even the personal will be explored in order to shed light on the news 'product' we see everyday.

This work is unashamedly about something; it will comment on a body of output which is both huge and diverse. From the ephemeral flow, emerging 24 hours a day from screens around the world, it will attempt to define fundamental underlying patterns beneath this constant flux. The work will use several case studies, combining these with background chapters analysing new developments both in technology and, more importantly, in working practices, which have led to significant changes in news grammar. These background sections inform the case studies, which include material from a wide range of contemporary events, including a major breaking story. A comparative approach will be used, with significant reference made to both practice and product. Finally, the question is asked: is the news better reported, with more understanding, as a result of the new technologies and the working practices they bring with them? Technologically driven change and institutional competition may have altered the nature of television news significantly and viewers certainly have more information faster and from a greater variety of providers than they have ever had before, but do they have a greater understanding as a result? The gradual evolution of the electronic media from the mass communications broadcasting model to a more diverse ecology has led to an unprecedented diversity where to speak of *'the* news' is anachronistic. This work will outline this new world where news must now be spoken of in the plural: a world where some intriguing things are happening.

Global video howl round

During the democracy riots in Thailand in 1992, events on the streets of Bangkok were reported by an international team consisting of the BBC's Hong Kong bureau led by reporter Brian Barron, his staff crew, a crew from the Australian Broadcasting Company and two local Thai crews. Material shot in the streets was edited locally and sent by satellite back to London where it was transmitted by the BBC domestically and by World Service Television which could be received in Bangkok. Within 20 minutes of this transmission, VHS copies of the reports were on the streets in the hands of the demonstrators. Television news, shot, edited and transmitted using new communications technologies, had created a global video howl round, a late twentieth century television hall of mirrors, with news itself entering the equation of events, and not for the first time. This case is interesting as an indicator of change. It is the story of news reported quickly from half way round the world by a team from two allied broadcasting organisations supplemented by local crews and as such is an indicator of changing institutional arrangements in foreign reporting. Edited in the field and sent back to base by satellite, the material returned to its source, carried on Star

Television's satellite service for whom BBC World Service Television were then programme providers. New technologies for newsgathering used by a team of new institutional alliances feeding into new output arrangements for transmitting the news and new reception conditions had led to a situation where the news itself had entered into the unfolding chain of world events. Foreign correspondents who once packaged up their work and despatched it to the nearest airport and rarely saw the finished story can now see their own work literally come back on them.

George Bush ended a presidential press conference saying that he had to leave and call the President of Turkey. In Ankara, Turgut Ozal turned off CNN, walked into his office, picked up the ringing phone and said 'Hello, Mr President' (Tracey, 1995, p. 146). Anecdotes of this kind circulate among news professionals and CNN press officers, evidence of the almost uncanny way in which the live and instant nature of 24-hour rolling news does more than simply report events.

During the Gulf War, a family in New York were to see a CNN report that Scud missiles had been launched, targeted on Haifa. They instantly phoned their relatives in the Israeli city who said that there were no signs of any rockets and they would know as there was a Patriot missile battery just up the hill from their house. As they spoke, however, the Patriots fired, confirming the reports fed back to them from half way round the world via rolling television news (conversation with playwright Trevor Griffiths).

Soon after Bill Clinton had CNN installed in the Presidential bathroom he was able to watch the storming of another White House live as CNN had 30 staff, including five reporters, present in Moscow. Four live camera positions relayed events from the Russian Parliament and, when the first shots were fired, the Reuters newsflash that went around the world credited CNN (Culf, 1993, p. 3).

On 18 April 1995 a catamaran ferry went aground off the coast of Jersey. No one was killed and it was hardly the story of the century. Nevertheless CNN had a live feed from the scene as the Harbour Office, the local lifeboat, a Customs helicopter, the police, fire and ambulance services together conducted the rescue of the 300 passengers. The local emergency services used the live CNN pictures from the scene to coordinate the rescue work.

CNNization

In 1990, Ted Turner, CNN's charismatic founder, perhaps feeling bullish after events in central and eastern Europe the year before, predicted that there would be no totalitarian states anywhere in the world in 10 years time such was the democratising power of transnational news services such as CNN (Flournoy, 1992, p. 2). His global rival Rupert Murdoch was quick to echo these noble democratic sentiments until it threatened to affect his business in China (Shawcross, 1995, p. 12). Murdoch has spoken openly of his plans for a global television network, building on his American, European and Asian holdings: 'Our activities include the creation of new channels with world-wide reach. We aim to *create* and cover global events' (Williams, 1993, p. 1, emphasis mine). This phenomenon has been called the CNNization (Turner, 1991, pp. 49–50) of the world, meaning not just the advent of globally available television services, but the fact that such services have begun to play a role in international politics. This development has also been called telediplomacy (Gurevitch, 1991, p. 187) and it can be seen to a certain extent taking place on the television screens of the world.

Iron curtains and walls come tumbling down

Both Murdoch and Turner might be understood for overestimating the power of their news empires, but there can be no question that the electronic media clearly can enter the international political arena as players as well as spectators. One need look no further than the dynamic of the 1989 revolutions in Eastern and Central Europe. That summer Hungary opened its borders and East Germans crossed *en masse*, providing television pictures of long lines of that quintessential symbol of East bloc shabbiness, the two-stroke, oil-burning, fibreglass parody of a car, the Trabant, queuing up for freedom in the West. Meanwhile party bosses in Berlin discussed 'a Chinese solution', hoping to copy the Tiananmen Square example in maintaining a totalitarian regime in the face of popular protest and international media coverage. Events, however, were to be taken from their control.

Later in the year, after a party shuffle, the new East Berlin party secretary Gunther Schabowski told a live press conference that East Germans would be allowed to cross directly to the West. The message was heard by Berliners, some of whom decided to do just that. Crucially, it was also heard by border guards who indeed let them through. This small event was duly recorded and transmitted on West German television, seen on both sides of the border. The crowds came out from both sectors of the city and the Berlin Wall came down on that particular night in November 1989 because of media-transmitted messages and media-received messages (Kent, 1996, p. 97).

From then until the end of the year, there followed a veritable domino effect as citizens, watching other countries' revolutions on TV, decided they should have one too. Romanians saw the Wall come down on Bulgarian television, then they heard of events in Timisoara and finally they took to the streets themselves. Indeed the events in Romania at Christmas 1989 took place in some part actually on television. As a result of the 1989 revolutions the world has changed utterly, but no sooner had these dramatic and historic events faded from our television screens than they were succeeded by another big story, the reporting of which was to tell us much about the rapid evolution of television news.

'Reporting live from ground zero'

With the words 'something is happening outside' CNN reporter Bernard Shaw told the watching world that the Gulf War had started as the first bombs fell on Baghdad. But CNN were neither first nor, arguably, the most accurate to report the story. Both ABC and NBC filed voice reports from Baghdad, with Gary Shepherd on the air first for ABC, and NBC's Tom Aspell providing the most insightful report (MacGregor, 1993, p. 26). However, both the traditional networks were reliant on the public telephone system which was soon destroyed and only CNN were left to report 'live from ground zero' (Wiener, 1992) using their own independent communications link.

In the White House George Bush tuned in, as did the Pentagon, while in the basement shelter of the Al-Rashid, CNN's Baghdad hotel, Iraqis and foreign journalists alike listened to BBC World Service Radio which was relaying the description of events outside given by CNN's John Holliman, Peter Arnett and Bernard Shaw nine floors above them. The first-night voice-only reports of the CNN team travelled on a dedicated landline to Jordan, from there by satellite to Atlanta to be transmitted by CNN globally and were then picked up and transmitted by various television and radio services, including BBC World Service, returning to their source, travelling halfway around the world and back to go nine floors downstairs.

The triumph of the 'Baghdad boys' put the letters CNN on the front pages of newspapers and on the lips of people who had never seen it. Within hours, the dramatic material from the Iraqi capital was used in CNN's on-air promotional material. Their ex-Baghdad reports became a media event in their own right, in many ways more real than the real world event covered. When pictures emerged some days later they were added to what were originally voice-only reports, creating something that had never actually been broadcast. Yet many people still remember the night of 16–17 January 1991 as being a live television event with pictures, the oft-repeated commercial and the fog of memory helping to muddle rhetoric and reality.

At one point Holliman (03:57:57 GMT) asked Atlanta for news from the Pentagon and Saudi Arabia. Intriguingly, the man with seemingly the best seat in the house, the eyewitness to history reporting live on global television, is asking for information. Clearly, reporting the news is not just a matter of a live link, a fast-talking reporter and a good view out the window.

Is this case symbolic of all television news and its status to reality? An undeniable real world event of great import is reported live on television, but such coverage is mediated by the physical (the limited view out of the hotel room window), technological access (voice only) and the at times self-dramatising commentary. The viewer nevertheless witnesses the event on screen in what appears to be a first-hand way and then assimilates that perception into their own set of beliefs, prejudices and biases. Some who watched the event no doubt reacted strongly, pronouncing it to be an act of militaristic, neo-imperialist obscenity, perpetuated against an already oppressed people, while others saw it as evidence of a hi-tech, low-damage conflict necessary for the maintenance of civilisation and world order; some may have seen it as both at once. While it may tell us something important about the changing nature of television news, the dramatic events of 16–17 January 1991 were not isolated and unique, but part of a bigger story.

Gas-mask journalism

Disaster, however, followed the first-night triumph of CNN. The next night, as reports came through that Iraqi missiles had fallen on Israel, Larry Register, Bureau Chief in CNN's Jerusalem Office, went on the air live to report the widening of the war. Register and his staff reported while wearing gas masks, the camera panning wildly around the office, occasionally looking out of the window to see cars going by. At times these less than informative visuals were kept on screen as CNN Atlanta put other voices over these shots, adding to the sense of confusion. Viewers saw a close up of a face in a gas mask on screen but the voice they were hearing was coming from another source in another part of the world. This live reporting was hardly informative and at one point (00:56:30 GMT) Register asked his base 'Have you any information you can pass on to me?' At the time the most reliable information on events available to CNN viewers was coming from Washington, where defence correspondent Wolf Blitzer at the Pentagon regularly reported both American and Israeli official comment which was more informative than the live material coming from Jerusalem. Later (01:28:28 GMT) the BBC's Middle East correspondent Michael Macmillan walked into the CNN Jerusalem office wearing protective clothing. With him was his cameraman who had a tape in his hand. Register instantly began to interview Macmillan who had clearly been out in the streets filming. As this impromptu dialogue with a reporter who had actually been engaging in orthodox newsgathering began, ITN in Britain, who were at the time rebroadcasting CNN, instantly cut away rather than transmit material from their domestic rival. CNN too cut away from Jerusalem.

These surreal events were yet another instance of video howl round in the world of global television and of what should certainly be called gas-mask journalism, knee-jerk grandstanding, which is live satellite newsgathering at its worst. In all the frenetic 'coverage' no voice, either from Atlanta, Tel

Aviv, Washington or from Jerusalem itself asked if the Iraqis would send missiles into the heart of what is after all a Muslim holy city. Knowledge, calm analysis, stop-a-minute-and-reflect journalism, might have saved CNN some embarrassment as they sought a second night of exclusive live broadcasting. The electronic global village has clearly arrived and the events of the early Gulf War showed it to be as prone to error and confusion as its unwired real world equivalent.

Nevertheless, broadcasters around the world took the CNN coverage, sometimes with grave reservations. At the BBC,

> the're'd be rows going on in the control room as to who we went to next. It was incredible. . . . On day two there were some people saying, don't take CNN, don't take that showbiz, and other people were saying it may be showbiz but it's there and it's happening and it's a part of what is happening and therefore we've got to take it, almost to the extent where I was left there wondering what . . . absolutely not knowing what the hell was going to happen next.

The confusion that reigned on the second night was widespread and CNN were not the only news organisation caught out by the fog of war. As Scud missiles fell on Israel, confusion arose as to whether they had chemical warheads. NBC announced that they had and this was duly reported by other networks, beginning a chain reaction, with news organisations dutifully second sourcing each other, creating a giddy whirling of 'facts' described by one senior BBC news-gatherer:

> I think we reported at one stage that there were at least reports that a chemical attack had been launched, which was wrong. One of the reasons for that which we discovered, was something we hadn't quite come to terms with yet, was what I call a public information howl round, a bit like feedback or something. We all work off computers. We all have instant access to news agency reports. We all monitor CNN, Sky and all the rest of it, and there'll be one unconfirmed report of something which will come up on a news agency. Suddenly it appears on CNN. CNN are then reported on a different news agency reporting that. We report CNN. We are then reported by yet another news agency and suddenly there are apparently five sources of this information. People think 'well it's on five sources it must be true'. In fact all it is, is one unconfirmed report that has gone round everybody very quickly, in 15–20 minutes sometimes. Everybody was on a heightened state of alert, everyone was looking to broadcast or publish whatever they could, and we had one rumour which suddenly multiplied and got picked up by a number of sources because it was appearing in a great number of places. You have to really check your sources and be very much on guard for that kind of thing not to happen.

Live war?

Television is ephemeral and gas-mask journalism was quickly forgotten, soon to be replaced by the dynamic on-screen heroism of the 'Scud Studs'. As the air-raid sirens sounded, brave reporters stood their ground in front of the cameras as CNN and other news services reporting from Saudi Arabia and then Israel showed audiences Scud missiles being destroyed by Patriot missiles. At last we were seeing the live, real time, actual war that had been promised. Viewers no longer just had to accept the military line, they could see for themselves actual events courtesy of satellite television.

The dramatic mid-air explosions, the hi-tech bombs bursting in air, were not quite what they appeared to be. George Bush stated categorically in February 1991 that the Patriots had hit 41 of the 42 Scuds they were fired at. By as early as April of that year, it began to emerge that the Patriots were not the technological miracle they had seemed. First it was suggested that they had only partly destroyed the incoming Scuds, with large pieces of falling debris from both missiles hitting the ground. The result, according to the *International Herald Tribune,* was that 'the Patriot may have caused as much damage as it prevented' (quoted in Frank, 1992, p. 10). Later the official position was modified when the military claimed that only 24 of 86 targeted Scuds were hit. Reporting this statistic in May 1992 *The Economist* cautioned that 'the jury is still out' (2 May 1992, p. 78) and sure enough, by the time of the fifth anniversary of the Gulf War in January 1996, no less a figure than Moshe Arens, the Israeli Defence Minster during the war, could be seen on the BBC admitting that not a single Scud was intercepted over Israel (*The Gulf War,* BBC, January 1996; Fairhall, 1996, p. 42). Kellner, in his book on the war, records a CBS item on night two which quoted former American air force general Michael Dugan to the effect that 'the Patriot system would not be adequate to defend Israel' (1992, p. 151).

The spectacular live coverage has since been the cause of much criticism from inside the news professions. A senior BBC executive interviewed for this study has remarked:

> If you go over live, then you have your correspondent standing there, you're in the middle of the air raid and you don't know whether he's going to get blown up in front of you or not. And it's a great temptation because it's absolutely gripping TV. In one way you're tempted to say this is extraordinary let's stay with it. In another way you're saying this could be absolutely horrific let's get away from it. You have to cut through that and say editorially are we justified in staying with this. Editorially, are we learning anything from it? Quite often the answer is no, in which case you're not really justified in sticking with it. CNN had people with gas masks standing there for what seemed like hours jabbering on about nothing, simply because it was

compelling to watch, but in the end that's not really journalism, that's not telling you anything about the situation.

These views are echoed by print journalist Max Hastings:

> the biggest danger facing television is that the technology simply takes over. Here you can have a reporter on the spot describing as it happens the shells landing, the bombs being dropped, the Scuds flying overhead. But images are being transmitted much quicker than any reporter, however brilliant, can possibly sensibly interpret them. In other words viewers are in danger of being given the idea that they're being told what is going on whereas actually they're being given a wildly misleading impression of what's going on (source: Pearson, 1995).

Other journalists are less likely to be dismissive. One senior BBC figure admits to being very ambiguous about CNN and all it has come to stand for:

> I think probably [it] will prove to be a turning point, professionally and personally. It was marvellous. I see it as a triumph of logistics. Most of what actually appeared on CNN in the guise of journalism, struck me as being crass, and not very well informed and slightly confused, but you were there, you were experiencing it in real time, and so consequently it's irresistible. You don't see pictures of what's going on; you only see a not very good reporter making remarks about the guy who was in Baghdad, quite often not a very good reporter either, not quite telling you what's happening, because it's happening to him at the same time, and he hasn't got a clue what's happening, but the whole thing had a sort of excitement about it, and the immediacy of that is absolutely irresistible . . . to be the only television organisation on the air with the indisputable opening of a war in which your country is involved, has to be a good story and accuracy was not at issue. Journalistically we were all pasted to the wall, however sniffy one should be about CNN, it's an immensely impressive exercise.

Another producer who actually publicly predicted much of what CNN was to accomplish remarks:

> I think just on the technical side it was brilliant, just the sheer operation of getting stuff onto the screen so quickly, it was just amazing, and I think that they've shown the way . . . they've changed the rules of the game for everybody.

In his opinion, these changes are not just cosmetic professional ones, involving more live links and 24-hour coverage, but permanent and structural alterations with wider political implications.

> I just think it daft to think you can keep the Genie in the bottle. It's got to happen. Maybe it can be done in a better way; maybe it can be

handled a bit more responsibly, not in such a gouache way, but they did it with a lot of style. They did it, which is the main thing. They managed to get things on the air from all the main places in the world; to be able to be going live out of Baghdad as the bombs were dropping, and I think in the end it's got to be much more a force of peace really, because it can bring wars to much speedier conclusions. It possibly can resolve situations quicker, simply because you have the immediacy of the communication. . . . I don't think there was any chance of America getting bogged down like in Vietnam while CNN was around.

Certainly CNN reporting of the Gulf War quickly entered oral legend and popular culture. A *Doonesbury* cartoon strip at the time depicts a wounded American GI being rescued by a helicopter. On being congratulated on being the first of his unit to be wounded, the soldier asks if he'll 'make CNN'. 'How do you think we found you?' comes the reply (Allen *et al.*, 1991, p. 236). The implication that a news network knows more and sees further than the hi-tech military is not entirely satiric comic-strip exaggeration. On the fifth anniversary of the Gulf War, a veteran phoned into CNN's *Larry King Live* (16 January 1996) to report that CNN had regularly been 40–60 seconds ahead of the military warning sirens in announcing Scud attacks on American bases in Saudi Arabia – yet another instance of a near instant communications loop with events folding back on themselves.

Live from Kuwait City

At the end of the Gulf War there was literally a race to see who would be first into Kuwait City. CBS reporter Bob McEwan with cameraman Dave Green won the race, the exclusive made possible in part by his crew's totally independent communications system of 'flyaway' satellite transmitter/receiver, a satellite phone and generator which took only 20 minutes to set up before broadcasting live to a worldwide audience. There was global television gridlock as stations around the world all took the feed that effectively declared the Gulf War to be over. Reporter McEwan engaged in a live two-way with the world, answering questions with everyone. As he spoke some Kuwaitis brought a pair of US marines to him. McEwan cheerfully interviewed these down-home boys who exhibited a certain degree of folksy charm and promised to put the coffee on for their soon-to-arrive military colleagues. McEwan didn't ask them how they had got there. Why and how were US marines in Kuwait City already? Had they arrived by sea, parachuted in or come over land? How long had they been there? When would they be joined by other American forces? There are journalistic skills other than the logistics of getting there first, setting up the kit and injecting live into the wired world. Nevertheless the situation was clearly a long way from Falklands when tapes from the front line took up to 23 days to get on the screen and when Max Hastings, the first journalist into Port Stanley at the end of the conflict, had to go to the local bar and ask to use the telephone to contact his editor (Harris, 1983, p. 139).

In a very real sense, the Gulf War began with CNN in Baghdad and ended with CBS in Kuwait City. These two very visible, high-profile exclusives tell us a lot about the development of television news. Both were acts of unilateral journalistic enterprise and pluck but both depended on technological self-sufficiency. Both stories had their own hardware and both were able to report independently of either a communications infrastructure or any other organisation attempting to control them. Both were events reported live in real time by reporters in front of microphones or in front of cameras; both were reported instantly around the world. There was no background; there was no preparation; there was no extensive production, editing, voice-over, commentary or structuring of the story. There were no helpful newspaper cuttings to consult, no wire service copy to rip and read, no other media to monitor. The open line to the outside world was there and the reporters began speaking. It has happened before; it will happen again; the issue at question is what are the implications of such journalism? Being live, in the right place, at the right time, letting the viewer see allegedly historic events for themselves is still no guarantee of accuracy or understanding, both of which often arise from a vantage point further away in time and place. It can, however, make for exciting television.

Chicken Noodle News scoops the world

In one estimation, 'the Gulf War became the story to confirm how wired the universe is' (Turner, 1991, p. 45). CNN Vice President Ed (no relation) Turner, reflecting on his network's high-profile performance during that conflict, sensed that the event was indeed emblematic, dramatically highlighting developments already well in progress. The story really started on 1 June 1980 with the first transmission of CNN. Dubbed 'Chicken Noodle News' by the networks, Ted Turner's 24-hour service was the first specialist service to challenge the traditional dominance of the senior American network news services. One observer has gone so far as to state that the launch of CNN was 'the single most important development in the history of non-fiction television' (Tracey, 1995, p. 146). The new service made its first major impact with the shuttle explosion on 28 June 1986. Alone of all news services, the brash newcomer broadcast the launch of the *Challenger*, which was deemed to be dull and routine by the existing news providers. When the unthinkable happened and only CNN had the dramatic, historic pictures, Ted Turner's Cinderella service had arrived. At the BBC in London, television news was not officially taking the CNN feed, but a keen trainee videotape editor just happened to be recording it for practice. In Washington, ITN correspondent Jon Snow saw the explosion and instantly booked a satellite line to London. Within 15 minutes of the event, a news-flash with pictures was transmitted on ITV and a substantial three-and-a-half-minute piece was aired in the early evening news only 45 minutes after the explosion. In the words of the reporter himself 'this was absolutely unheard of'. A man in Washington, using a satellite feed, had reported to London in record time on an event taking place in Florida which had been recorded by an upstart, third-party 24-hour news service. CNN had joined the big boys and the game they were all playing was changing as both the technology and the world they were reporting altered radically.

Moscow coup

The story headlined in the Gulf War was confirmed with the Soviet coup attempt later in 1991. Late on the afternoon of 19 August (CNN 17:00) a press conference was held by the leaders of the Soviet coup. They were lit-erally grey men seen against a grey background, giving a rather uncharis-matic performance, seemingly trying to convince themselves it was all necessary. One of the plotters was visibly much the worse for wear from drink, another's hands were shaking. One wonders why they called such a conference in the first place. It was clearly something they felt they had to do. The plotters may have received a certain message about using the media, but they neither truly understood it nor could they act on it.

Moscow's huge television tower was still seen by some as a vast hypo-dermic for administering ideological injections to the Soviet people, hence the need for the coup to begin in classic fashion: a Soviet television news-reader not seen for some time returned to announce the momentous news in front of bland curtains. The newsroom background behind the announcer, a convention clearly cloned from the West, and therefore itself a sign of liberalisation, was obscured. The attempt to turn back the politi-cal clock was expressed in media terms. Russian Federation TV, only on the air since the previous May, was taken off and the new liberal papers and radio stations were closed down. Troops surrounded the main televi-sion transmitter as in every classic coup. There were signs of a recognition by the *putsch* leaders that controlling the means of communication was important.

Serious mistakes were made, however, owing to a radical misunderstand-ing of how developments in communications have changed the nature of global politics. Links to the outside world were left open. Western reporters could work and CNN could broadcast live from a Moscow rooftop, show-ing tanks in the streets of Moscow. The BBC could broadcast from inside the threatened Russian Parliament, while back in London BBC 'expert' Carrie Schofield could phone Soviet generals inside the Kremlin and get news from the very heart of the situation. Boris Yeltsin could speak to President Bush and Prime Minister Major, and, when he stood on a tank, shook hands with its crew and read a statement of defiance, Yeltsin knew he was creating an instant icon to be seen around the world within minutes. Bush in Kennebunkport and Major in London could see evidence from the scene faster than any diplomatic despatch. Soviet citizens could watch CNN and Sky News and see what was happening in Moscow, and the troops in the streets knew they were going to be seen around the world.

Away from the centre of things, in the Crimea, President Gorbachev undertook two media-conscious acts. His KGB guards quickly altered Russian radios designed only to receive domestic programming and tuned him in to the BBC World Service and the Voice of America so he could get information on events in Moscow. The video camera that had been used to film such innocent domestic joys as his granddaughter's ballet practice was used to record a presidential statement to be smuggled out. Later Mikhail Gorbachev was to hear on the radio that his chief opponent had been shaking at the press conference. He knew then they would fail. Once again modern communications links and electronic news had played a part in the dynamic of events. Another major player, Eduard Shevardnadze, was to remark:

> Praise be to information technology! Praise be to the reporters and announcers of CNN! Those who had parabolic antennae and could receive this station's broadcast were getting a full picture of the developments, while the obedient TV of Leonid Kravchenko was pouring forth the murky waves of disinformation and lies (Shevardnadze, 1991, p. 21).

The August events in Moscow were even more revealing about the changing nature of reporting and modern communications technologies than at first sight. The first news of the Soviet coup reputedly came into Britain not through a wire service, not through the monitoring service of the BBC, not on a 24-hour satellite news service, but as electronic mail:

> Moscow is full of tanks and military machines, I hate them. They try to close all mass media, they shutted up CNN an hour ago, Soviet TV transmits opera and old movies. But thanks heaven, they don't consider Relcom [e-mail] mass media or they simply forgot about it. Now we transmit information enough to put us in prison for the rest of our life :-) (quoted in Perry, 1992, p. 31, reproduced as sent).

The classic *coup d'etat* is perhaps not possible anymore. Loyal troops can surround the television station and solemn music can be played on the radio, but this is no longer enough when the fax machines still work, when computers are wired to the Internet, when desktop-published newspapers can be circulated in spite of the official presses being closed and, what is more important, when you can see what is really happening on global television networks which cannot be taken off the air by any coup. Not just spectators, the media have become players.

The Netanyahu principle

Larry King Live is a CNN programme which is reputedly watched by Saddam Hussein. During the Gulf War the programme created a classic global village situation: Benjamin Netanyahu, then Israeli Deputy Foreign Minister, was answering questions from phone-in viewers in the United States, watched by people in over 100 countries around the globe at a time when the world was waiting to see if Israel would retaliate after the first Scud attacks. Diplomacy was being conducted on television with Larry King, not Boutros Boutros Ghali, as the interlocutor. Netanyahu answered a question with a statement:

> Maybe they are listening to us in Baghdad, in fact I'll delete the maybe, I'm sure they are. They are listening to us in Moscow and Washington, everywhere else. So the impact of what is seen and said on television is an integral part of the war effort on both sides. . . . But what it means is that television is no longer a spectator. You know in physics, in sub-atomic physics, there's something called the Heisenberg principle which basically says that if you observe a phenomenon you actually change it. Well we now have the Heisenberg physics of politics: as you observe a phenomenon with television instantaneously you modify it somewhat (*Larry King Live*, 23 January 1991).

What we might call the Netanyahu Principle is one that global television itself is keen to encourage. CNN regularly run several ads for themselves. One used during the Gulf War period is particularly revealing. As still pictures of recent events flash onto the screen at a blinding rate, the words 'World Leaders Use It' are repeatedly superimposed. This is the self-image of CNN, as a conduit of diplomacy, providing not just information for the people, but a global network used by leaders themselves. When he doesn't know what's happening the President of Egypt reputedly sits down and watches CNN: 'I waited all the time watching on the CNN [*sic*]' says Hosni Mubarak in another of the stations's commercials for itself. When they start to bomb Baghdad, George Bush and Dick Cheney tune in to CNN to find out what's happening. The message is 'Watch us and you won't just see 24-hour news, you'll see history being made'. This on-screen rhetoric has been articulated off the air by CNN executives:

> we continue to collect evidence that television news does have an impact on the conduct of foreign policy, but no one knows how much. Some things we do know: heads of state and their aides do most certainly watch CNN and our fellow broadcasters; leaders of institutions

such as other networks, newspapers, think-tanks, academia, corpora-
tions are close and careful viewers of the news product. We believe we
are a factor in the decision-making, but of course, to what extent is
unclear (Turner, 1991, p. 42).

The notion that the new global media might enter into events and help to
prevent tyranny is an attractive one, but not entirely realistic. Cynics might
ask what happened to the Kurds. Were they not wired up? Couldn't they get
CNN? What Internet service provider did the Chechens use? And what of
the opinion that 'the failure of Tiananmen Square was a failure of the distribution of data' (Perry, 1992, p. 31)?

The interaction of television news with the events it covers is a complex
dynamic not amenable to any one simple explanation. The analysis which
holds for discussing the Kurds in northern Iraq after the Gulf War where
television pictures had the effect of changing American policy clearly
doesn't apply to later events in northern Iraq. The secret diplomatic discussions away from the cameras in Norway which led to Arab–Israeli peace
talks were the very opposite of telediplomacy. In one case, television news
and the global village it reputedly creates entered the equation of events
while in another it had no effect whatsoever, being left to report events that
had already happened out of its gaze. But then when the Arab–Israeli talks
did take place in Madrid, most of the 4600 journalists present had to watch
proceedings on CNN (Henry, 1992, p. 19). The clear message to observers,
in whatever profession, is to avoid simplistic explanations; never to say
always.

We now have the possibility (or the threat) of instantaneous postmodernist real time realpolitik. There is a danger that that diplomacy will now
be conducted in public, under great unnecessary and unhelpful pressure.
More importantly there is a danger of overrating the media, a danger of
believing its own rhetoric, of buying its self-image. Dick Cheney may have
used CNN for bomb damage assessment during Desert Storm, but the voice-
only reports from the limited vision afforded by a hotel window were hardly
the full extent of the Pentagon's intelligence about the state of Baghdad.
CNN would have been just a small part of his jigsaw. The illusion is created
that the only way that anybody, be they soldier, statesperson or citizen,
knows anything is by watching television.

Events in Moscow went the way they did because the Red Army
remained in barracks. The Russian military were the kingpins in August
1991 and again in October 1993, not CNN. Tiananmen Square was wired
to the global village and, in spite of tottering on the brink, orthodox methods of repression worked in the maintenance of the *status quo.* When it
comes literally to the crunch, a fax machine will not stop a tank. Certainly
the new global media and their predecessors are a factor, but a factor
among many. To return to the physics metaphor, Heisenberg may have
revolutionised theoretical physics, but Newton still holds sway in most

instances. We shouldn't allow ourselves to mistake image for actuality, rhetoric for reality.

There has been a period of unprecedented hyperactivity in crisis news reporting since 1989 with Tiananmen Square, the fall of the Berlin Wall, the subsequent changes in the former Soviet bloc, the Gulf War, the failed coup in Moscow leading to the break up of the Soviet Union itself, the storming of the Moscow White House, the long-running Bosnian crisis, the changes in South Africa and the horrors of Rwanda and Burundi. Beneath the surface flux of such a period of concentrated conflict reporting, it is possible to perceive fundamental developments with lasting significance for the way in which events are reported on the television screens of the world. The emergence of the 24-hour satellite news services, particularly CNN and, to a lesser extent, Sky News, the BBC World Service and *Euronews* have permanently changed the news map. In addition to these conspicuous and often hyped changes in the delivery of television news, there have been crucial advances in the actual technology with which news is gathered and produced. These technological developments have had a considerable effect on the working practices of journalists using the medium of television and these new methods in turn have changed the actual product transmitted to the public.

From Morse code to the satphone

Soon after the outbreak of the Gulf War, most foreign journalists were expelled from Baghdad. Famously, Peter Arnett of CNN was allowed to stay and became 'the only Western television journalist in Baghdad'. CNN's 'exclusive' was portrayed in part as the result of a technological advantage. Arnett was equipped with a satellite phone, the use of this was denied other journalists and, along with the actual reporting of the news, CNN viewers heard a rhetoric, not just of exclusivity, but also of technological superiority.

Among the archive of CNN's voice-only transmissions from Baghdad in January 1991 we find a quiet reflective Peter Arnett late one night talking about the conditions under which he was working. Viewers heard from him what it was like to be reporting to a global television audience live from an enemy capital under fire. Arnett compared this situation with reporting from Indonesia in the 1960s when he had to file reports in Morse code. In the 30 intervening years, tremendous changes have occurred in communications technology, to the point where viewers could hear Arnett reporting live from outside a Baghdad hotel using an independent portable communications system beaming up to a satellite linking into a television system which itself was then distributed around the world to over a hundred countries by satellite technology, to be watched alike in Iraqi command bunker and the White House. From the telegraph to the satphone, the technology of

location-based crisis news reporting has changed utterly and, with it, journalistic working practices and the product ultimately seen by the public.

The reading of news texts

Given the ephemeral nature of television news and of current affairs production in particular it is all too easy to ignore the screen product, the endless flow of text which is outdated and useless soon after broadcast. When
it is no longer new, the news is of little, even academic, interest. It is also
very hard for academics or anyone else to write about the close details of
even the simplest media texts. Critics analysing a time-based, audio-visual
medium must often expend great energy describing broadcast materials to
readers who have never seen them or who are unable to remember them. As
one experienced commentator has remarked: 'This kind of analysis is difficult and arduous to undertake' (GUMG, 1995, p. 23), often requiring
detailed and time-consuming transcription. No doubt in the much hyped,
soon to arrive, multimedia future, studies like this will arrive on the succes-
sors of CD-ROM, including both the audio-visual material under study and
the written commentary upon it, copyright problems permitting. Failing this
hi-tech annotation method, often critics are reduced to using phrases such as
'there seems to be a case', which is usually a clue that the writer has seen little actual output. There is a constant danger of unsystematic impressionistic
viewing leading to skewed findings. I was present at a conference which discussed the media coverage of the Gulf War. In support of his case, one academic present showed a clip of an Iraqi woman who spoke straight to
camera very eloquently questioning the Allied bombing of her country. The
woman in question had been identified some time before on two news services as being a member of Iraqi Foreign Minister Tariq Aziz's staff. This
fact undercut somewhat the case being made, a situation that might have
been avoided had the speaker actually seen more of the television coverage
about .∕hich he spoke with such apparent authority.

If the traditional disciplines of sociology and politics, which gave birth to
media and communications studies, provided models for analysing the institutions, organisations and working methods of media production and the
nature of relations between the media and the state (what might be called
media contexts), they were not so good at providing methods for examining
the texts produced in these contexts, with the comment and theory resulting
all too often neglecting the realities of the media text itself.

Researchers have always been able to conduct quantitative content analysis, systematically recording occurrences of different acts and actors, and
then drawing conclusions from these statistical data. This form of research
is expensive to conduct and is potentially a crude instrument. Researchers
need to know which questions to ask, which categories to record and be prepared to alter these in response to on-screen evidence. Patterns must then be

recognised and interpreted. The fact that the single most frequent occurrence in British television news during the Gulf War period was BBC anchor Martyn Lewis reading to camera (Morrison, 1992, p. 69) may or may not be a useful piece of statistical information to have. In any case, such evidence must be used as part of a wider discussion. It can be seen as an indication that in spite of all the promises of live location reporting, television news is by necessity predominately a studio medium. Such information, arising from close attention to the details of broadcast material, then needs to be taken a step further. Whether this studio bias is a good or bad thing is a further evaluative issue for academic debate or professional polemic. In addition, questions should be asked about research methodology, not in order to attack it but to understand fully the results. Almost all items are introduced in the studio, therefore one would expect a one-to-one, or very nearly, ratio between the studio newsreader and other items, especially if one is counting occurrences and not duration. A normal non-crisis sample would be needed as a control to see if such a pattern were atypical. The finding may tell us something of the BBC's duty rota or be evidence of a conscious policy to employ a certain anchor. Certainly it is open to interpretation. In an interview with Lewis himself, he suggested it was simply a function of having lots of short items from a wider range of locations than normal, with crews and correspondents deployed in a wide number of locations, with all providing frequent updates.

Early in the Gulf War, journalist John Pilger attacked the television presentation of the bombing campaign in a typically combative piece called 'Video nasties', in the *New Statesman*:

> Television's satellite and video game wizardry merely reinforces our illusions. The system of 'sound bites', perfected by CNN, means that if truth intrudes, it is quickly rendered obsolete. Genuine, informed analysis is out of the question. There are few salient facts and no blood. An emotional screen is erected between us and reality, and our sensibilities are manipulated accordingly (1991, p. 7).

Pilger was far from alone in making such comments and these images quite rightly attracted the attention of journalists and academic commentators alike. Statistically speaking, however, the Gulf War was not a video game with endless tapes of smart bombs being constantly repeated. Air attack footage actually represented only 2.3 per cent of the picture content in the study (Morrison, 1992, p. 73). These powerful images were remembered by the audience, though not to the same degree as either the pictures of allied prisoners of war or the surrendering Iraqi soldiers (Svennevig, 1991, p. 22). Nevertheless, the striking 'video game' images need to be examined closely and the statistics of both content analysis and audience research borne in mind when discussing them. All too often empirical research ignores less quantifiable approaches to the text and, equally, close readers using various methods from the plain angry to the systematically semiotic are unable to

lift their gaze from the text to take account of the conditions of its production and consumption.

The point at issue here is that something seen on the screen was novel,
memorable and certainly evidence of the military attempting to sway public
perceptions by releasing arresting visual material never seen before. It is
equally interesting that the images that the audience found most memorable
had greater human content and, interestingly, showed suffering on both
sides of the conflict. Far from being fascinated by the hi-tech images of the
clean, casualty-free war, viewers remembered images which contradicted
the message that smart bombs had no human effect.

Systematic empirical research and 'semiotic guerrilla warfare' (Hartley,
1982, p. 191, quoting Umberto Eco) can equally be applied to the same text
and the results examined together. Like the television reporter duly interviewing both sides in an industrial dispute, there is no reason why both sides
of an academic debate should not be seen alongside each other without the
need to take sides and declare winners. John Pilger's polemic reading of the
television text needs to be seen alongside the statistical evidence on the
broadcasting in question. Neither approach invalidates the other with each
providing evidence for the reader to consider. Examining the two together
leads to important questions being asked, and comment of whatever kind
should be seen for what it is. Empirical work has both its strengths and its
weaknesses and they need to be taken into account. Equally, Pilger's work
is a known quantity, part of a richness and variety we should applaud rather
than dismiss as we seek simplistic explanations under the influence of whatever shade of political or methodological predisposition. Truth, be it academic or journalistic, is a jigsaw puzzle. Given the various pieces which may
or may not fit together, the journalist, the academic researcher and the
viewer each need to assemble a vision from the diverse views. Pilger's oppositional reading and empirical audience research are not contradictory with
the viewer response proving him wrong. Taken together, they show that in
spite of military efforts to portray the war as being a clean and casualty-free,
hi-tech affair, people on both sides did suffer, the media did depict such suffering and the audience not only percieved this but held it in their memory.
In one sense the news media colluded and are guilty as charged by Pilger for
they did show the video game material, but nowhere near as much as some
observers might imagine. Such material, however, was far from the entirety
of output and the viewers who consumed the television news were not
totally swayed by it.

In this work I will attempt to avoid overly simplistic explanations and will
not reject substantial bodies of previous research simply in order to set up a
new, allegedly definitive, analysis. It is possible first of all to acknowledge
the accomplishment of scholars who have gone before and to assert that a
certain amount of the work doesn't ever have to be done again because it is
so fundamental, even obvious now. We have certain givens; the foundations
have been laid. Anybody doing news studies is going to be building on a

certain foundation of assimilated knowledge. In acknowledging this legacy, this book aims to update certain aspects from certain perspectives. It is based on four and a half years of participant observation undertaken as a television professional, a continuing dialogue ranging from over 60 formal recorded interviews to over-coffee asides, recent formal observation in a range of news organisations, membership of various on-line groups and forums and a lifetime of viewing as a self-confessed information junkie. Its close readings arise from an academic background in English literature and from experience as a professional maker of audio-visual text. These close readings are professionally and technologically informed. Having worked in television and seen institutional pressures and working decision-making procedures from the inside and understanding certain technical considerations mostly unknown outside the media professions, I have then observed from a distance and interviewed key figures from a much more informed point of view than many academics might have done. This of course raises a variation on the perennial methodological pitfall of 'going native', when the investigator was himself at one time a native of sorts. It would be more accurate, however, to describe myself as an academic to begin with who took up a brief media career always with an eye to returning to academe but it would be severe self-dramatisation to say I was a kind of undercover participant observer with a notebook ever at hand. There is some precedent here. Tuchman describes such 'retrospective participant observation' (1991, p. 81) in the work of the American sociologist Robert Park who had himself been a journalist, and it is certainly common in America for communications scholars to have a professional background in the media. Such methodological concerns obviously don't disappear simply by acknowledging them, but such acquired experience enables one to comment in a way that many media scholars cannot. The point surely is to make a unique contribution, perhaps biased in its own way, to the understanding of the subject under study.

This book is not a textbook as such, solely consolidating and re-presenting existing work, but it is a book that is meant to be accessible and one which acknowledges, comments and draws on what has gone before. This does not stop it from trying equally to make an original contribution to knowledge which will be read by students of television at whatever level, in whatever profession. It eschews, no, avoids, the use of needlessly complex language for its own sake, seeing no value in the facile demonstration of the mastery of certain kinds of abstruse academic discourse. The use of professional and technological terminology is not avoided, however, but used deliberately in what I hope is an educative way. In a previous publication, I was criticised for the use of jargon when I had used (and explained) the term ENG. Electronic newsgathering has been a daily reality in television for over 20 years and I was somewhat surprised that an academic who had in fact written about news technologies would think such a phrase to be needless jargon. It is more than mildly ironic that a world where the word diachronic might be in commonplace usage would find it hard to accept a term in daily use in their area of study. I also believe that academic or journalistic comment on any form of television should give some evidence of the writer having regularly watched it. Close attention to the increasingly diverse details of television news as seen on the screens of the world yields much evidence which must be recognised and theorised; therefore, as a general rule, this work attempts to alternate detailed case studies of various lengths with wider ranging theoretical and historical discussion.

Chapter 1 offers a series of specific examples of news content which raise questions about the nature of the form. This is followed in Chapter 2 by an overview of academic research on news. Chapter 3 is a closely observed case study of how a major breaking story was covered by a range of news services on both sides of the Atlantic. A history of broadcast news in Britain and in America follows in Chapter 4 before the second case study in Chapter 5. Reflections on the development of newsgathering technologies, in Chapter 6, frame the final Chapter which undertakes the perilous task of discussing the future before arriving at conclusions.

|1|

More news, less understanding?

This section consists of a diverse collection of examples, mini case studies if you like, which provide evidence to be considered in length in the chapters that follow. The constant flow of news that fills our screens 24 hours a day can never, by its very nature, be fully grasped in any systematic way. The news is now increasingly diverse, so much so that even to use the definite article is inaccurate.

The news is plural

Newsgathering is not the only part of the news chain that has undergone radical change. Paralleling the dynamic evolution in news intake, output has altered in a way unimaginable 10 years ago. CNN, Sky News, MSNBC, BBC *World* and CBC *Newsworld* are all dedicated rolling news channels. Perhaps the most radical example of this new phenomenon is *Euronews,* a multilingual service which has no visible presenters of any kind. Eight times a day it runs a segment called *No Comment* which transmits raw news footage with only its natural sound and literally no comment of any kind save the date. Ordinary viewers across Europe can see the raw materials of which the news is made.

Live TV, a British cable channel owned by a large newspaper group and managed by a former tabloid editor, attracts attention to itself with programming such as *Topless Darts*. Female viewers are served, not by the perhaps obvious strategy of transmitting bottomless billiards, but by *Lunchbox Volleyball,* a programme where young men in strategically marked shorts lunge around beaches. The channel also has a news service. A female newsreader sits in a newsroom reading copy to camera and introducing location reports. The agenda is unashamedly tabloid with an upbeat music bed playing throughout the bulletin. Behind the newsreader, an adult (sized) person in a rabbit costume nods approval or gives a thumbs up, unless the story bores him, in which case he mimes yawning. News Bunny sometimes appears in location-recorded pieces; he features in the station's promotional material and, for a time, was part of a sub-plot in *Canary Wharf*, *Live TV*'s soap opera which is set in a television station. News Bunny signalled his enthusiastic approval of one story recorded for this study. A woman in Pennsylvania who had claimed damage to her back in a car accident had been filmed wrestling, barely clad, in coleslaw. This fraud by the 'salad-loving scammer' had been found out by the power of television investigative reporting, and viewers of course saw footage to prove the case.

Bloomberg Information Television's newscasters appear in a window in the top right-hand corner of a screen which features a myriad of other information, from stock prices to horoscopes and weather, all displayed as text in various boxes. Originally a 'wholesale' service available to the financial world, a retail version is now offered to broadcasters around the world. For a time *Live TV* gave news bunny the morning off, running Bloomberg at breakfast. Sky News also take short segments of Bloomberg financial news early in the morning, while some cable companies transmit it 24 hours a day. The company's staff also provide a syndicated radio service going out all over America, with scripts written in New York read by desk staff in London.

The news is now plural. It comes in many variants: broadsheet and tabloid, rolling and fixed-point, global and local, public service and commercial, specialist and general, live and recorded, delivered by cable, satellite, the Internet and over the old-fashioned airwaves. It can be gathered by one organisation, packaged by a second and transmitted by a third to a niche market audience viewing 'out of home'. Table 1.1 lists the news available to an ordinary cable television subscriber in suburban West Yorkshire in the north of England, neither the centre of the world nor a provincial backwater. The listing confines itself to material broadcast in English. If you add only one European language, French, the material available increases significantly to include six bulletins from four countries.

Output

This output is clearly substantial and diverse, with some services, such as Sky, offering material from a range of sources. If one adds up the hours of broadcasting involved one finds that in addition to the 24 hours provided by CNN, Sky News and Bloomberg Information Television, *Euronews* broadcasts for 20 hours a day. Of the terrestrial services the BBC provides roughly five hours of news per day, while ITN provides ITV and Channel 4 with around two hours. Add the programming on NBC Super Channel, Reuters' service for GMTV, one hour of local news, *Live TV*'s News Bunny, and you have over 100 hours of news programming in a 24-hour real time day. It would clearly be impossible to watch it all, let alone analyse it in any detail.

Table 1.1 Fixed-point (fp) bulletins and 24-hour rolling news

CNN: 24 hr	Sky: 24 hr	Bloomberg: 24 hr	Euronews: 20 hr	BBC1: fp	BBC2: fp	ITV: fp	CH4: fp	NBC Europe: fp
	0430: CBS News							
	0530: ABC News							0600: NBC
24 hr	0630: Bloomberg	24 hr	20 hr					0630: ITN
	0700–1100: Sky			0700–0900		Reuters		
	1130: CBS							
24 hr	Sky	24 hr	20 hr	1300		1240		
				1800		1740		1700: ITN
	Sky		20 hr	1830: local		1800: local		
							1900	
24 hr	Sky	24 hr	20 hr	2100		2200		2030: ITN
24 hr	2330: CBS	24 hr	20 hr		2230			
	0030: ABC	24 hr						

Running orders in Britain, line-ups in America, agendas for academics

Nevertheless, what does this enormous output consist of? What makes up the news line-up, the running orders, of the traditional fixed-point news bulletins? If you take the running order of three ordinary days selected over a period of a decade and compare the output of the traditional news services in Britain and America one sees quite quickly an interesting pattern. The three days chosen were based on existing work on British television (Duncan, 1987; Gallagher, 1996; Stephenson, 1987) which was supplemented by material on the American networks drawn from the Vanderbilt University Television Archives, a marvellous service available over the Internet. These results are presented in Figure 1.1.

A pattern clearly emerges. Between three and four stories in a network running order of about 13 items are universally covered. Add these to the stories carried by more than one bulletin, but not universally, and about one half of any running order is covered by more than one service, meaning that as much as half of many bulletins consists of unique material. Some of these would be genuine exclusives, but most would be stories that other services simply just didn't carry. This represents clear evidence drawn from a longitudinal sample over a decade that the news is not an immutable, fixed entity out in the world waiting to be gathered, for, if it were, the news would be pretty much the same in all running orders. Thorough academic researchers will no doubt say the sample is too small, while some journalists will say 'I could have told you that'. This information is offered here not as a definitive analysis but as food for thought, one of many observations that the reader is asked to bear in mind when reading this work.

Mapping the news

These running orders can also be represented to indicate geographical predisposition or bias (Figure 1.2). These results are hardly surprising, with each traditional news service having a clear domestic bias. Even CNN, who claim to cover the world, come close, but they are alike their competitors in seeming to neglect the southern hemisphere. This overview tells us much about the general nature of television news content, but it must also be seen at closer range by looking at a variety of specific examples.

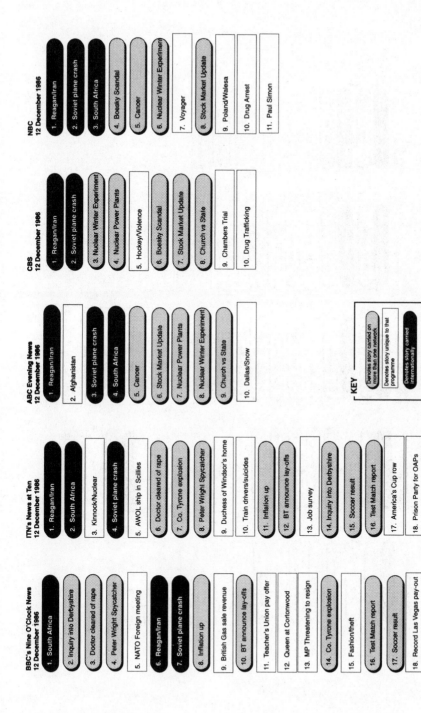

Fig. 1.1 Running orders of main evening news bulletins in Britain and America: (a) 12 December 1986.

BBC's Nine O'Clock News
12 December 1986

1. South Africa
2. Inquiry into Derbyshire
3. Doctor cleared of rape
4. Peter Wright Spycatcher
5. NATO Foreign meeting
6. Reagan/Iran
7. Soviet plane crash
8. Inflation up
9. British Gas sale revenue
10. BT announce lay-offs
11. Teacher's Union pay offer
12. Queen at Cortonwood
13. MP Threatening to resign
14. Co. Tyrone explosion
15. Fashion/theft
16. Test Match report
17. Soccer result
18. Record Las Vegas pay-out

ITN's News at Ten
12 December 1986

1. Reagan/Iran
2. South Africa
3. Kinnock/Nuclear
4. Soviet plane crash
5. AWOL ship in Scillies
6. Doctor cleared of rape
7. Co. Tyrone explosion
8. Peter Wright Spycatcher
9. Duchess of Windsor's home
10. Train drivers/suicides
11. Inflation up
12. BT announce lay-offs
13. Job survey
14. Inquiry into Derbyshire
15. Soccer result
16. Test Match report
17. America's Cup row
18. Prison Party for OAPs

ABC Evening News
12 December 1986

1. Reagan/Iran
2. Afghanistan
3. Soviet plane crash
4. South Africa
5. Cancer
6. Stock Market Update
7. Nuclear Power Plants
8. Nuclear Winter Experiment
9. Church vs State
10. Dallas/Snow

CBS
12 December 1986

1. Reagan/Iran
2. Soviet plane crash
3. Nuclear Winter Experiment
4. Nuclear Power Plants
5. Hockey/Violence
6. Boesky Scandal
7. Stock Market Update
8. Church vs State
9. Chambers Trial
10. Drug Trafficking

NBC
12 December 1986

1. Reagan/Iran
2. Soviet plane crash
3. South Africa
4. Boesky Scandal
5. Cancer
6. Nuclear Winter Experiment
7. Voyager
8. Stock Market Update
9. Poland/Walesa
10. Drug Arrest
11. Paul Simon

KEY

Denotes story carried on more than one network

Denotes story unique to that programme

Denotes story carried internationally

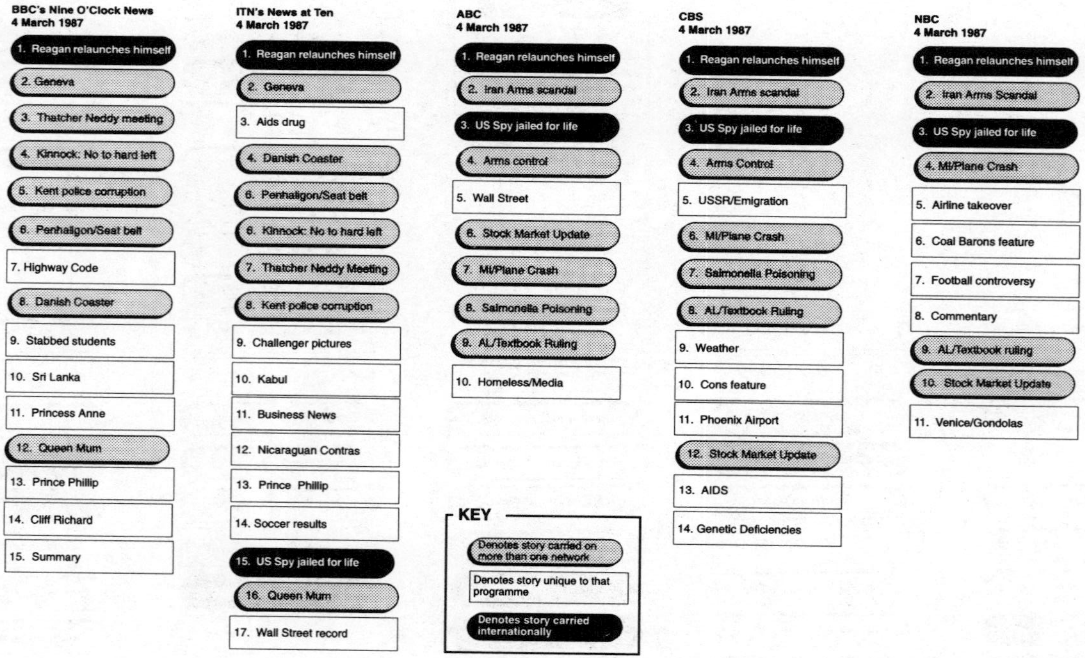

BBC's Nine O'Clock News
4 March 1987

1. Reagan relaunches himself
2. Geneva
3. Thatcher Neddy meeting
4. Kinnock: No to hard left
5. Kent police corruption
6. Penthalgon/Seat belt
7. Highway Code
8. Danish Coaster
9. Stabbed students
10. Sri Lanka
11. Princess Anne
12. Queen Mum
13. Prince Phillip
14. Cliff Richard
15. Summary

ITN's News at Ten
4 March 1987

1. Reagan relaunches himself
2. Geneva
3. Aids drug
4. Danish Coaster
5. Penthalgon/Seat belt
6. Kinnock: No to hard left
7. Thatcher Neddy Meeting
8. Kent police corruption
9. Challenger pictures
10. Kabul
11. Business News
12. Nicaraguan Contras
13. Prince Phillip
14. Soccer results
15. US Spy jailed for life
16. Queen Mum
17. Wall Street record

ABC
4 March 1987

1. Reagan relaunches himself
2. Iran Arms scandal
3. US Spy jailed for life
4. Arms control
5. Wall Street
6. Stock Market Update
7. Mil/Plane Crash
8. Salmonella Poisoning
8. AL/Textbook Ruling
10. Homeless/Media

CBS
4 March 1987

1. Reagan relaunches himself
2. Iran Arms scandal
3. US Spy jailed for life
4. Arms Control
5. USSR/Emigration
6. Mil/Plane Crash
7. Salmonella Poisoning
8. AL/Textbook Ruling
9. Weather
10. Cons feature
11. Phoenix Airport
12. Stock Market Update
13. AIDS
14. Genetic Deficiencies

NBC
4 March 1987

1. Reagan relaunches himself
2. Iran Arms Scandal
3. US Spy jailed for life
4. Mil/Plane Crash
5. Airline takeover
6. Coal Barons feature
7. Football controversy
8. Commentary
9. AL/Textbook ruling
10. Stock Market Update
11. Venice/Gondolas

KEY

Denotes story carried on more than one network

Denotes story unique to that programme

Denotes story carried internationally

Fig. 1.1 (*cont.*) (b) 4 March 1987.

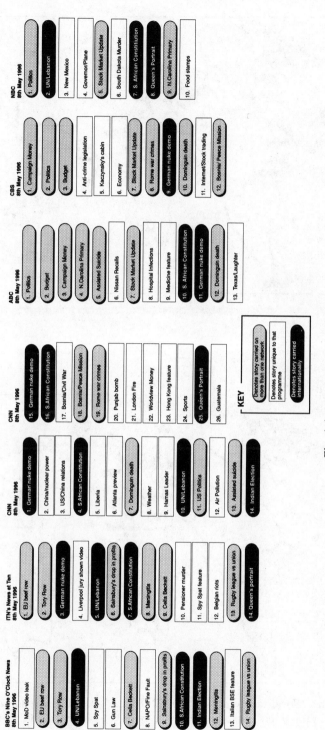

Fig. 1.1 (*cont*) (c) 8 May 1996.

BBC's Nine O'Clock News
8th May 1996
1. MoD video leak
2. EU beef row
3. Tory Row
4. UN/Lebanon
5. Spy Spat
6. Gun Law
7. Celia Beckett
8. NAPO/Fine Fault
9. Sainsbury's drop in profits
10. S.African Constitution
11. Indian Election
12. Meningitis
13. Italian BSE feature
14. Rugby league vs union

ITN's News at Ten
8th May 1996
1. EU beef row
2. Tory Row
3. German nuke demo
4. Liverpool jury shown video
5. UN/Lebanon
6. Sainsbury's drop in profits
7. S.African Constitution
8. Meningitis
9. Celia Beckett
10. Pensioner murder
11. Spy Spat feature
12. Belgian riots
13. Rugby league vs union
14. Queen's portrait

CNN
8th May 1996
1. German nuke demo
2. China/nuclear power
3. US/China relations
4. S.African Constitution
5. Liberia
6. Atlanta preview
7. Dominguin death
8. Weather
9. Hamas Leader
10. UN/Lebanon
11. US Politics
12. Air Pollution
13. Assisted suicide
14. Indian Election
15. German nuke demo
16. S.African Constitution
17. Bosnia/Civil War
18. Bosnia/Peace Mission
19. Rome war crimes
20. Punjab bomb
21. London Fire
22. Worldview Money
23. Hong Kong feature
24. Sports
25. Queen's Portrait
26. Guatemala

KEY
Denotes story carried on more than one network
Denotes story unique to that programme
Denotes story carried internationally

ABC
8th May 1996
1. Politics
2. Budget
3. Campaign Money
4. N.Carolina Primary
5. Assisted Suicide
6. Nissan Recalls
7. Stock Market Update
8. Hospital Infections
9. Medicine feature
10. S.African Constitution
11. German nuke demo
12. Dominguin death
13. Texas/Laughter

CBS
8th May 1996
1. Campaign Money
2. Politics
3. Budget
4. Anti-crime legislation
5. Kaczynsky's cabin
6. Economy
7. Stock Market Update
8. Rome war crimes
9. German nuke demo
10. Dominguin death
11. Internet/Stock trading
12. Bosnia/Peace Mission

NBC
8th May 1996
1. Politics
2. UN/Lebanon
3. New Mexico
4. Governor/Plane
5. Stock Market Update
6. South Dakota Murder
7. S. African Constitution
8. Queen's Portrait
9. N.Carolina Primary
10. Food stamps

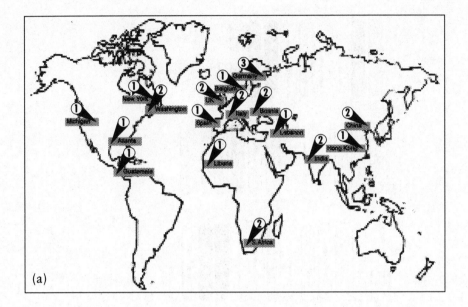

(a)

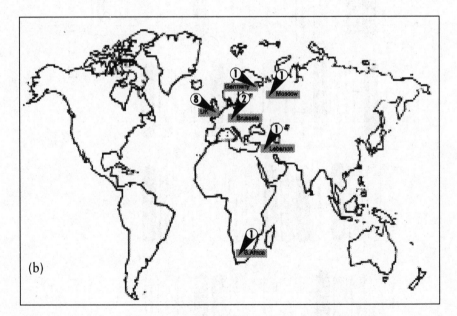

(b)

Fig. 1.2 The World according to (a) CNN and (b) ITN (*News at Ten*).
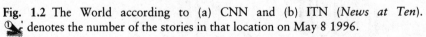 denotes the number of the stories in that location on May 8 1996.

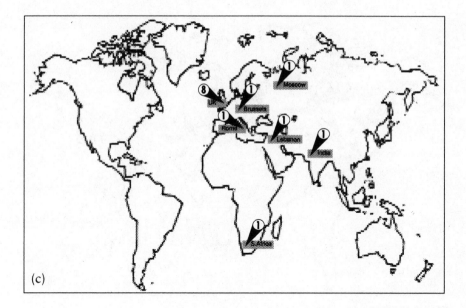

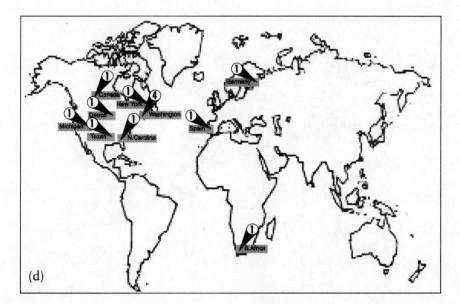

Fig. 1.2 (*cont.*) The World according to (c) the BBC (*Nine O'Clock News*) and (d) ABC on May 8 1996.

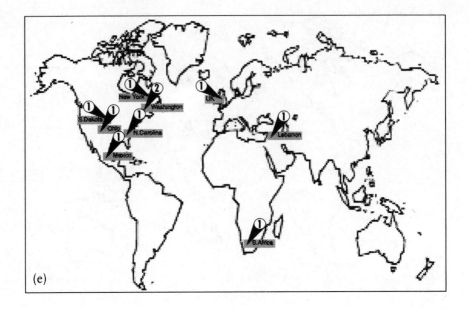

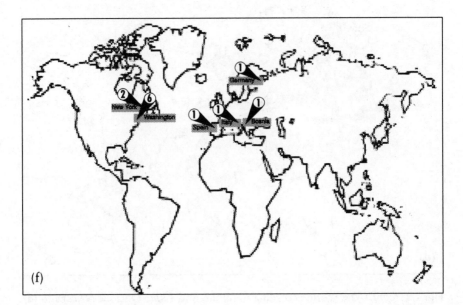

Fig. 1.2 (cont.) The World according to (e) NBC and (f) CBS on 8 May 1996.

Events in Moscow seen from London

As the dramatic events of the Moscow coup attempt in August 1991 drew to a climax, things were far from clear. Events were not happening in convenient range of CNN's rooftop camera. At the BBC in London, anchor Anna Ford and Foreign Affairs Correspondent Brian Hanrahan prepared to do the *One O'Clock News* on 21 August, the third day of the coup. Lunchtime bulletins are far from tranquil even in normal times. Satellite feeds are often booked for the period just before the programme, with packages often arriving (or not) after transmission has begun. Given the time difference and the fact that many of the events of the time took place in the streets at night, there would have been certain congestion on the satellite links out of Moscow that morning. This fluidity was signalled by the first words of the bulletin: 'Reports are coming in'. Rather than the normal lead package, the first item was a discussion between Ford and Hanrahan, the kind that would normally end a bulletin. It was a sure sign that some reports hadn't come in and that others had been left behind by events. Hanrahan relayed a number of reports from Tass and other sources and discussed possibilities with Ford. A conventional ENG package from reporter Martin Sixsmith in Moscow followed, including footage shot earlier that morning and the night before. A round-up of events in various Soviet republics led to a live two-way with John Simpson in Moscow. Like London, he began with the warning 'We've just been getting reports' and related some of the same stories that London had already reported about tanks leaving the city. To this he added that there were reports of limousines making their way to the internal airport. A second ENG package, voiced by David Shukman in London, followed in which he discussed the attack the night before on the Russian Parliament and outlined how British expert Carrie Schofield had telephoned Moscow from the BBC in London and spoken with a Russian commander who told her of the withdrawal of his forces. Pictures from Moscow showed that indeed tanks were on the move. A live two-way with a Glasgow University academic provided comment and analysis until it was interrupted by the arrival of further pictures of military vehicles in the streets of Moscow, which were discussed by the studio team as they were played out. Hanrahan spoke of his own experience in the Russian capital, which added authority to the running commentary, and when a brief shot of a black limousine moving slowly down a highway caught his attention he was able, as a former Moscow Correspondent, to interpret its significance. Large black Zil limousines full of party officials normally speed down the centre of the highway, and to see one virtually crawling told the whole story of the coup in one emblematic shot. The picture was there, but it still needed comment as the coup crumbled before viewers' eyes.

This was television news at its best, live, studio-based reporting that depended for its impact on a back-at-base perspective, itself informed by knowledge arising from years of on-the-ground experience. Incoming picture feeds mean literally nothing unless they can be interpreted properly. This analysis included a two-way with an academic commentator and made predictions subsequently proved accurate. The concentration of skill and resources into a fixed-point bulletin created a back-at-base synthesis impossible from any reporter in the field. None of the bulletin was live from the scene and some recorded material was hours old, but the story was told clearly, calmly and dramatically. It was also, as we know in retrospect, told accurately. The caution shown was justifiable under the circumstances, but did not stand in the way of the reporting of what have turned out to be historic events.

Somalia

Few Americans would have known or cared much about Somalia in December 1992 when George Bush's parting attempt to restore hope burst onto their screens. Marines came ashore to find neither hostile warlords nor grateful Somalis, but a fully deployed international media circus awaiting them on the beaches. One hundred still and video photographers turned the amphibious landing into a photo opportunity. ABC had 65 people present and NBC had freighted in half a ton of gear (Pilkington, 1993, p. 20), while CBS had five times as much kit and a rollerblading reporter (Rosenblum, 1993, p. 29) who hired two trucks full of gunmen to protect him so he could exercise safely in the streets of Mogadishu (Glaister, 1996, p. 17). Months later, with hope far from restored and the prospect of a military quagmire looming, pictures of a dead GI being dragged through those same streets shifted American public opinion overnight (Pringle, 1993, p. 21). The horrifying pictures were shot by Reuters Television's Somali driver who had been quickly trained when the agency pulled out after the death of three staff. American public opinion and policy were being swayed by television material recorded on an amateur camcorder. Only eight journalists remained in Mogadishu to confirm the story, for the media circus had moved on and, in the words of one commentator:

> despite the state-of-the-art technology, despite the satellite links and instant commentary, the Western viewing public will be as ignorant of the Somali people and the causes of their tragedy as they were when the whole sorry charade began (Pringle, 1993, p. 21).

When American troops were sent to Haiti, President Clinton had to ask CNN and the networks not to go there first, but they had already been deployed. 'When we landed we saw a bunch of press, which was good' said a young sergeant on CNN. 'I assumed, if the press was here, the enemy probably wasn't' (Banks-Smith, 1994, p. 24). Such media events are a long way from the 1958 American landing in Beirut which had been filmed by a local dentist (Cox, 1995, p. 139).

Bosnia: a faraway place of which we know nothing?

There were 700 reporters in Sarajevo for the expiry of the ultimatum for Serb withdrawal. The city had substantial broadcasting facilities as a result of the 1984 Winter Olympics, and reporters lined up to do live two-ways from the roof of the television station. Peter Arnett did 14 live shots for CNN in one day, with no more than 40 minutes in between to witness anything (Bell, 1995, p. 208). In terms of broadcasting infrastructure and coverage, Sarajevo was a long way from a third world story like Rwanda in the summer of 1994 when portable satellite equipment was sent in only when it was decided that the story had got big enough. The tragic dissolution of Yugoslavia didn't start at the top of the news agenda, however, or even within handy reach of a major broadcasting installation. Events began as early as April 1987 when the then unknown Serbian politician Slobodan Milosevic visited Kosovo to reassure Serbs in the area that they would be protected from the majority ethnic Albanians (Vulliamy, 1994, p. 51). In October of 1988 all three American networks ran pieces on the possibility of ethnic unrest in the former Yugoslavia, with NBC and ABC returning to the story the next spring. BBC World Service reporter Misha Gleny reported in 1990 that trouble was brewing and was told by his editors that he was exaggerating (Keating, 1993, p. 15). On 6 April 1992, when snipers shot 11 demonstrators in Sarajevo and the Bosnian conflict began in earnest, NBC didn't carry the story.

Even after the regular shelling of Sarajevo began on 21 April 1992 and when it was clear that a big story was breaking, journalists arrived slowly. In the summer of 1992 an American network anchor, introducing a live two-way, announced that their reporter was 'the only Western journalist in Sarajevo'. The veteran correspondent blushed almost imperceptibly, a fact noted by the two American print journalists and the British radio reporter watching from the next room in the television centre. The anchor in question may have genuinely believed his words to be true but this was a clear case of the rhetoric of live exclusivity that infects so much television news.

A British reporter working in the former Yugoslavia, about the same time, returned to Sarajevo to find a television colleague and his crew away on a story. Wishing to avoid any undue duplication in the dangerous circumstances, he phoned the London desk to ask what his colleague had been doing in his absence. 'Great stuff', came the reply. 'Yes, but what?' asked the reporter. 'Great stuff', came the echo from the desk-bound editor, for London simply couldn't remember the details of the marvellous output obtained at great risk. If those making the news don't often get much feel for it what chance has the viewer? The constant flow of events that constitute the news can overwhelm even the professional, as it apparently did one NBC assignment editor who couldn't tell a questioner which countries bordered on the former Yugoslavia even though he regularly sent staff there

(Kent, 1996, p. 204). As with Vietnam, too much reporting may have made for too little understanding. Nevertheless, out of the constant flow, certain images appear which have become emblematic, telling hard truths which may themselves in turn affect events.

On ITN's *Lunchtime News* on 7 August 1992 a report from former Yugoslavia ended with credit being given to the cameraman, the sound recordist and the producer who had collaborated with reporter Penny Marshall in an exclusive story about Serbian concentration camps. Two days earlier the ITN team, together with *The Guardian* reporter Ed Vulliamy, had been allowed into Omarska to reveal horrors not seen in Europe since 1945. Writing some years after the event, Ed Vulliamy points out that the story of the camps had been in circulation for some months and had been reported in *Newsday* as early as 19 July that year. Various officials in the UN, the Red Cross and the American State Department had knowledge of the camps long before these first newspaper reports appeared (Vulliamy, 1996, p. 16). Vulliamy, Marshall, producer Ian William and the crew didn't roam the countryside looking for latter-day Dachau's. They used great journalistic skill and negotiated access to see and report that the unthinkable was happening (Vulliamy, 1994, pp. 98–117). Afterwards they were taunted by the Bosnian Serb leader Nikola Koljevic:

> Took a long time didn't it? All that happening so near Venice! All you people could think about was poor multicultural Sarajevo. None of you ever had your holidays in Trnopolje did you? No Winter Olympics in Omarska! (Vulliamy, 1996, p. 16).

Physical access and the skills required to acquire it are still more fundamental to the journalistic process than any technology. The story took two days to reach the screens, but was worth 10 000 live two-ways.

As events in former Yugoslavia progressed, the media spotlight came to focus more intensely and the communications infrastructure developed further. In September 1995, BBC reporter Clarence Mitchell reported live on breakfast television from the Bosnian Serb capital of Pale. This in itself was nothing remarkable, but the link was used for more than interviewing reporters in the field. Mitchell explained that journalists, receiving incoming information on their satellite link, were able to tell Serb officials what NATO was saying about the cruise missile strikes launched against them (BBC1, 0710). In time, covering the fragile peace was to become so routine that the CBS office in Tuzla could be reached on a telephone extension of their London bureau (Hurt, 1996, p. 22). With American troops on the ground, the story became more than an incomprehensible foreign event and CBS anchored their main news from Tuzla.

The duration of the war of the Yugoslavian dissolution has meant that the vast flow of coverage has been difficult to analyse. The British Film Institute has helped in this task, sponsoring first a conference and then a comparative study of output, pointing out the unique multidimensional nature of the coverage when compared with the relatively simple model of the Gulf War (Gow *et al.*, 1996). Television itself has provided a range of documentary and comment both on the war itself (*The death of Yugoslavia*, BBC2, September 1995) and on the issues raised by the media coverage (*Tales from Sarajevo*, BBC2, January 1993). From this flow interesting material has emerged.

Late one night, during the long Bosnian war, *Euronews* broadcast a seven-minute item which explained the historical background to the crisis. Events such as the assassination in Sarajevo of Archduke Ferdinand, an event which sparked off the First World War, were outlined and set in context. This act by a Serb nationalist was only part of the discussion of the powder keg of the Balkans. Events in the Second World War were also related, and the German recognition of Croatian independence as seen in its proper perspective. The long-forgotten Ottoman empire and its treatment of its conquered subjects was discussed. Seven minutes long and not a single 'talking-head' interview was seen in the piece. A rolling news service with hours to fill was using the time to its advantage. Not padding live two-ways or engaging in long studio discussions, *Euronews* was giving viewers something traditional news did not, so that the next time they saw picures of yet another shelling they would at least know the difference between a Serb and a Croat.

O.J. Simpson and helicopter journalism

Everyone saw the white bronco on the freeway (17 June 1994), whether live on CNN and other networks, endlessly repeated throughout following days or on recordings sold in supermarkets. The coverage became a form of inter-active television, yet another example of howl round, as people watching the chase on television phoned into the radio station O.J. was supposedly listening to on the car radio. Across North America live television coverage of the chase took over the airwaves as a squadron of helicopters followed the pursuit. In newsrooms staff stood transfixed in front of monitors dis-cussing what they would do if O.J. got out of the Bronco, held the gun to his head and committed suicide on live television. Who would cut away knowing that the opposition might not? Years later, at an international con-ference, a CBC editor had the temerity to question the decision to take over the main networks when specialist news channels were covering the story. She was practically laughed out of the building. It was an important story, insisted one network journalist. It must have been because it was still being discussed such a long time afterward. 'We ran it because it was important and it was important because we ran it', was effectively the argument.

Of the millions who saw the prime-time chase, many may not have seen coverage carried earlier the same day on CNN. In the period between Simpson's disappearance and the discovery of the Bronco, KCAL, KTTV and KLTA fed CNN material from Los Angeles. Some came from outside the home where the murders had taken place days before. KLTA's 5Live skycam hovered above the Brentwood condominium where the police had been called by the victim's father. Over shots of the building and a van parked behind it, viewers heard the helicopter-based reporter:

> We don't know what this van is and I may have jumped to cor·clusions. . . . It is difficult for us from the helicopter as we have no contact with the ground at this point to get any definitive information as to what is going on.

Once again the privileged eyewitness professional reporting live from a technologically enabled unique point of view is at a loss to tell us what is happening as he is out of contact with base. Some minutes later, KTLA's studio team, speaking over the helicopter shots of the same van, remark to each other and the viewers:

> *Anchor one.* That tan van is certainly an intriguing element. Someone went out of there and went into the house.

> *Anchor two.* It looks like the County coroner's van. Apologies for overreacting. It certainly resembles it. They could be laying carpet in the town house next door, you don't know. You don't know exactly what that's all about. There was a lot of attention paid to the van as it pulled up. You've been on these scenes a lot too Stan. I know that every time some little titbit of information or something comes rolling in as a reporter you immediately respond therefore you have a tendency to react to things on a moment's notice, of course we are live here, so that's what we are doing.

Of course, the culprit was elsewhere and the helicopters eventually found him, and O.J. was brought to trial.

The O.J. Simpson trial was a major media event reported by over 1000 journalists reporting via 121 video paths including 14 satellite uplinks. The logistics included 80 miles of sound and vision cable, 650 phone lines and 10 portable toilets (*International Broadcasting*, 1995, p. 19). When the verdict was announced on 3 October 1995, 21 channels in New York City alone went live to Los Angeles for the result. The time difference meant that the story broke in the middle of the British early evening bulletins. ITN linked to Bill Neely who was outside the courthouse holding a small portable television in his hand so he could watch the result himself, just as viewers would. His experience was no different from theirs and when the verdict was actually announced ITN did not go back to their location reporter. The BBC carried the verdict live in their bulletin, only going to the scene for the actual announcement and then linking afterwards with a location reporter before running a substantial background piece. Back in Los Angeles, no riots broke out outside the courtroom, but CNN had blanket coverage from a variety of locations. The helicopters flew, and in an uncanny echo of the beginning of the long story, CNN and Sky News viewers saw a white car followed along the freeway from on high. The gavel-to-gavel coverage of the trial, which had been a boon to rolling news services as a very cheap way of filling the hours and paying for such expensive adventures as the Gulf War, was over. However, coverage did not end with the verdict and for weeks afterwards lawyers from both sides, and certain jurors, could be seen telling their story on CNN's *Larry King Live*. The big interview, however, was missing until an NBC executive, a golfing partner of Simpson, arranged for him to tell all to Tom Brokaw. This exclusive was not to be, however, as Simpson's lawyers advised against such exposure. As one, hardly disinterested, ex-NBC employee remarked of the chain of events, 'The News Division had come a long way from the Berlin Wall and Tiananmen Square. A long way down' (Kent, 1996, p. 290).

Oklahoma City

The tragic events of 19 April 1995 when a large bomb exploded outside a federal building in Oklahoma City were reputedly first reported on the Internet by a man in a building near the scene. Most of the public, however, depended on more orthodox sources. Channel Four in Oklahoma City went on a roll. Their live coverage was fed to other services and could be picked up directly by amateur satellite watchers in England tuning in to the Brightstar feed. This material tells us much about the strengths and weaknesses of such rolling coverage. Over pictures described as 'unedited video from our live truck', viewers were warned by the out-of-vision anchor, 'there will be blood' and that they should keep children away from the television. Basically, they did not know what they were about to see and warned viewers to that effect. At one point, the anchor described a shot of the damaged building as being like Beirut. Nevertheless, viewers were told there were no fatalities. It was accurately pointed out that it was the second anniversary of Waco and that some of the federal agents who were involved in that event had their offices in the federal building in question. The mixture of live and unedited recorded video from various locations gave a general impression of chaos but told the viewer little of any substance. While the studio anchors did reasonably well with very little to go on, it is arguable whether there was any point in going live. The memorable still image of a fireman carrying a child from the ruins, which captured the event for all time, was only to emerge later as were the full horrific details of the many deaths.

Live from Greenpeace at sea

Everyone has seen dramatic footage of Greenpeace activists at sea, attempting to sabotage the dumping of waste or occupying the Brent Spar oil rig. The organisation is a master at getting such images into the news. Not only do they stage such events, but Greenpeace runs its own 24-hour operation with camera crews, editors and satellite dishes at sea. They spent £350 000 on equipment and links keeping Brent Spar on the screens. For the French nuclear tests in the South Pacific, Greenpeace took journalists on board but not camera personnel (Culf, 1995b, p. 5). However, no pictures shot by anyone emerged despite all the technology after the French navy confiscated the ships. On 10 July 1995 ITN reported French commandos boarding the *Rainbow Warrior*. The reporter was identified, both in the studio introduction and in her sign off, as being in New Zealand, where journalists in Auckland to cover the Commonwealth Conference suddenly found that their beat had become the whole South Pacific. Even with the Greenpeace dishes in protective custody, the coverage of the French tests was much advanced from those in the 1970s when telephone quality sound from Moruroa had to suffice (Schlesinger, 1987, p. 266). As the French military created an effective news blackout in the area, teams based in Tahiti were left without the big story and viewers suddenly heard about independence movements in French Polynesia that had previously escaped media attention. The nuclear tests slid down the agenda according to Greenpeace (Culf, 1995c, p. 3). This was an access issue, partly determined by technology, partly determined by the efforts of a pressure group keen to cover the story, but it was an issue ultimately decided by the French government's decision to deploy commandos rather than press officers. Access, whether to information, people or places, is essential to any journalism and this is inevitably controlled and rationed on certain terms. The contract that inevitably arises is a compromise between the public need to know and the official predisposition to control the flow of information in a way that is favourable to them. The French reaction, in this case, was absolute and effective.

Rabin assassination

The assassination of Israeli Prime Minister Yitzhak Rabin on 4 November 1995 was recorded on video, but those pictures did not emerge for some weeks. Rolling news nevertheless had the story in its own way. Reuters reported the shooting soon after 9 pm GMT and by 9:14 Sky News had a live two-way with Keith Graves answering questions from London. As he spoke, an out-of-vision figure told him they had heard an announcement on Israeli Forces Radio that the Prime Minister had died. Thus assisted by another media outlet, Sky beat CNN by some four minutes, but by 9:42

they had only an audio link when they next went to their reporter. Satellite traffic out of Israel would have been heavy in the hours following the shooting, and the consortium that Sky and CBS belong to used 155 minutes of satellite time that night and nearly seven hours the next day (Hurt, 1996, p. 28). NBC transmitted the pictures of the actual shooting on 19 December.

Let's have that exclusive, everyone else has it

In its Saturday magazine on 13 July 1996 *The Guardian* ran a story about global warming which previewed a conference about to be held in Geneva. Concrete evidence of the alleged warming was given in the form of the snout of the Trient glacier in the Swiss Alps which has retreated yearly, a fact marked by local people who have painted rocks to show each year's deterioration. Four days later the BBC ran the same story, taking full advantage of the visual possibilities of television to show viewers that global warming was a demonstrable fact. The next day ITN ran the story. One reading that could be put on the chain of events is that a specialist print journalist used his or her extensive knowledge and a few days walking in the mountains to illustrate his or her feature-length piece tied to the conference. A BBC reporter and crew followed, cutting in one hand and a map in the other. After transmission, the phone lines to ITN's Geneva hotel would have been white hot as London asked why their team had missed the story which indeed followed one day after the BBC. NBC and CNN both covered the conference and the issue, but there was no mention of the glacier in question. Were the British media chasing each others' tails? The location in question was in easy reach of Geneva, with most of the drive on excellent Swiss autoroutes; a road ran very high up into the mountains and a well-prepared long-distance footpath led almost to the glacier snout. Helicopters fly frequently in the Alps, supplying alpine huts in the summer. The whole story was a journalist's dream, especially if the conference organisers had provided a mini bus and driver and juggled the facility so everyone was happy. All three teams could have been taken, along with other journalists, to the story. Some form of embargo might have existed, with weekend papers allowed to use the story first. One organisation or the other might have broken the embargo, either deliberately or by accident. A team in the field may have filed their story with instructions that it be held until a certain date, but output editors may have simply ignored the embargo or not even known of it. Whichever scenario transpired, most British viewers saw an interesting item which graphically illustrated an undisputed fact. Few would have known that the story had had several incarnations and most wouldn't object to this diversity. Whether the retreat of one alpine glacier constitutes proof of global warming is yet another question.

A mission to explain

'Freedom and flowers for Benazir Bhutto' (BBC *Six O'Clock, News*, 9 September 1986).

'Brickbats and bouquets for Benazir Bhutto in Bradford' (BBC *Look North*, 1 December 1994).

The mission to explain seems to have led to an advancement in alliterative aptitude over the years, but does the audience in either case understand the complexities of Pakistani regional politics or grasp why Bhutto had been jailed and why she might be unpopular with Muslim groups in Britain?

And finally, global squirrels and news bunnies

Playing with her young children in a Vancouver park, a young mother was shocked when a squirrel, expecting to be fed, bit her two year old who had not offered the desired nuts. Upset by this, she complained that the sale of food for the express purpose of feeding the animals had led to them becoming aggressive and dangerous. This story entered the news chain, appearing in local papers, on the radio and eventually on the local CBC television news. The story was then taken up and transmitted nationally by the CBC. But it did not end there, as CNN took the story and broadcast it around the world. A local event had become global. There was another instance of the squirrel virus, some months later, in northern England, when a child was bitten in a school playground near Leeds, but this outbreak was confined to the local papers, Yorkshire television and BBC Leeds. For the time being, the global village had had enough of cheeky squirrels.

On the BBC's *Six O'Clock News* on 18 July 1986 the body language of anchor Nicholas Witchell indicated that he was less than happy presenting an item about Hoppy the rabbit escaping the mid-Western American heat by lounging in a tub of water wearing sunglasses: 'no longer a hot cross bunny because Hoppy is looking on the bunny side of life' were the words that came up on his autocue. The Birtian reforms at the BBC have, of course, banned bunnies and they now have their own news service in the multichannel world. A brave new world which has not been without its critics.

Hostile prints

Interestingly, today, extreme criticism of television news often comes from inside the journalistic profession itself. John Dugdale, writing in the Media

Guardian on the occasion of the 40th anniversary of ITN, judged that 'Broadcast news is its own worst enemy'. He compiles a long list of charges, characterising news as:

> Essentially radio with pictures . . . It's formulaic. Alongside the visual clichés are the stylistic ones . . . . It's incessantly repetitive . . . . It's fraudulent . . . . It's a lousy experience. Compared to other factual and fictional genres news as narrative structure is cussedly unsatisfying. Each show is miscellaneous and unpatterned, and yesterday's storylines disappear without explanation or resolution (1995, p. 12).

Other print journalists evince similar statements:

> For all its flash and promise, much of the coverage of news from beyond our borders is hardly much better than in the days of Morse code (Rosenblum, 1993, p. 2).

These sentiments were echoed when the television news coverage of the Oklahoma City bombing (19 April 1995) prompted television critic John Naughton to remark:

> We now have news round the clock, produced by organisations which have at their disposal unimaginable banks of information, visual material and expertise. And yet we seem to be getting less hard news and more vacuous speculation. I saw nothing on Wednesday night which would not have been more thoroughly – and more graphically – reported by a Fifties print journalist (Naughton, 1995, p. 25).

This otherwise astute observer is perhaps guilty of falling for the self-publicising rhetoric of certain television news organisations. One has to ask what such 'unimaginable banks of information' are likely to be, to see an instance of rhetoric triumphing over reality. The substantive point remains, however.

Journalistic sniping at television news is the most visible, and very often the most critical, form of comment on a subject which has generated a considerable body of literature from observers, most notably academics. The next chapter discusses academic research on news in an attempt to set the present and future state of the form in its proper theoretical context.

|2|

Theories of news production, from 'Mr Gates' to market-driven journalism

Television news might at first sight appear to be a straightforward subject of study. The ephemeral result of daily industrial production under great time pressure, news is but one of the many disposable artefacts of modern mass culture. Studying it would appear to be far simpler than, say, decoding *Finnegan's wake*, unravelling the mysteries of human consciousness or charting the fate of the modern family. Even the most cursory literature review of academic research, however, reveals a myriad of conflicting methodologies and diverse final conclusions. Clearly it is possible to study various aspects of television news and to arrive at diverse theoretical conclusions as a result. News has been extensively studied and heavily theorised, which is not surprising considering its perceived importance as the locus where relations between the state and the media are most often played out, particularly in times of crisis, such as war, industrial disputes and civil unrest. Crime and deviance are given considerable attention by the electronic media, which thus play a central role in shaping public attitudes. News is one of the starting points of the public information equation, providing an essential forum for an informed citizenry in a democratic society with the routine electoral process and long-term democratic evolution of the contemporary world depending in part on healthy, properly functioning news media. Television news is the means by which people increasingly get their information about the world and as such reputedly sets the public agenda. It needs therefore to be examined carefully and to be understood fully.

Academic hyperactivity in the field over a period of nearly half a century has created a 'contested field of theory' (Cottle, 1993, p. 2), which is not surprising given the nature of the beast under study:

> media texts are produced under determinant ideological, institutional, commercial, technological, statutory and professional conditions and arrangements, all of which inform the production, organisation and

delivery of media texts. These texts do not escape the condition of their production, and inevitably bear the traces of their professionally and socially informed construction (p. 7).

Looking thoroughly at one of the above aspects alone would be difficult enough. This situation is further complicated as there are by now several generations of examination, layered accretions of theory, among the different approaches scrutinising any one of the above categories. Equally, the context of television news has changed from a mass communications model to the diverse multichannel media ecology of today and, as this context evolves and with it content, so too must the theory.

One might ask why bother with theory at all? Theory is often seen as the opposite of practice, which can too easily be caricatured as abstract speculation which leaves behind its real world starting point. It should instead be the outcome of reflection on close observations which attempts to understand the studied phenomenon. Theory should be used 'to ferret out the unapparent import of things' (Geertz, 1993, p. 26); to 'make the invisible visible' (Blumler and Gurevitch, 1995, p. 76) and hence to aid understanding; in short, to explain. Academic fashion and publishing economics have led in recent years to a shift towards excessively theoretical work which often gives little evidence of any real world starting point. Too often this tendency has stood in the way of any meaningful dialogue between media academics and practitioners, with the latter so put off by excessive theorising that they take no part in debates to which they have much to contribute and from which they might themselves learn.

There is a need in some way to offer something of an overview of academic research and theorising by way of framing this particular study. It is crucial that such theory is not simply speculation on the subject in question, but rather that it grows from close contact with the day-to-day reality of television news itself. In this regard the discussion that follows will not so much offer answers as pose a series of questions that the reader might bear in mind when reading this study and when watching television news output.

Perspectives, unique and otherwise

One of the first academic studies of the television coverage of a news event was the now classic work by Lang and Lang (1953) which focused on General Douglas MacArthur's visit to Chicago on 26–27 April 1951. On this occasion the television stations of the city cooperated to produce outside broadcast (television remote) coverage of the parade. The Langs' research based itself on the contrast between the actually recorded experience of participant observers on the scene, on the one hand, and the picture which a video viewer received by way of the television screen and the way in which the event was interpreted, magnified, and took on added significance on the other (Lang and Lang, 1953, p. 187).

The research pointed to notable discrepancies between the experience of trained participant observers in the street and the televised version of events, with concern being expressed about 'how the picture of the events was shaped by selection, emphasis, and suggested inferences which fitted into the already existing pattern of expectations' (p. 188). The key finding, that television offered a perspective different from that of the eyewitness, perhaps seems rather obvious today. The television viewer at home watching an outside broadcast event clearly has a better overview than the streetside observer. Crucially, however, these increased points of view are themselves selected and commented upon. This commentary was seen to have the effect of dramatising the event in order to fulfil the expectations created around it by the media themselves. Included in this was a form of self-publicising rhetoric frequently describing the 'unique co-operative effort of TV' (p. 192) required to arrange the coverage. This rhetoric culminated at one point in a crescendo of mediacentric commentary:

the General now enters his car. This is the focal point where all the newsreels . . . frankly in 25 years of covering the news, we have never seen as many newsreels gathered at one spot. One, two, three, four, five, six. At least eight cars with newsreels rigged on top of them, taking a picture that will be carried over the entire world, over the Chicagoland area by the combined network of these TV stations of Chicago, which have combined for this great occasion and for the solemn occasion which you just witnessed (p. 194).

The result was television coverage which gave 'a very specific perspective which contrasted with that of direct observation' (p. 193). The Langs saw this negatively, when in fact each perspective had its own advantages. As one member of the public observed tellingly: 'I bet my wife saw it much better over TV' (p. 195). For the researchers, however, the conclusions were clear:

assumed reportorial accuracy is far from automatic. Every camera selects, and thereby leaves the unseen part of the subject open to suggestion and inference. The gaps are usually filled in by a commentator. In addition the process directs action and attention to itself (p. 195).

The foregrounding of the very activity of coverage is something that seems to have remained constant to this day, though there were clearly very different circumstances operating over 40 years ago. The then infant medium of television had a need to establish itself and attract viewers and hence was perhaps inclined to overdramatise events in its attempt to increase its audience: 'a drama it had to be, even at the expense of reality' (p. 196). The coverage itself was an event requiring the extensive deployment of hi-tech equipment. The commitment of these expensive and inflexible technical resources, necessarily well in advance and well publicised, meant that once it had been decided to cover the visit, the story had to be used and it would be difficult then to say that the said event was not very interesting after all. Such logistical considerations still apply today, with the decision to commit expensive resources often leading to their automatic use almost regardless of the value of the material thus covered.

The circumstances of broadcasting output have changed considerably since the early 1950s. The Chicago event would have been broadcast by all the cooperating channels, interrupting normal programming and taking over the airwaves. Today, media attention would take a more diverse form. Dedicated news channels would have the airtime to cover such an event if they chose, while news services transmitted on general programming channels would probably devote, at maximum, five minutes to the story. In competitive markets, local stations might make more of such an event, but it would, in any case, be less of an occasion than the MacArthur day broadcast. The Gulf War commander General Norman Schwarzkopf received a similar kind of attention on his return, being given both a Washington parade and the traditional New York ticker tape parade. The New York event on 10 June 1991 led the network news bulletins that evening, with CBS devoting a substantial 4 minutes and 30 seconds to the story, ABC 3 minutes and NBC 2 minutes and 10 seconds, but the world did not stop and the airwaves were not cleared for the returning hero who admittedly was not in conflict with his President.

The Langs' conclusion from their study was basically pessimistic: 'A general characteristic of the TV presentation was that the field of vision of the viewer was enlarged while, at the same time, the context in which these events could be interpreted was less clear' (p. 197). Television's 'unique perspective' was less than ideal, leaving the viewer 'completely at the mercy of the instrument of his perceptions' (p. 197). In this view, a real world event mediated by television meant increased vision for the audience, but decreased understanding.

This assertion assumes that the viewer uncritically accepts the vision and particularly the commentary offered. This might have been more likely to have been the case in 1951 than today. In the case studied, the alternative to the view offered by the television coverage was no vision at all for the viewer at home. For the eyewitness the very limited point of view available in the crowd was certainly very different from that offered by television, but it did not necessarily have greater status. In events unfolding over time and space, such as parades and races, television creates a unique perspective by adding a chain of viewpoints which constitute an overview impossible otherwise. This view, however, is not definitive for it has its own limitations. When the first naive assumption that the camera never lies is removed, it is important to understand that it does not automatically follow that the camera always lies. In fact it tells its own truth, from its own perspective, and the viewer needs to know what that is and allow for it, to take what it offers, all the while remaining fully aware of what it does not or cannot provide.

In the Langs' research there were in fact three accounts of the event: the television version, that of the eyewitness public and that of the social science researchers. Each of these had their own perspective on the event, none of them definitive. Great care was taken to control for personal factors in the research observations, as stated in this footnote:

> Analysis of personal data sheets, filled out by participants prior to MacArthur Day, revealed that 'objectivity' in observation was not related to political opinion held, papers and periodicals subscribed to, and previous exposure to radio and TV coverage of MacArthur's homecoming. The significant factor in evaluating the reports for individual or deviant interpretation was found to reside in the degree to which individual observers were committed to scientific and objective procedures. Our observers were all advanced students in the social sciences (Lang and Lang, 1953, p. 269).

Objectivity was offered as a research ideal which would guarantee the accuracy of the findings. The sought-after objectivity on the part of observers was seen as coming from professional values, held in spite of personal attitudes and opinions. Interestingly, this interplay of personal and professional values and the evocation of objectivity as a professional goal was to be the focus of much subsequent academic research on the news media.

Selectivity, bias and the personal realm

In another classic ground-breaking study, David Manning White, writing in 1950 (reprinted in Dexter and White, 1964), reported the means by which an editor selected which wire service stories to use in a mid-Western American newspaper. This editor, 'Mr Gates', was a man in his middle 40s with 25 years' experience both as a reporter and copy editor, whose job was to fill the front pages from the vast mountain of copy available to him from three news agencies. In White's study 'Mr Gates' chose to print about one-tenth of the material at his disposal. Every night after his paper had 'gone to bed', he would spend up to two hours recording his reasons for rejecting stories. Analysis of this data led White 'to begin to understand how highly subjective, how reliant upon value-judgements based on the "gatekeepers'" own set of experiences, attitudes and expectations the communication of "news" really is' (p. 165). Explanations such as 'He's too Red' (one case), 'propaganda' (16 cases), 'Don't care for suicides' were advanced as evidence of this subjectivity. A large number of stories (168 cases), however, were rejected as there was no space for them (p. 165), while others were judged on the quality of writing (p. 169) and on the basis that 'Sensationalism and insinuation seemed to be avoided consistently' (p. 169). 'Mr Gates' also made reference (when asked) to his audience: 'I believe that they are all entitled to news that pleases them (stories involving their thinking and activity) and news that informs them of what is going on in the world' (p. 170). On the effect of his own prejudices on selection 'Mr Gates' wrote:

> I have few prejudices, built-in or otherwise, and there is little I can do about them. I dislike Truman's economics, daylight saving time and warm beer, but I go ahead using stories about them and other matters if I feel there is nothing more important to give space to. I am also prejudiced against a publicity-seeking minority with headquarters in Rome, and I don't help them a lot (p. 170).

At this distance one can detect a slight hint of irony, with the journalist sending himself and his researchers up a bit, but more importantly he also seems to be stating overriding professional and institutional values when he claims: 'My other preferences are for stories well-wrapped and tailored to suit our needs (or ones slanted to conform to our editorial policies)' (p. 170). As well as evoking the culture of his paper, 'Mr Gates' also replies to one of the researcher's inquiries by articulating a different professional standard: 'the only tests of subject matter or way of writing I am aware of when making a selection involve clarity, conciseness and angle' (p. 171). 'Mr Gates' certainly articulated certain personal values that might be expected from a man born before 1910 and who was speaking in 1949 mid-Western America, but he also evoked certain technical professional issues, his audience's interests and his paper's editorial line. His reasons for his choices were perhaps more complex than White concluded. Certainly, subsequent scholars have been ambivalent about the work: 'its essential naivety is not difficult to identify or pillory . . . but the research was easy to conduct, conceptually simple, readily quantifiable, and not without a useful conclusion, that news production was often mechanical, routine, passive and systematic' (Golding and Elliott, 1979, p. 12).

The result of this research was that public information was seen to be determined by editorial gatekeepers who chose what news to use, with this selection procedure inevitably being a reflection of the personal background and beliefs of those individuals. This grounding of the editorial process in the realm of the personal ignores the wider organisational context of newsmaking, and subsequent research has certainly focused attention elsewhere, but 'Mr Gates' should not be forgotten and one may today find instances where this model still applies. A violent male-on-male attack described by one local television station in northern England as a 'serious sexual assault' was less euphemistically called 'rape' by its competitor news programme. Remarking on this seeming difference in house style to a newsroom insider, I was told that the news editor in question was openly gay and had strong views on the subject of male rape, believing that such cases should be more openly reported. Both competing stations had run the story, so this was not a selection issue, but instead one of emphasis and detail, with personal factors clearly entering the news-making process. Whether this intervention compromises the quality of the journalism is another issue, but this case serves to illustrate in a small way that the lessons learnt from 'Mr Gates' are still in some part pertinent today. A senior British journalist with experience of print and broadcast media at a senior management level who has subsequently become an academic certainly concurs: 'Journalists may often be unaware of the way their own social or personal backgrounds affect their judgements or their phrasing' (Hetherington, 1985, p. 21).

The changing media ecology from the days of 'Mr Gates' working on a mid-Western daily newspaper with a local circulation of 30 000, to the age of global television news services which are themselves part of enormous corporate concerns, would seem, on the surface, to point away from the individual and towards the organisation and other wider contexts. However, the increased diversity of media outlets, in part technologically enabled, may have the effect of shifting significance back onto the individual. A small handful of people can now programme and transmit a cable or satellite channel, selecting and commissioning material from third-party producers, and it is not unknown for small local radio stations to have a 'rip-and-read' news service, with one person creating and presenting short regular bulletins from agency material without leaving the building. Whether such contemporary situations support the gatekeeper analysis would need detailed research.

Such a personal perspective might have been applied to CNN's Peter Arnett during the Gulf War. Did the fact that Arnett was not a native born American make any difference to his view of events? Certainly he was to come under attack on personal grounds, including reference to his marriage into a Vietnamese family (MacGregor, 1993, p. 29). Of course, neither Arnett nor 'Mr Gates' are representative cases, and any sensible researcher would insist on studying more than a few selected individuals. One only has to imagine a newsroom full of 'Mr Gates's to see a major problem with the research, for such an organisation could not function unless all the individuals were identical in their beliefs or entirely autonomous in their actions.

News is what newspeople make it

A subsequent study with a wider sample (Gieber, 1956; 1964) effectively contradicted White's findings based on 'Mr Gates', locating the core of the selection procedure elsewhere from the realm of 'personal evaluations'. Starting from the assumption that 'news is what newspapermen make it', Gieber laments 'the paucity of literature on the newsgathering process' (Gieber, 1964, pp. 173–4) and attempts to work 'within the walls of the newsroom' (p. 173), using 'the techniques of the depth interview and participant observation' (p. 174). His conclusions point away from subjectivity as a determining factor. The 16 editors studied exhibited a remarkable, even predictable, consistency in selection, while differing in their explanations (p. 175). Nevertheless:

> Common to all the telegraph editors were the pressures exerted by the reality of the newsroom bureaucratic structure and its operation. The most powerful factor was not the evaluative nature of news, but the pressures of getting the copy into the newspaper; the telegraph editor was preoccupied with the mechanical pressures of his work rather than the social meanings and impact of the news. His personal evaluations rarely entered into his selection process; the values of his employer were an accepted part of the newsroom environment.
> In short, the telegraph editor was 'task oriented;' he was concerned with goals of production, bureaucratic routine and interpersonal relations within the newsroom (p. 175).

In this view there is still a process of choice, but its essence is to be found more in routine and the professional relationships inside a news organisation than in individual, personal value judgements.

Gieber also studied reporters and the dynamics of covering civil rights stories in the late 1950s. In this study he found that 'the reporters, with few exceptions, *personally* held the same values as the sources, but publicly did not so convey them' (p. 177), instead 'they appeared to be oriented primarily to problems of the craft and the newsroom' (p. 177) and at times were prevented from reporting as they wished:

> They charge that their employers did not allow them sufficient time to write full reports, often because they were preoccupied with a frantic gathering of trivia, failing to distinguish items of broader social significance. The reporters could, then, only discuss these issues among themselves and, in a few instances, write on them for magazines of small circulation (pp. 177–8).

This research pointed to a much more complicated dynamic than that offered by the simple gatekeeping model personified in 'Mr Gates'. Gieber pointed to the need for more work, but felt himself able to make one important generalisation: 'News does not have an independent existence; news is a product of men who are members of a newsgathering (or news originating) bureaucracy' (p. 180). Subjectivity is a factor, but 'the reporter's individuality is strongly tempered by extrapersonal factors' (p. 180).

Certainly, anyone who has ever worked in a newsroom will tell you that news values are 'in the air' and it is an essential part of the professional development of any young journalist to acquire a version of the same skills and values possessed by older colleagues. In this view the shared professional aim of creating news output under great pressure for the most part supersedes personal viewpoints. One senior television news editor spoken to for this study remarked that even his own family could not discern what his personal views were. Here objectivity becomes a sought-after professional goal, part of the self-image of certain journalists. Such an ideal may be the result of well-institutionalised professionals conventionally adopting organisational aims or indeed the very opposite; a defence against pressures of various kinds either from within or without news organisations. Interfering proprietors and proactive editors can bring pressure to bear on individual journalists, as can press officers, politicians, their spin doctors and public relations people. It is a matter of professional pride with many journalists that neither these diverse forces nor personal preferences are allowed to dominate. This articulation of objectivity has been styled a 'strategic ritual' by Gaye Tuchman (1972), who characterises it as a protective device against external attack (p. 661). Interestingly, Tuchman (1972, p. 677), quoting Gouldner, also speaks of 'sociological objectivity as *strategic ritual*' (emphasis in original), an observation which could be applied to the footnote of the Langs quoted above, where their evocation of 'scientific and objective procedures' and their statement of the advanced status of their observers can be seen as a pre-emptive defence against attack on methodological grounds. For social scientists and journalists alike, objectivity becomes a defence against any questioning of their reports. Suggestions that they are creating a social construction, a man-made product, are almost always seen by journalists as a criticism of their professional abilities rather than an explanation of what they do.

The institutionalisation process whereby journalists are first recruited, then trained and by which they advance their careers is hard to chart, but it is clearly important. Professional values are trained in by a variety of subtle formal and informal processes and, generally speaking, as in other professions, atypical mavericks don't advance. An important element in this process is what might be called intellectual metabolic rate. Certain temperaments thrive in the pressure-cooker environment of news production where the daily need to make quick judgements and to keep one's nerve leaves no room for the reflective, the self-doubter or the perfectionist. The competitive ethos that manifests itself in relations with other news organisations also permeates the internal working environment, and those who excel in this respect very often advance. There is certainly scope for the psychological study of news professionals and no doubt much can be said about the personality types attracted to and selected by the profession, although one can hardly imagine the archetypal hard-bitten hack (if indeed such a creature actually exists) agreeing to cooperate with such psychological profiling. Interestingly, however, the only journalists to refuse to do interviews for this study actually conform in some part, in their public persona at least, to that stereotype.

One such psychological study has been undertaken by Lichter *et al.* in their 1986 study, *The media elite*. Using thematic apperception tests

(TATS), they identified certain characteristics across their sample. They found that journalists hold an ambiguous relationship with power, being fascinated with it yet still being very sceptical, particularly about those that exercise it. Ambivalence was also evident in other aspects of the journalistic personality, which appeared to be at once narcissistic and lacking in high levels of achievement motivation, with a reduced capacity for intimacy (p. 130). This duality enabled the media elite 'to live the insider's life while holding onto the outsider's self-image' (p. 131). Lichter *et al.*'s conclusion 'is that personality can influence a journalist's work, in both direct and indirect ways, no less than ideology or social structure' (p. 131). Such findings take us back to the 'Mr Gates' model, but with more diverse psychological data. One wonders, however, if the collective personality identified in these tests was not simply the result of effective socialisation and institutionalisation. A profession pre-socialises young lay people who may be drawn towards it by certain expectations, personality predispositions and affinities. Once selected, the socialisation process progresses, institutionally reinforcing and rewarding certain personality traits. Certainly, there is a complex dynamic of factors at work, including personality, but to ignore other factors would be simplistic to say the least.

Talent and fixers: two news cultures

There is also a need to bear in mind how institutionalisation in journalism is different from that in other professions. One commentator (McQuail, 1994, p. 198) suggests that media occupations are 'weakly institutionalised' compared with traditional professions such as medicine, law or accountancy. Journalists share no common educational path, have no required formal qualifications and don't have watchful professional bodies shaping their professional formation. Their core skills are hard to identify other than by nebulous notions such as 'rat-like cunning' and 'a nose for news'. Even rigorous academic definition can only come up with: 'news judgement . . . the sacred knowledge, the secret ability of the newsman which differentiates him from other people' (Tuchman, 1972, p. 672), while Stuart Hall (1973, p. 181) simply admits that '"news values" are one of the most opaque structures of meaning in modern society'.

This manifest difficulty in characterising news practitioners and their value systems arises in part because the television news profession is far from uniform. There are at least two separate cultures definable in terms of their primary working space. Reporters and crews work away from base a substantial proportion of the time, dealing with the unusual real world events that constitute the news. They develop relationships with sources and contacts and with the ordinary people about whom they may make the news. They routinely engage in guerrilla-like activities, negotiating access, dealing with minders, living on their wits often in extreme and difficult circumstances. Sometimes, by necessity, they enter, in varying degrees, into the world on which they are reporting. Whether dealing with politicians in the lobby or guerrillas in the jungle, the access needed requires the establishment of some kind of relationship. Crime reporters drinking with the police is an oft-quoted example of this bonding phenomenon where an unwritten contract exists. Whatever the source of their story, journalists have to enter into often complex negotiations with their editors about the nature of their piece, and often tension arises. The reporter is by nature adventurous and enterprising, whereas the editor back at base is cautious. Everyone has their own version of the sad story of the BBC foreign correspondent phoning London with an exclusive story, only to be told by cautious editors that they could not use the story as there was no second source. This confirmation is duly provided by the reporter walking down the corridor to the Reuters office to give the story to a grateful news agency colleague who puts it on the wires for the world to see. A former network correspondent recalls his dealings with New York:

> There are two kinds of producers. One says, 'Hey what's going on out there?' and when you come up with a story that's news, he doesn't say, 'how come I haven't seen this in the *Times?*' That kind is in short supply. The other kind calls and says, 'At the morning meeting today' – and you know you're in trouble (Mayer, 1987, p. 201).

Some reporters think of the producers who accompany them as 'fixers', only along to book satellite feeds and hotel rooms. The feeling can run both ways. One such 'fixer', a senior producer with vast experience, was full of praise for her crews, but was less keen on reporters, remarking suspiciously that only a 'certain kind of person' would want to go in front of the camera. Certainly, in American television news that certain kind of person, the on-screen 'talent', often takes on a role that the humble British reporter can hardly imagine. Their perceived status and their pay set the network correspondent apart, apart at times from their own producers who claim, in some cases, to do all the work while the 'talent' merely reproduces the results. One disgruntled former network producer told me that he got tired of untalented 'talent' arriving late, demanding an all-too-brief briefing, before jumping in front of the camera to give a reputation-enhancing performance. Whether such a producer was badly institutionalised himself, or simply jealous, his views were witness to significant diversity inside the television news profession. That said, both my own experience and a set of complemetary interviews obtained for this study point to the possibility of a different, more supportive, model of long-term producer–reporter relationships which may be the lingering result of the current affairs tradition of location reporting.

Meanwhile, back in the newsroom, editors, whose professional life has hardly required them to leave the building, rise up the editorial and management ladders by displaying different traits from journalists in the field.

They are more easily institutionalised, more likely to adhere to the norms of their organisation. They are susceptible to pressures from government, other media and from the public. They become cautious, whether simply checking facts or thinking of the long-term future of the organisation, be it public service or commercial. Taste and decency are issues with them, as they have final editorial responsibility for what is seen in the living rooms of the world. Theirs is a culture of 'responsible carefulness' (Blumler and Gurevitch, 1995, p. 181). As one veteran correspondent, now anchoring, remarks with characteristic brevity on the subject of managerial caution: 'they're on their way up and they want to make sure they don't blot their copy-books', with the result that 'there has been a wide cultural divide, between the people out on the field and the people here in the office, and the two really haven't crossed over, reporters don't become executives by and large, almost inevitably'.

The editor's perspective on events is very different from that of the journalist in the field. In the newsroom they receive all the information from a wide range of sources and locations; they know more than anyone else; they select and they reject. They can see the opposition's output, often chastising their reporters and crews for missing something the competition has got. They read all the papers, aware not only of their substantive news content, but equally of any attitudinal shifts attacking their programmes or organisation.

Particularly abroad, reporters can be surprisingly isolated, having only their individual point of view on events which can in fact be limited by the very proximity and unique perspective which makes their reports valuable. Speaking of his experience of the fog of war at Yom Kippur in 1972, one senior British reporter remarks:

> we were going to the front, across the desert, and you'd be away for 36 hours or something, and you'd come back and do a piece . . . but of course the truth of the matter is, you've had 36 hours in the back of a beaten-up Volvo. You've gone to a one or two mile section of the front, you haven't the faintest idea. People tell you the sort of things that could be bullshit. You've seen something – a few Egyptian prisoners – you can make your own view that at this corner of the front, the Israelis are winning hands down, the fact that everybody seems to be going back, you can draw some general conclusion, but actually in terms of accuracy, you can only tell what you've seen, and there is a sort of institutional compulsion, now much more than then, to start drawing interesting conclusions from your observations.

Instead of being at the centre of a newsgathering web, the journalist in the field has a literally different position with regard to events. As BBC foreign correspondent John Simpson has written of his work:

> It is rather like an account of a football match written from a seat
> near one of the goals. Whenever play was down my end I had a
> superb view of it. But when it moved to the far end of the pitch I only
> knew what was happening when I heard the crowd roar (Simpson,
> 1991, pp. xv–xvi).

Simpson's comments were reflections on his time in Baghdad at the
beginning of the Gulf War. One of his colleagues, who reported from the
same locale later in the conflict, reports an interesting interaction with
London:

> I sensed there was something up because more and more senior editors
> who normally I wouldn't speak to were coming across the line. One of
> them said 'we have a thousand per cent confidence in your reporting'.
> A fair comment and that often doesn't happen, you know. I'm sure
> they always had a thousand per cent confidence in my correspondence,
> but they don't normally bother to say it.

He took this overt praise as a sure sign there had been criticism of him and
his organisation. Although the tabloid newspapers were not delivered to his
Baghdad hotel, nevertheless it didn't take much imagination to know that
something was up and the office were worried. And well they might have
been concerned, with questions asked in Parliament and one print media
commentator being of the opinion that 'the BBC's future could depend on
its Gulf coverage' (Thynne, 1991, p. 6).

Not surprisingly, tension often arises between the field force and their
bosses back at base. As one senior British news executive acknowledges,
'Editors are not ex-correspondents. Correspondents never move on to
become editors – this causes problems' (Duncan, 1996, p. 17). This talent
versus fixers, correspondent versus editors, location versus base, in-front-of
versus behind the camera, distinction can possibly be overstated, but nevertheless tension exists. As one senior British anchor remarks:

> you're in your little box and you stay there, and management are in
> their little box and they stay there, and the editorial side are in their
> little box, and it's basically a load of boxes, and for an organisation
> that believes in communication, I do find it quite extraordinary that
> particularly when you have newscasters who have been on the road as
> reporters and who are working journalists, . . . I just find it extra-
> ordinary that we don't have a formal position in there at the heart of
> policy making discussions. . . . I think it's based on nothing more than
> sheer envy, they say you newscasters, you are recognised by the pub-
> lic, you are paid huge sums of money, you are on-screen, that's your
> little bit, you've got to leave something important to us here in man-
> agement and they totally underestimate the contribution that we can
> make.

Editors and executives are particularly wary of anchors, who, it is thought, can become too powerful, exercising undue editorial influence. American precedent and one particular case in Britain has led to caution, and while no one wants automaton newsreaders, there is a fear that a powerful on-screen figure could come to concentrate editorial power unduly.

To some, such tensions are endemic. One third-party commentator, himself a print journalist and broadcaster, writing about the debates at a major television news convention, remarked on the journalistic 'capacity for wingeing about the boss that makes bitchy theatrical luvvies and professional footballers look models of disciplined loyalty' (Fiddick, 1995, p. 10). Substantial recent changes in all broadcasting organisations have led to falling morale and a culture of quiet, constant complaint that has become a background hum in all newsrooms, so much so that some managers simply ignore it: 'You only have to change the opening hours of the canteen and they scream it's the end of the BBC as we know it' (Engel, 1996, p. 3). To some, such tension may be creative, the inevitable result of the specialisation of function which arises in any large organisation employing large numbers of people to do different aspects of the same job.

Meanwhile, the crews, the camera(mostly)men, sound recordists, and picture editors who actually make the programmes sit in the middle, bemused by it all. These technicians and craftpeople constitute a third culture, from different backgrounds again. Without wishing to sound like a variant on a typical Oscar acceptance speech, one needs to say that technicians (for want of a better word that is less condescending and which more accurately describes the difference between them and journalists) play an important role which is hardly researched at all. The role of picture editors and their emergence from the different cultures of film and videotape technology particularly is one which would bear analysis, given the prominent role such craftspeople play in the actual construction of the visual material which is one of the defining characteristics of television news.

This diversity inside the news profession is not simply a question of function. Gender factors are certainly under-researched in news organisations, which are clearly ruled by a male-dominated ethos. Stereotypically, newsrooms are full of what one female news editor described as 'ambitious young men in crisp white shirts', though clearly some change is occurring behind as well as in front of the camera. Nevertheless, the fact that until the mid-1990s no BBC national news programme had been edited by a woman is significant. Staff on one award-winning programme report a notable change in atmosphere since the recent appointment of a female editor and deputy. There is clearly an opportunity here for research to track any difference in the nature of output at a time when two national bulletins are for the first time edited by women and when one American network news division has appointed a woman as its European Vice President.

I asked a female news anchor with a wide range of experience in several British news organisations if she found her profession to be male-dominated. She deflected the question:

> I think I've always felt an outsider anyway, and I think it's a very useful thing to be, I think most journalists feel – by the nature of what they are – that they're outsiders, because they are standing on the sidelines looking on.

Interestingly, she evoked a *professional* ideal which may, or may not, have been used to hide a *personal* viewpoint which might have been critical of the *institution* for which she worked. Unravelling these complex interactions is never easy. From the beginning, with 'Mr Gates' and his choices, media research has had to deal with how the individual interfaces with the institution and decide which factor is most important: the personal or the professional.

Twin traditions: organisation and ideology

Selection, particularly of wire service material in newspapers which formed the basis for the early gatekeeping studies, is far from the entirety of the news-production chain and, as the study of the news media developed, emphasis shifted away from the personal, the issue of selection and from reliance on newspapers as the only subject of study. Two broad traditions of media research evolved, running in parallel. These approaches could be crudely characterised as applying, respectively, the methods of sociology and political science to the news media and as such they reflect the development of communications studies as a coherent area of academic study, itself growing out of several older disciplines. Simply stated, one approach is organisational, the other ideological. Having moved on from the personal realm, researchers had to decide where to locate the driving force in determining news values. Whether in terms of organisational working, institutional ownership and regulation or in the dynamics of the wider body politic, a wide range of possibilities were to be examined and, hardly surprisingly, one of the first places to be studied was the newsroom itself.

News organisation and production studies

In 1963, Wilbur Schramm, commenting on the gatekeeping issue which by then had been central for over a decade, remarked, 'participant observer studies are clearly called for' (quoted in Dexter and White, 1964, p. 161) and it seems that the advice of this respected figure was taken to heart by a number of academics. There appears to have been a golden age of television news studies in the late 1960s and 1970s, with the research often being the

PhD work of young scholars rather than of established figures. One such scholar, Gaye Tuchman (1991, p. 92), comments that participant observation is a 'method for the young', with doctoral students possessing the energy and, perhaps more importantly, the time not available to older scholars.

Newsrooms are easy to study. It all happens there, or certainly it appears to. All researchers need is permission, an extra chair, a note book and a tape recorder for interviews. Such work certainly gets academics out of the ivory tower and near to the process behind the screen product. Whether employing the ethnographic methods of social anthropology or those of management and organisational studies, such work looked at individuals working in institutional settings in order to understand better the conditions of what can be seen as a form of industrial production. Schudson (1991, p. 149) particularly distinguishes two kinds of these studies: 'social constructionist' and 'organisational or bureaucratic'.

Social construction of news

In the first analysis the news is a depletable consumer product that must be made fresh daily (Tuchman, 1978, p. 196), the result of a process of routinisation which clearly creates a social construction. The relation of this construction to external reality is not a question of distortion or bias, for 'the concept of "distortion" is alien to the discussion of socially constructed realities. Each socially constructed reality necessarily has meaning and significance' (Tuchman, 1973, p. 129). In this view 'it might be valuable to think of news not as distorting, but rather reconstituting the everyday world' (p. 129). Unlike the Langs' pessimistic view that television distorts, Tuchman offers the analysis that it is but one of many possible social constructions, no more or less valid than any other, including the sociological.

Organisational theory

The other view, represented by Edward Jay Epstein in his *News from nowhere* (1973), which grew out of work on organisational theory in political science, puts more emphasis on the way in which the news organisation functions within certain technical, logistical and economic parameters. In this research

> the working assumption was that members of such organisations eventually modified their own personal values in accordance with the requisites of the organisation and that therefore the key to explaining the output . . . lay in defining the basic requirements which a given organisation needs to maintain itself (p. xiv).

Epstein's work adopted 'the approach of treating a news service as a business organisation rather than as a collective faculty for highly independent newsmen' (p. xiv). Interestingly, his study was metropolitan, based on access to network television news rather than the local news operations that had been used in many previous studies. It also clearly distinguishes between the print and electronic media (p. 40) which much earlier work had not always done.

Epstein dismisses a number of previous explanations of television news offered both by professionals and by academics. He makes short work of what he calls the 'mirror metaphor' frequently advanced by professionals in reply to external criticism. NBC Vice President Robert Kasmire is quoted as evidence of this widely held belief: 'There is no doubt that television is, to a large degree, a mirror of society' (p. 13). Epstein replies to this notion with a number of well-documented cases demonstrating that, far from merely reflecting the external world, television news shapes its output in a number of discernible ways:

> Unlike a mirror, which is automatic, both an informational and a value premise shape the image in television news. To describe network news as mirroring events thus necessarily involves seriously neglecting the importance of the chain of decisions made both before and after the fact by executives and newsmen, or, in a word, the organisational process (p. 25).

Neither the personal nor the professional predominate, but instead organisational values are central. In Epstein's analysis, 'correspondents are under some pressure to focus their reportage on the elements of stories which best fit the needs of the organisation, even if it conflicts with their own news values' (p. 33). News studies had come a long way from what would appear to be the simplistic personal analysis of the 'Mr Gates' model.

Epstein delineates the economic logic (p. 100) of news coverage which he sees very much as a function of financially determined logistics. With film crews costing $500 000 each per year in 1968, one network could afford to employ only 10 crews in five selected major centres who were responsible for producing 80 per cent of the network news in his sample (p. 102). Their deployment therefore determined what was in the news as much as any other news value. Epstein also outlines the enormous cost of getting material back to base. In his study, between 30–40 per cent of programme budgets went on the landlines then used to send pictures back from remote locations (p. 106). These two related factors reveal the manner in which 'the fundamental economic structure compels producers to select a large share of their film stories from a few locations' (p. 109).

Today all news organisations are under even greater financial pressure than the American networks were in the 1960s. Film has been replaced by much cheaper videotape, and landlines have been supplemented by microwave and satellite links, the costs of which have come down as a result of telecommunications deregulation but which are still substantial. Rather than pay for expensive crews and links there is a tendency to make greater use of pooling and agency pictures, which can result in everyone having the same pictures. Soon-to-be employed new technology promises to make crews smaller and therefore cheaper, allowing news-gatherers to deploy more crews for less money or, more probably, the same number of cameras for less money. Logistical discussions such as these can become circular. Network executives might be justified in saying that crews have to be stationed in Washington or Chicago as that is where the stories are, while observers would say that the allocation of resources determines that the material such crews produce will be used at the expense of other material originating from outside major metropolitan centres. The development of a broadcasting centre in Millbank to cover British politics has meant that a substantial amount of technical and staff resources have been committed which must therefore be used. Some would say that this logistical predisposition leads to undue attention being given to the minutiae of parliamentary life at the expense of wider political issues in the country (Bolton, 1995). Although over 25 years have passed since Epstein's fieldwork, and although certain surface details have changed, many of his insights apply equally today.

By centring his analysis on the organisation, Epstein claims he is able to explain why news seems to be *pro status quo*. Network producers simply don't want to offend the mass audience by being anything other than conventional: 'Newsmen therefore avoid radical arguments not because they are politically committed to supporting "the system", but because they do not satisfy the audience requisites of network news' (p. 271). This argument can of course become circular, with the audience only accepting what they are given and producers only giving the audience what they supposedly want. Innovative, imaginative alternative approaches might be accepted by audiences, but no editor is going to risk their job finding out. Instead, 'they always tell the people what they think the people are already thinking' (Miller, 1988). The audience is constantly evoked. I took part in a radio discussion programme which dealt with the blanket coverage of the TWA Long Island crash. The moderator was critical of the long hours of CNN coverage, including the filming of grieving families at Paris airport. The CNN case was put by a senior figure in their London bureau who said simply that the coverage was just giving the audience what they wanted.

Epstein is not as pessimistic as some analysts, but neither is he optimistic. He insists that 'alternative sources of national news are necessary for balance' (p. 272), for in his view:

> the prognosis for change is severely limited. The systematic distortion of events which journalistic critics, conservatives, radicals and social scientists point to will not be remedied by more enlightened executives, the education of journalists, different personnel, the politicisation of recruitment – which, ironically both conservatives and radical

critics advocate – or the availability of data from the academic world. As long as the [organisational] requisites remain essentially the same, network news can be expected to define American society by the problems of a few urban areas rather than by the entire nation, by action rather than by ideas (p. 272).

He goes on to elaborate a long litany of well-articulated failings of television news, all of which he attributes to the organisations which produce it and which cannot easily be changed.

Mapping the world

Epstein concludes 'the point is not to change news, but to understand its limitations' (p. 273). He likens news production to map-making. No mapping system can reproduce reality, and the 'distortion' that results should not be lamented, but understood. This analogy clearly bears some attention. Map-making produces an accurate representation of an external reality which is expressed in a stylised symbol system, observing certain conventions, which requires a degree of literacy on the part of the user. The map is as accurate as possible, but in no way can it be mistaken for its real world starting point. It makes sense of that world, provided that the mapping convention is appropriate to the task for which it is required and that the map has been rigorously made. Three lines on the back of an envelope may suffice as a map to guide a motorist on a journey of several hundred miles, while a large and detailed three-dimensional survey may be needed to lay 100 metres of utility cable in an urban area. Television news is a mapping of the world which charts certain domains in its characteristic style. There is no point in complaining that the map is not a landscape painting, although you can certainly say that a particular map is badly made or indeed that you prefer the painting as an account. Decoding any symbol system requires literacy, in the case of television news, viewer competence, and the map must be both well made and properly used if it is to assist in the navigation of the complex reality of which it is necessarily a stylised simplification.

Epstein's work made great use of internal directives, notably a long (32-page) memorandum from a senior network news executive setting out certain (p. 42) principles which were to be applied to all news coverage. One wonders if such a method of analysis would shed light on the Birtian BBC with its top-down directives, internal reforming zeal and emphasis on management and (re)organisation. Such a study would need to have an historical dimension, possibly comparing the contemporary situation with that found in earlier British studies.

Stopwatch culture

The BBC, as a unique public service organisation with an international reputation, was an obvious subject for a newsroom study which could offer interesting comparisons with the work based on American commercial television. Philip Schlesinger's *Putting 'reality' together* (1978; reprinted 1987) resulted from three periods of observation in both BBC radio and television news in the years between 1972 and 1976. His research reveals the importance of pre-planning in the organisation of news production. Schlesinger describes attending weekly forward-planning meetings which were 'a mixture of news judgement and logistical talk' (p. 71) which resulted in 'a routine agenda of predictable stories' (p. 79). This logistically determined and pre-planned production chain meant that 'most news is really "olds" in a sense that it is largely predictable' (p. 80). Schlesinger observes that most stories originate from agency or newspaper sources and approvingly quotes Epstein, offering cross-confirmation for the insight that television news is reactive, rarely investigating its own stories. He found 'an inbuilt tendency to caution' (p. 80) resulting from organisational and ideological factors which are seen in fact to be 'mutually reinforcing' (p. 47).

Schlesinger, in a seminal chapter entitled 'A stop watch culture', discusses 'the way in which newsmen's production concepts are shaped by the constraints of time' (p. 83). Temporal factors impinge on news production in a number of ways. Great value is placed on the up-to-dateness and immediacy which is signalled by live broadcasting, and success is defined as beating the competition by getting a story first. Time is a factor in other ways as well. Schlesinger points out that in television bulletins duration is clearly an indication of news value (p. 98). The more important a story is deemed to be, the more time it is given in the bulletin running order. In addition to considerations of length, the substantial time pressures of the daily production routine create a product that is temporally thin. Schlesinger finds that 'news is virtually all foreground with very little background' (p. 104); it is 'ahistorical' (p. 105) with no context provided.

My own experience was that in daily news and current affairs there was rarely enough time in which to do the task in hand. The output created so quickly was further time-dominated in that there was very little airtime available for the finished product on transmission. In short, you have no time to do your job and the result is determined by the time slot available. Programmes such as *Newsnight* and *Channel 4 News* are fortunate in having more airtime than the main fixed-point bulletins and they work to different agendas, running fewer items, at greater length. Whether this makes for a properly contextualised form of television journalism is a question which would need systematic long-term research. Certainly staff on such programmes do fewer 'on-the-days', having longer than simply the day of transmission to research, shoot and edit their pieces, which may therefore provide in depth what they might lack in immediacy.

Context, historical or otherwise, is most readily available to television journalists in two forms. Newspaper cuttings and the film and videotape library are available to provide background information effortlessly. The ease with which journalists in major news organisations can take advantage of such facilities can be dangerous, as they become authoritative, with yesterday's mistakes being repeated endlessly. I have often seen a set of cuttings where at a certain point an error has crept in which is then repeated time and again, becoming canonical. One senior news executive spoken to for this study pointed out to me that a commonly held view of his organisation's performance with regard to the reporting of a certain major event was untrue, but try as they might to make the truth of the matter known they 'couldn't get it into the cuttings'. It was accepted by this experienced figure that setting the record straight was a matter of breaking into a media cycle that rolled on regardless of the facts of the matter.

Resources such as newspaper cuttings and well-indexed picture and moving-image libraries are part of the standard equipment of major national and international news organisations, but many local and regional services are less well provided for. The information infrastructure of newsrooms mostly concerns itself with acquiring contemporary material and getting it on-air as fast as possible. Where necessary, the media recycle their own output, but there is very little attempt to provide supplementary information which might give events a wider context. Even when alternative sources are available there is not always time to research contexts, particularly the historical. During discussion of a shooting by security forces in a South African township, a colleague mentioned the Sharpeville massacre (1961). 'Has there been another one?' came the reply from a journalist not yet born when that crucial event happened. Similarly, the word 'Sarajevo' rings in the historically primed memory, not just because of the 1984 Winter Olympics, and if one's understanding of the complexities of former Yugoslavia extends geographically to include Kosovo, fourteenth century events (Bell, 1995, p. 102) enter the equation of contexts needed in order to explain today's news. Even in the realms of the contemporary, the flux of events tend to blend into one another. How many journalists, indeed academics, could properly date and differentiate the run of mortar bomb incidents in Sarajevo? One hit a water queue, or was it a bread queue or a queue outside a bank? Another hit the market place, or was the market place hit twice?

The major incident which led to NATO air strikes was the market place shelling of 5 February 1994 when 68 were killed and 200 wounded. The market was hit again on 23 December 1994 just as a ceasefire brokered by former US President Jimmy Carter was about to take effect. Two were killed and seven wounded. Other Sarajevo mortar incidents involved the bread queue on 27 May 1992 and the water queue on 12 July 1993. Martin Bell (p. 143) gives January 1993 as the date for the water-queue attack while

Vulliamy (1994, p. 82) mentions a bank queue in June 1992. A funeral, a school, a football match and sledging children were other mortar targets which warranted individual news stories (Shrock, 1994) while the Vanderbilt Television News Archive lists 34 mortar incidents reported on American network news in the period 1992–95.

A recent spate of American military helicopter crashes may be a series of random isolated events or part of a pattern either of mechanical shortcomings or operational ineptitude. Faced with the need to write 30 seconds of words to a dynamic picture sequence quickly, a young desk-based newsperson is unlikely to be able to do more than ask a question. The long-term investigation into equipment procurement policies, defence funding cuts, military training and operational procedures has to be done by someone else or not at all. There is no systematic way for newsroom journalists to extract pattern from the flux of daily events. Use of the cuttings, sometimes supplemented by specialist publications, can help, as can computerised on-line searches (Koch, 1991). Since the days when 'Mr Gates' trawled through the wires, the amount of information in all forms coming into any newsroom has grown exponentially and with it the demands placed on journalists to be able themselves to understand the flow of events. Present time has become wider, with less possibility of depth being provided.

Time is not just part of the news professional's working conditions. It is highlighted to the audience. Perhaps as a result of its all-determining role in news production, time is part of the iconography of television news, and clocks regularly feature on-screen, particularly in bulletin title sequences. The BBC's *One O'Clock News* used to have an animated title sequence which took the viewer inside the face of the clock as the second hand raced towards the top of the dial and the ever-punctual bulletin itself. Currently, ITN use a not dissimilar animation which moves around the face of Big Ben in a clockwise direction, arriving likewise at the top of the hour. Not only is the bulletin up-to-date and professionally punctual, but it comes from the heart of events in Westminister.

An atomic clock culture?

It is interesting to compare Schlesinger's findings with the situation today. My colleague Simeon Yates, who accompanied me on a recent period of observation in an international newsroom, remarked that in the intervening years Schlesinger's stopwatch culture had changed to an atomic clock culture, with margins even tighter than before, partly the result of advances in technology. One of the anchors of the service in question supported this view with her exasperated hope that we had 'reached the limits of how fast you can get'.

The move towards real time television, facilitated by advances in technology and the parallel institutional development of rolling news services,

appears to have done little to remedy the lack of historical perspective identified by Schlesinger in the 1970s. Detailed content analysis carried out on
the coverage of the Gulf War (Morrison, 1992, pp. 68 and 76) revealed that
there was a demonstrable lack of historical perspective provided for an
event which in part had its roots in the tangled web of Middle Eastern and
British colonial history. Paddy Ashdown, leader of the Liberal Democrat
Party and a frequent interviewee during the period, had actually been part
of a previous British military intervention in Kuwait, mention of which was
for the most part absent from the coverage of events.

When presented with such criticism, news professionals inevitably have
two answers. In many cases they legitimately reply 'we did an item on that'.
An instance is given and no doubt the archive does contain the back-
grounder on Yugoslavian history which does clearly explain the difference
between Serb and Croat. During the Gulf War period, eight items on the history of Kuwait and Iraq were transmitted on the six English-language channels analysed. This was out of a total of 3954 stories, representing less than
one half of one per cent of coverage (Morrison, 1992, p. 67). The coverage
of such issues was there, but it hardly intruded on the popular imagination.

Another reply professionals give to such remarks is something to the
effect 'we're not the Open University; teaching history is someone else's
job'. To some extent this is true. Particularly in British television, the full
range of current affairs and other factual programming does tend to give a
wider view. If the cliché is true and news is indeed the first rough draft of
history, it should be noted that it is both rough and a draft. A chain of
explosive events such as that which has transpired in former Yugoslavia can
be best understood when some kind of pattern has emerged. A documentary
series such as *The death of Yugoslavia* produced by Brian Lapping
Associates for BBC2 relied for much of its visuals on news material, but
equally was able to use video material that the news could not have had at
the time. Such a series can offer an overview that the day-to-day run of news
coverage cannot possibly provide. Rightly described as 'magnificent television' by Martin Bell, one of the major players in the news coverage of events
in Bosnia, it discussed the fourteenth century battle of Kosovo and illustrated how that defeat is imprinted on the Serb memory. Such an exemplary
series did a certain job that news could not, but to say that viewers would
have to wait years before being told anything is palpably absurd. News does
its immediate job, sometimes well, sometimes not so well. It operates under
tremendous time pressure and the worldwide newsgathering apparatus of
agencies and picture exchanges is in some ways little short of miraculous. It
does not necessarily follow that news thus produced is automatically without flaws. In fact in some ways its weaknesses arise from its very strengths.
The ability to get live pictures from anywhere in the world means that you
use them, and visual values are often said to dominate television news.
There is no denying that in certain instances seeing history being made live
on television is both an exciting and important experience for the viewer.

However, it doesn't happen every day and even in the rare instances when it does it still needs to be put in context subsequently. Only time will tell if the bombing of Baghdad in January 1991 which CNN reported so memorably will turn out to be more important than events happening at the same time in Vilnius, Lithuania. The beginning of the end of the Soviet Union was captured by amateurs on VHS and was reported on all major news services, but no journalist or academic speaking on television could have said then that within months Gorbachev would fall and with him the Soviet empire.

The advent of rolling news has meant that although more airtime is available other factors militate against increased discussion of historical perspectives. One such factor is the perception that the audience find such background material boring. Another is that news is simply not set up to do the job. The news is new and journalism deals with the daily and if television is to provide such historical background analysis it has to be done in other forms of programming. Certainly, in this context, there is an argument for maintaining the distinction between news and current affairs which, although managerially merged in the BBC, are mercifully still distinct types of programming. That is not to say that the Birtian reforms haven't changed the nature of BBC news, for they clearly have, but just how much and in which ways the mission to explain has been realised is a topic for extensive research. One aspect of such investigations would have to be the extent to which 'individual personalities can indeed make a considerable impact on their environment, but within an historical and organisational context which they inherit and unavoidably confront' (Golding and Elliott, 1979, p. 7).

The news of the world

This uncanny anticipation of the impact of John Birt on the BBC predated his appointment as its chief journalist by nearly a decade. In 1979 Peter Golding and Philip Elliott published a much needed international comparative study which confirmed some of the findings of earlier news-production studies with American and British samples. Based on observations in Irish, Swedish and Nigerian newsrooms, these researchers found news production to be: 'a strongly patterned, repetitive and predictable work routine, essentially passive in character and varying only in detail from country to country' (p. 83). In this analysis, news is 'a highly regulated and routine process of manufacturing cultural product on an electronic production line' (p. 137). They detected bias (p. 17), which they found, very like Epstein, to be 'the inevitable, but unintended consequence of organisation' (p. 208). However, Golding and Elliott interpret this finding somewhat differently, seeing broadcasting as basically passive, relaying the values of news-producing groups in society and therefore ideological in nature (pp. 18, 169 and 208). Whereas Epstein had stressed technical and logistical factors in

explaining slants, they conclude that news is the transmission of an ideology, inevitably representing the world-view of particular social groups arising from the production process and 'the presumed demands of its expected
audience' (p. 138). News is an ideology creating a particular world-view
resulting from 'the exigencies of organised production' (p. 208); necessarily
a partial view whose alignment with ruling ideology 'is more than acciden-
tal' (p. 209). In order to reach the largest possible audiences, news becomes
consensual. Attention is focused on 'the arenas of consensus formation'
(p. 211) where social conflict is managed. Professional and regulatory
demands for objectivity and neutrality militate against alternative views,
pushing instead toward consensus. Television news does not properly portray power relations in society, nor does it give any indication of the possibility of change, instead creating a world-view of endless events with no
historical dimension which does not portray the real power relations in
society (p. 210).

Golding and Elliott offer suggestions that aim to 'improve or refashion'
(p. 211) television news. The first is to lengthen news bulletins: 'by extending the news even further, perhaps to an hour, most of the limitations to
broadcast news will disappear' (p. 212). They also urge producers to provide more background information (p. 212) and to use a more active and
less reportorial style of journalism (p. 215). There is a call to break down
the distinction between news and current affairs (pp. 81 and 218), which is
of course an echo of the Birt/Jay analysis. Indeed, Golding and Elliott's call
to combine news and current affairs has subsequently been implemented by
one powerful figure, a development which could be said to be a clear example of the great-man theory of history that they pointedly reject (p. 7).
Interestingly, rather than agreeing in part with the Birt/Jay thesis which
seems at times to echo their own analysis, Golding and Elliott dismiss it:
'their views were far from radical, merely popularising a critique which had
been familiar for many years' (p. 218 no. 1).

Writing from a different temporal point of view, it would seem hard not
to apply something very like a great-man theory of history to recent developments in the BBC. Had a different Director General from Michael
Checkland been appointed in 1987, there might have been no perceived need
to bring in an outsider such as John Birt to deal with the journalism of which
the accountant Checkland had no experience. Had David Dimbleby, Brian
Wenham, Jeremy Isaacs or indeed Michael Grade been appointed, the development of the BBC and its news output would have been very different.
Blumler and Gurevitch (1995, p. 199) quite rightly make the point that there
was a perceived need to transform BBC television journalism, for a number
of pressing reasons, and that the changes do not arise simply from Birt's 'personal philosophy' (p. 199). To some, nothing less than the future of the BBC
was at stake and reforms were much overdue; to others, inside the organisation particularly, Birt was an unwelcome saviour, not unlike the American
soldier who set fire to a Vietnamese village with the explanation that he had

to 'destroy this village in order to save it'. Certainly, the evolution of the BBC would have been very different if, for example, Marcus Plantin had been appointed Deputy Director General in 1987 with a mandate to make the corporation's output more populist, or if respected journalist and historian John Tusa had succeeded Checkland as Director General.

The same form of personal analysis could be applied to a very different figure to explain how reporter John Pilger has worked for over 20 years in commercial television, offering a number of oppositional readings which could hardly be described as ideology in support of the *status quo*. Pilger has not, of course, worked in news, in fact his work has very often been in conflict with the version of events offered by the orthodox news media. His work in current affairs documentary making with producer David Munro, in the face of considerable odds, offers empirical evidence to balance any theory that television is exclusively taken up by messages in maintenance of the *status quo*. Whether Pilger is the exception that proves the rule is a point open for discussion, but it is clear that the separation of news and current affairs can have its advantages, giving scope for powerful investigative reporting not even conceivable in orthodox news organisations. One only has to imagine an encounter between the two Johns – Pilger and Birt – to see how the former could never have done his television work within the confines of the BBC. Personal, committed, consistently oppositional reporting in the context of commercial television under various regulatory regimes would seem impossible in an organisational analysis, yet the fact remains that Pilger has worked for two decades in a commercial system that made profits for its shareholders. The recent television work of *The Guardian* journalist Maggie O'Kane on topics such as the Gulf War and former Yugoslavia is a testament to the fact that such work is still possible in the post-1990 regulatory environment and that Pilger is not some relic of the 1960s and an IBA-regulated ITV system long buried by market forces (for example, O'Kane, 1996).

Given the events since Golding and Elliott published their findings, does their analysis stand the test of time? Philip Elliott is alas dead. I met him when I was a young television researcher working on a programme about television and we engaged in the very opposite of a dialogue of the deaf across the professional divide. I was impressed by his sensitivity to the pressures under which programme makers work and his appreciation of the subtleties and diversity of the British broadcasting system of the time. Peter Golding's later work shows the same professional thoroughness evidenced in *Making the news* and appears to result in the delineation of a slightly more subtle relationship between vested interests, the news media and the public. His work with David Deacon (1994) on the media coverage of the poll tax points to a complex dynamic of public opinion formation, with the media both leading and following wider societal views (p. 197). News-producing groups in society which might once have been seen as using the media as a conduit in the furtherance of their interests are now revealed as having less power in defining public opinion. A much more subtle and dynamic model of source–media relationships (p. 9) emerges:

> The power to create and distribute meaning still resides with centres of material and political power, both within the state and amongst the higher reaches of corporate and financial authority. But this power is exercised dynamically. It is fought over, challenged, and abused, both within and without (p. 203).

The poll tax represents a clear case where radical change from above was resisted by a number of sectors in the body politic. In this respect there has been a subtle refinement and development from Golding and Elliott's 1979 position.

'New world disorder'

Equally, their notion that television news portrays a world that is unchanging should perhaps be examined in the light of events since 1989 when enormous change has clearly taken place and has been duly reported by the news media. It may well be that such developments are clearly convenient for the *status quo*, marking as they do ideological and economic victory in the Cold War and, indeed, in one view, the end of history with the triumph of certain established values. Nevertheless, change has taken place and been reported, indeed some would say overreported. Nowhere can this be better seen than in former Yugoslavia where the turbulent events of 1992–95 represent cataclysmic change of a kind not seen in Europe since the Second World War. Much of the coverage of events in the Balkans could be said in some ways to be oppositional, with the news media being an inconvenient reminder of events that Western governments would really rather not have to deal with in public. Those journalists that then British Foreign Secretary Douglas Hurd called 'the something must be done brigade' (Bell, 1995, p. 138) could hardly be seen as transmitters of a *status quo* perpetuating ideology. Neither were the news media simply relaying a consensual view on events in Bosnia, because for the most part the only commonly held public view was confusion, and while at times the news media themselves appeared confused they were clearly less confused than either the public or the politicians.

In the chaos of the post-communist world, in what BBC correspondent Martin Bell calls 'the new world disorder' (1995, p. 225), traditional sources of information no longer function as they did when the lines were more clearly drawn. In certain circumstances, enterprising reporters can now tell the diplomatic and intelligence communities unpleasant truths they would not otherwise know. During the summer of 1992, as Yugoslavia descended into chaos, the Foreign Office was informed at a press conference that Bell was about to go to Goražde to report on the state of that city's beleaguered Muslim inhabitants. The Foreign Office spokesman with quite un-British candour replied '. . . that's all the f ∗∗∗ we need'.

One must be careful not to try and extract universal principles from such a case. For every instance where the news media act as an oppositional thorn in the side of a blinkered *status quo* or expose a government policy-vacuum, there are equal examples where events happen well away from the camera and where journalism only enters the equation of events when given access by the powers-that-be on their terms.

In domestic coverage, much of the coverage of privatisation of utilities has hardly been supportive of the *status quo*. Well before the much publicised water crisis in the summer of 1995, well before Yorkshire Water executives were summoned to London to see the Secretary of State, regional television services in Yorkshire were running frequent stories on the water company and its long-running tendency to manage by drought order. Certainly, the job of press officer in the private utility sector has hardly been an easy one of late, as even the attention of *Panorama* (4 November 1996) and *World in action* (15 July 1996) has been brought to bear. This is surely a clear case of 'the higher reaches of corporate and financial authority' (Deacon and Golding, 1994, p. 202) being challenged. There is scope here for research which could build on the work of Deacon and Golding and on work done on the reporting of environmental issues which has always to some extent been oppositional.

Whether Golding and Elliott's 1979 hope that by extending news output to very nearly an hour 'most of the limitations to broadcast news will disappear' (p. 212) has come to pass remains an open question. Since 1982, *Channel 4 News* has provided a longer bulletin and less of a distinction between news and current affairs values, but even this excellent programme cannot single-handedly have answered all of the objections raised by Golding and Elliott which grew out of newsroom observations in a very different world.

Problems with method

The news production studies which replaced the gatekeeper research at the top of the academic agenda were not universally accepted even in the scholarly community. Schlesinger (1987, p. xliii) reports criticism of his work from the Glasgow University Media Group who attacked such an approach as doing 'little but regurgitate professional notions of production', thus creating 'academic journalism which pessimistically accepts that no real change is possible under present society' (GUMG, 1980, p. 479).

Closely reasoned theoretical objections are raised by John Corner in an article in *Screen* (1995a) discussing a wide range of knowledge problems in media studies. He warns against what he calls '*descriptivism* rendering ever thicker accounts of process, but being unable to make any clear connection upwards to explanation because of a gravitational commitment to ground level phenomena' (p. 152, emphasis in original). Observational methods can lead to two related faults. Like the news itself, such reports can lose sight of their 'own constructed authorial character' (p. 152), either insisting on objectivity and naive empiricism or, more fashionably, stressing authorial presence, with the postmodernist Professor Gates confusing himself or herself with Joan Didion, Hunter S. Thompson or Umberto Eco, intruding between the reader and the object of study. Certainly, reflexive theoretical discussions of ethnographic methodologies are something of a growth industry, with fieldwork seemingly more discussed than achieved.

Whatever the theoretical issues, practical concerns are also crucial. Access can be difficult to negotiate and the day-to-day routine of observation can put 'great strain on tolerance and hospitality' (Golding and Elliott, 1979, p. 14). 'Are you writing down everything I say?' asked one news producer rather aggressively as he watched me watching his workplace. For the most part, however, my own experience has been one of friendliness and openness, with newsroom personnel now being very familiar with being observed by everyone, from professors to teenagers. Indeed, some current professionals spoken to in this sample began their own careers as student visitors to newsrooms.

That is not to say that there are not practical problems with such a research method. A variant on the well-known Stockholm syndrome can develop, with researchers sharing the same space and interests as practitioners and all manner of relationships can develop. Personnel with a beef sometimes turn instantly to newly arrived outsiders, providing a torrent of criticism which can skew results. Often, interviewees, who themselves might include interviewing amongst their professional skills, can be quite cagey. Sometimes they cannot remember certain things, which is not surprising given the torrent of events and facts which flow through their professional lives. This can sometimes be a convenient excuse, at other times a genuine reality. Some respondents can be exceedingly indiscreet, using researchers as a mouthpiece or a sounding board. Although journalists are in many ways quite sophisticated, some can be unintentionally revealing. Equally, I know for certain that I have been lied to on a few occasions. It is possible to know this simply by cross-reference with other substantiated sources, although I never confronted such informants as they themselves might have done. Other interviewees were totally scrupulous both on and off the record, exhibiting an attention to detail, clarity and the interests of truth that would embarrass the most painstaking academic researcher. In many cases I was struck by their limited viewpoint, particularly of reporters who have spent a lot of time on the road, but equally of some newsroom personnel who knew very little of other news organisations, including their rival's output. Not surprisingly, given the demands of their working life, journalists do not watch a lot of television.

Observing the invisible

A lot of what goes on in the newsroom is invisible to the observer. The increasing use of newsroom computers – electronic newsroom systems – now virtually universal, highlights this. The 'Mr Gates' of the 1990s would sit in front of a computer screen scrolling through wire service copy using one finger. He could search for keywords, finding every reference to warm beer or Rome, effortlessly removing any chance of these topics appearing in his newspaper. I have watched a programme editor going through the wires and compiling a bulletin running order in a similar manner. When his staff arrived, they logged on and viewed the running order before they spoke. The morning meeting, part of the traditional ritual of news production, no longer exists on this particular programme. Text which was once dictated to news typists is now written by individuals working in silence, who can then pass the script to colleagues who can alter it and comment without words being spoken. Even when given access to a computer terminal, the job of the newsroom observer has changed now that less is in the open oral domain than was once the case. Less actually happens in the newsroom.

Taking decisions and making pictures

The actual construction of the pictures that constitute television news takes place in edit suites near the newsroom where rewinding tapes produce a cacophony of high pitched sound and fast-moving, flashing pictures which are almost purpose designed to produce migraine headaches. Under great pressure, picture editors regularly take decisions that even the journalists producing the item might not notice or understand. I have spoken to editors who very often find themselves trying to make transmittable material out of indifferent visual material provided by reporters and crews. It is not unknown for picture editors to work on their own, taking decisions of jour-nalistic import. I sat with an editor who was assembling a short piece that had been shot by a stringer. Sent to film the arrival of a new lifeboat at a coastal port, the freelance cameraman had in fact shot the old boat. The pic-ture editor sensed something was not quite right and pulled a cassette off the shelves of his well-stocked personal tape library. Sure enough, the old had been confused with the new. The story, hardly a major one in any case, was about to be dropped when the picture editor, continuing his search of his archive, actually found material featuring the new lifeboat alongside the old. He took some pride in getting the story right so that the local people in question would not lose confidence in their preferred news service, though the keen-eyed amongst them might notice that strict immediacy had been sacrificed in the interests of accuracy. When asked about his private tape collection, this editor replied that he didn't like to rely on the institutional film and videotape library and therefore kept copies of all of his work.

At one time, part of the BBC's process in the recruitment of picture editors consisted of flashing pictures of world leaders on the screen and asking
interviewees to identify them. This practice no doubt arises from lessons
learnt the hard way. There is no journalistic sense in asking for 30 seconds
of Egyptian President Mubarak if the picture editor proceeds to supply a
sequence of a bodyguard or half a minute of the President of Syria. One
journalist I spoke to told me of being stopped from making basic factual
errors in the use of library pictures by a tape editor who knew the materials
used in one running story inside out.

Picture editors can be seen as the first member of the audience, offering a
dispassionate view of visual material that may have required great effort to
obtain. If material is weak they can and do say so. In addition to their editorial function, they have an important informal training function, introducing reporters newly arrived from radio or newspapers to the visual
grammar of television news (cf. Tuchman, 1978, p. 121). Tape editors often
travel abroad with reporters and the traditional camera and sound crew,
editing pieces *in situ* and thereby playing a significant and under-researched
role in the news production chain.

Computer-generated graphics are increasingly important in presenting
complicated stories. With some news services deliberately seeking to offer
more explanation of complicated economic and social issues, there has
been a greater reliance on graphics, not just for the traditional maps and
charts, but also for complex visualisations requiring detailed abstract
knowledge and a special kind of visual imagination. What is the public
sector borrowing requirement, and, more crucially, what does it look
like? A story discussing a run on a currency may typically show dealers
in front of screens shouting into telephones, but how is the dramatic fluc-
tuation in the price of money to be explained to a mass audience in a few
minutes? Such tasks often fall to art-school-educated graphic artists
working to the brief of sometimes totally unvisual journalists, and as
such they represent another cultural interaction in the newsroom which
needs examination.

Equally, there has not been much fieldwork with reporters and crews
on the road (see McManus, 1994, pp. 44–47, 138 ff. and 151 for recent
examples). At its most basic, in local news there isn't always room in
the car, while in foreign crisis reporting the problems preventing observation multiply exponentially. Imagine a reporter handing out the
Marlboros at a Serb checkpoint explaining to the edgy man with the
AK47 and reeking of slivovitch (plum brandy) that the man talking into
a tape recorder in the corner is Professor Gates, a harmless academic
who follows the crew everywhere doing ethnography. Even in the comparative calm of the newsroom there have not been many recent studies.
There has been no extensive analysis of the Birtian and bi-media BBC,
except by management consultants, nor of the rolling news services such
as CNN and Sky.

Professional visualisations

One recent exception has been Simon Cottle's excellent study of an English Midland regional commercial station (1993). Concentrating on the coverage of inner-city conflict, interesting findings are arrived at, which add considerably to the existing body of knowledge arising from the classic studies of the 1970s and 1980s. Cottle concurs with received wisdom up to a point, finding regional news to be 'a highly mediated product, a product which conforms to professional expectancies and known programme parameters' (p. 225). This last category, 'the general conventions of the news form under consideration' (p. 226), has become vital by way of explaining how, in spite of the widespread use of a similar production process, discernibly different news products result. On the legacy of news-production studies, Cottle remarks: 'What is arguably missing from such accounts is the manner in which despite all these [similar] features, news organisations can and do produce immediately recognisable differences of news output' (p. 226). Newsroom culture grows from a number of well-researched factors (p. 227) and from the basic fact that journalists know which programme they work on. Producers observe the conventions both of the genre in question and of the particular individual variant on which they work, guided by an 'informing professional visualisation' (pp. 160 and 228), which is in effect a professional target to be achieved on each transmission.

The local commercial news studied, the kind of programme, has an effect on the nature of reporting because of the perhaps obvious but crucial point that there are different kinds of news. Cottle acknowledges that the programme itself is the tip of an iceberg which emerges from routine production in a profit-making commercial organisation, itself affected by shifting ownership patterns, themselves determined in part by the regulatory framework set in place by legislation. The change in the regulation of British commercial television following the 1990 Broadcasting Act can in part be charted by the transformation of screen product. Cottle's analysis is offered as one further tool to aid in the understanding of the changing nature of news production.

Market-driven journalism

While Cottle's work noted the pressures at work in British commercial television, John H. McManus uses American local television as the basis for his study of what he calls market-driven journalism (1994). This work uses 'economic theory to understand how newsrooms are organised, and how events and issues are selected and reported' (p. xii). McManus feels such a study to be crucially important 'at a time when much of the news industry is moving to replace journalistic judgement with market judgement' (pp. xii–xiii) with the inevitable result that news 'becomes a commodity to fit the market demands of a collection of special interests' (p. 37).

McManus identifies three stages of news production: discovery, selection and reporting. In this first instance 'the business model of news discovery' (p. 100) is predominately passive, with substantial reliance on newspapers and agencies as the most economically viable sources of news stories (p. 99). Detailed analysis reveals that up to three quarters of all stories were passive in this way and 'the market model overwhelmed the journalistic' (p. 101).

As in many previous studies, McManus found the selection of news material to be determined by a series of factors which were similar across a range of outlets (p. 130). One reason for this conformity was the role of news consultants, while another was the move towards positive, uplifting stories. When asked to articulate the principles by which they selected news, the respondents in McManus's sample often evoked the needs of the audience (p. 133) just as 'Mr Gates' had done over 35 years before. While there may have been a legacy of public service rhetoric in such statements, the economic reality of commercial television demands audience building and revenue building.

McManus finds the production of news to be equally dominated by market forces, with very little time and effort given to the quality of journalism and no semblance of quality control existing. He witnesses numerous 'objectivity violations' (p. 147 ff.), the result of economically determined practice, the result of 'organisational and corporate self-interest' (p. 159). The case studies he witnesses seem to me to be shocking examples of unprofessionalism and generally slack reporting. That said, one must offer a reason for this seemingly widespread tendency which is perhaps more complex in origin than McManus allows. Given his evidence and sometimes omnidimensional explanation, he arrives at the pessimistic conclusion that maximising profits is incompatible with maximising public understanding (p. 90) and declares finally that market journalism is an oxymoron, 'a contradiction in terms' (p. 197).

Studies such as those by Cottle and McManus bring production studies up to date, dealing as they do with the deregulated commercial broadcasting environment resulting from the Thatcher and Reagan years. Their conclusions are not incompatible, given the very different systems studied. Cottle is perhaps best at articulating subtleties and avoids the trap of overstating his case by way of offering definitive explanation. McManus too claims to offer 'one important piece of the puzzle' (p. xiii), but does little to examine other parts of the jigsaw.

Changes over time

What has a generation of newsroom studies told us? Having conducted newsroom-based election studies at the BBC over a period from 1969 to

1992, Jay Blumler and Michael Gurevitch (1995) are in a unique position to remark on changes over those years, giving such investigations a much needed temporal dimension. Specifically addressing the developmental issue, they point to a generational change: 'many among this generation of news professionals have been socialised into the present-day technologically oriented, rule-regulated, hierarchically ordered and politically cautious work culture. They also appear more at ease with bureaucratic conditions than their predecessors' (p. 199). These changes are not attributed solely to the reforming efforts of the interventionist Director General John Birt. Blumler and Gurevitch suggest indeed that the pressures on the BBC were such that change would have occurred notwithstanding Birt's mission to explain.

This analysis is supported by a senior television news journalist:

> There's a generational change. When I left here for South Africa in 1983, there was lino on the floor, manual typewriters. Everyone was a lot older than me, about 45. They wore T-shirts, frayed jeans, drank about 5 pints of beer every lunchtime. They all smoked and there was fag-ash on the corner and so on. When I came back 4 years later, everyone was about 19, they all drank Perrier water, all wore collars and ties, there were deep pile carpets on the floor, flickering green screens, but, above all, there was a different culture of orthodoxy, which I think is generational, it's nothing to do with the BBC. Before, to be a journalist was somehow rather rebellious and fractious. . . . Both the BBC and ITN used to recruit from newspapers. Now, for all sorts of internal reasons, we have tended to recruit directly from universities. They are different kinds of people. Also I think there have been generational changes, broadly speaking. . . . There's more of a feeling of orthodoxy about both the BBC and I think ITN. . . . It's much more intellectually rigorous, in the sense of getting detail and context, but a much less vivid, instinctive, flexible view of these things, and also possibly a little less in touch with the mass of its audience.

Certainly the world is a much changed place since the Langs put television on the academic agenda and since sociologists first went into newsrooms, and one wonders what such pioneers would make of global television, the 1990s American networks and a Birtian BBC. The question that needs asking is, what has been learnt from over 40 years of news-production studies?

Cottle lists a baker's dozen of such work, remarking that they 'secured insights which simply could not have been sustained from a reading of news texts alone' (1993, p. 10). The main one of these is that journalism is 'the art of structuring reality, rather than recording' (Smith, 1978, p. 168). Gaye Tuchman, a leading practitioner of this type of research, has reflected on both the practical and theoretical issues involved (1991, pp. 84–6), ranging from questions of time and energy to notions of epistemology, concluding that certain such studies were 'implicitly political', with a radical outcome which did no less than 'challenge ideologies of facticity common to both news and American sociology' (p. 84).

One pragmatic response to such analysis might be to ask why bother at all if all this activity leads only into a reflexive cul-de-sac, with socially constructed academic comment on the social construction of television news creating an intellectual hall of mirrors far removed from day-to-day reality and the concerns of the viewer. One should perhaps not make the mistake of looking for a definitive answer delivered by one exclusive research method applied to a dynamic phenomenon, but instead see the insights offered as contributing to an understanding of wider issues. There is a need to interpret the interpretations:

> The largely consistent findings show the news product to be, in one sense or another, an artificial and very predictable symbolic 'construction' of reality. However, this conclusion was itself open to alternative interpretations, since it could result either from a hegemonic ideology or simply from the standardisation to be expected in any mass production process (McQuail, 1994, p. 187).

Ideologies, dominant and otherwise

The insight that the news is not merely relaying an objective truth waiting out in the world to be 'gathered' but is instead selecting, shaping and producing its message leads to an examination of what indeed that message is. There is a notion, in certain versions of the political economy school, of a dominant ideology which is passed on (consciously or unconsciously) by media elites, limiting the public's views of the world by excluding alternative perspectives. This approach can be open to caricature and gross misrepresentation, particularly when the notion of deliberate conspiracy is raised. Such theory is regarded as total nonsense by most news professionals, who claim it is hard enough to get a programme on-air without including any ideologically motivated message: conspiracies are just too hard to organise. The media, however, could be said to transmit dominant ideologies unconsciously. The reply from journalists to such a suggestion would be that their output is simply a reflection of reality, a mirror held up to the world, representing consensual views already existing in the body politic – a consensus that some academics would say the news media helped to manufacture. However, the notion of dominant ideology is far from universally accepted in the academic world, no doubt because of its lack of subtlety: 'analyses which see news as necessarily a product of powerful groups in society, designed to provide a view of the world consonant with the interests of those groups, simplify the situation too far to be helpful' (Golding and Elliott, 1979, p. 210).

Conflicts of cultures

Clearly there have been occasions when the academic and journalistic professions have not always seen eye to eye. Academics commenting on the media in general and on news practitioners in particular have often been accused of 'uninformed media bashing' (Cottle, 1993, p. xii), with news professionals 'dubious about sociologists telling them anything worth knowing about journalism' (Schlesinger, 1987, p. 47). While it has now pretty much entered common academic currency that news is not the unbiased representation of an objective truth but is instead a social product, the result of a process of selection and production, such assertions can still create contention and misunderstanding between academic researchers and media practitioners. The notion of the social construction of news has evolved over a period of decades as a result of academic observation, reflection and refinement, but its articulation still often comes as a shock to news professionals who reply that they aren't making up the news. Confrontation and misunderstanding of a sort is a well-known conference and public forum tradition experienced by many academics (Schudson, 1991, p. 141), for quite simply 'the yield of research about mass media does not always jibe with the personal experiences of people who work in the field' (Dennis, 1989, p. 132). The work of the Glasgow University Media Group in the 1970s, notably *Bad news* (GUMG, 1976), discussed in Chapter 4, is perhaps the most extreme example of this phenomenon and, interestingly, one which actually led to some dialogue. Given the different intellectual metabolic rate of the two professions (cf. Golding and Elliott, 1979, pp. 8–9), it is not surprising that these sprinters and marathon runners might have trouble communicating.

McNair suggests that relations changed in the 1980s, with academics and practitioners united in the common purpose of defending public service broadcasting from attacks from the right (1994, p. x). He also suggests that the equation has changed because of the rise of media-related courses in universities, many of them attended by would-be professionals and taught, in part, by former practitioners. Certainly there is some evidence of cross-enculturation. BBC newscaster Sue Lawley, speaking in a 1986 BBC schools programme *Inside TV: making the news* (30 October 1986), remarks: 'to a great extent the news is produced. It is not simply gathered in, written up, put in a certain order, slapped on the air and punched up, it is produced'. In the same programme Ron Neil, then Editor of BBC Television News, remarks: 'the fact is that the amount of information that comes into this building every day would produce five hours of news'. He goes on to list three selection criteria: importance, relevance and interest. In his view television news indeed offers a unique perspective: 'we put a telephoto lens onto the world. We only show in close-up the things which are newsworthy and they tend to be sad things. They tend to be events of disaster and gloom which is a fact of life'. Underlying all is 'news judgement', which he describes as: 'the way in which the journalists are trained to say that this is an interesting story; it's relevant, we ought to tell the audience about this'. Neil clearly acknowledges construction by selection and production in a way that earlier generations of his colleagues could not, and his articulation of importance and interest as criteria for news selection echoes Tuchman's (1973, p. 114) academic distinction, which was itself based on interviews with journalists.

A main bulletin anchor with significant experience of several news organisations who would agree with Neil that the news is often bad, also shows evidence that the news professional's understanding of their craft is much developed since academic comment questioned journalists' claims to simply report the news objectively:

> We all know there is no such thing as objectivity, there really isn't. Objectivity is like democracy, it's something that you strive for and seek for in its ideal form, but you know that you will never ever get there, because logistically it is probably impossible to achieve.

This is slightly more sophisticated than the view of some journalists that they are simply 'telling it like it is'. The use of the word *logistically* is interesting. If you substitute the word *epistemologically* for *logistically* you get some idea of the differences between practitioners and academics who are speaking something more like the same language but are still coming at the issues from their own professional perspectives.

Stuart Hood, who has been both a senior television news journalist and an academic, observes on the same question of objectivity:

> there is no such thing as objective news; there are only a number of verifiable facts – facts which can be corroborated. From these any news service culls a selection according to certain criteria of interest to the public or importance in the life of the citizens. The choice of these facts is, however, highly subjective, being coloured by the political, religious and social assumptions of the society in which the news editors are brought up. Editorial judgments will vary within that society from group to group and from class to class. There are, however, certain broad assumptions which guide the editorial process – beliefs in certain rights and freedoms, in certain moral values, and in certain conventions. Objective news is objective within these limits (1967, p. 120).

Whether the result of academic comment or not, some broadcasters are clearly more aware than others about the issues raised by their craft. Given the deadline-driven quotidian rush of the journalist's working life, most television professionals are remarkably reflexive about what they do. Although one can always find the hard-bitten hack who dismisses all analysis of his calling with a choice selection of four-letter words, such exceptions are rare and tend to prove the rule. Certainly, the journalists spoken to in this study were all perceptive and articulate about their profession and how it had changed, both for the better and for the worse, over the years. Many were extremely critical, in an internal professional way, while some were clearly aware of external criticism. That is not to say, however, that many routinely cogitated long and hard on the status of the truth claims they regularly advanced. They made the news every day like the bread, but don't perceive their calling as being the social construction of reality, for 'processing news leaves little time for reflexive epistemological examination' (Tuchman, 1972, p. 662). That is not to say that television journalists are all unthinking hacks. One can always find closet dons, writing articles in international relations journals and presenting papers at conferences. One senior news executive and former bulletin editor, referred to admiringly by one journalist (herself a graduate of universities on two continents) as 'planet brain', is well known for writing insightful and self-critical internal papers on the failings of news coverage. Blumler and Gurevitch (1995, p. 180) comment favourably on journalistic self-awareness, particularly after being allowed to attend a post-mortem meeting on election coverage, an event not in the normal run of academic observation. Their positive comments on the BBC's 1987 election coverage (Blumler and Gurevitch, 1995, p. 164) belie the notion that all academic comment is critical.

Attacks on television news and its values can also come from within the profession. BBC anchor Martyn Lewis put forward a case for the use of more 'good' news in bulletins. He articulated this view in an interview for this book before going public:

> we've actually got to change our thinking to make it more receptive of the positive stories that come through. . . . We're somehow getting it wrong, it's always the positive stories that are the first to be dropped from the bulletin, because it's felt that our main business should be conflict and controversy. . . . All the editors who are in place now are young dogs who have learned old tricks from old editors who were set in their ways, everyone has passed on the way of doing things right across the board and the present editors have been weaned on the student riots of the 60s, on two decades of trouble in Northern Ireland, on the economic disasters of the 70s, on the Gulf War, on the Falklands War. They wouldn't know a positive story. Instinctively they do not apply the same judgements to positive stories as they do to negative stories because their whole background had been with negativity.

This argument was not taken seriously by some of Lewis's colleagues. Whether one agrees with the need for uplifting news, the point is surely that there is a need to constantly re-examine the news agenda and the very givens of the news itself. A leader from *The Guardian* on the occasion of Lewis's remarks suggests that there is room for different agendas, as already proven by *Newsnight* and *Channel 4 News*:

Television ought really to be developing those differences as its outlets broaden and its viewers disperse. A Six O'Clock session of gloom with Snarling Sissons and Sunshine at Nine with dimpling Martyn? Probably not yet. But it is possible and there is, every day, the raw material of totally different, but equally valid, agendas of the unexpected (*The Guardian*, 1993, p. 26).

There is an undoubted need for the news media, like any other segment of society, to come under the same kind of scrutiny that they themselves devote to their subjects, with academics and other commentators taking on the same role towards the news as they themselves have towards politicians and other subjects. Cultures of criticism and accountability must be universal.

Jigsaw of truth

Academic 'intoxication with theory' (Collins, 1990, p. 251) can lose sight of the complexity of the issue. The search for an explanation, for a unified, coherent analysis of a dynamic cultural phenomenon, often leads to narrowness. There is an understandable tendency for researchers to overstress one aspect at the expense of other factors. There is nothing wrong with that in itself, but they mustn't then offer their analysis as totally comprehensive theory, for 'The complex nature of news production and its embedded existence within wider social processes and culture is unlikely to lead to a situation where any one theory suffices' (Cottle, 1993, p. 228). This is particularly the case, as the subject under study is constantly changing in content and in form. The study of news and its theorising is a complex dynamic of factors developing over time. The move outward from personal valuations, through professional rituals and institutional functioning, to business and competition issues and to wider political interactions reflects the nature of the subject under study.

Shoemaker and Reese (1991) identify five influences on media content, each operating to varying degrees. McQuail (1994, p. 186) summarises their position:

- Content reflects social reality (the mirror metaphor).
- Content is influenced by media workers' socialization and attitudes.
- Content is influenced by media–organisational routines.
- Content is influenced by wider social institutions and forces.
- Content is a function of ideological positions and maintains the *status quo*.

No one answer suffices to produce a comprehensive watertight theory. Like journalism, there is a jigsaw of truth that needs to be assembled, with reports from various sources being synthesised into an overview of a complex reality. A mapping takes place, using certain methods, conducting its survey with varying degrees of accuracy and presenting its results in its own unique, coherent language and symbol system. The truth presented is not absolute in any sense, but it is valid in its own terms. Criticism can come in two forms: the mapping is inaccuarate or it is the wrong kind of survey. The ultimate test of any mapping is its relation to its real world starting point. Does the theoretical survey help make sense?

If one takes a recent and relevant test case, that of Peter Arnett reporting from Baghdad for CNN when he was, in the words of a fellow journalist, 'in a position of influence perhaps unparalleled in the history of television journalism' (Thomson, 1992, p. 213), one can see the event in various lights. Arnett was accused on *personal* grounds of having been anti-war, anti-government and a Vietcong sympathiser by virtue of his Vietnamese ex-wife (*Washington Post Weekly,* 1991, p. 28). He was also compared to Lord Haw-Haw by British Conservative MP Robert Adley (*The Guardian*, 30 January, 1991, p. 2) and was also described as a 'feeler' (Smith, 1991, p. 35) with 'a seemingly inexhaustible concern for the welfare of the Iraqis' (*Washington Post,* 16 February, 1991). Such a view would hardly find acceptance with anyone who has met the man, with one Vietnam era contemporary describing him as 'as hard-boiled as a Chinese thousand-year-old egg' (quoted in Knightley, 1975, p. 406). There is a case to be made that Arnett stayed behind in Baghdad because of the chance of personal glory and fame, although Arnett himself denied that in on-air comment just hours before the war broke out. 'I've got nothing left personally to prove. It's just the greatest story in the world at this moment in time and I'd like to cover it as much as I can', Arnett told Walter Cronkite, apparently evoking *professional* values (CNN, 20:50 GMT 16 January 1991).

His world-beating exclusive was only possible because of *access*, as Arnett convinced the Iraqis to let him stay when almost all other journalists were expelled. CNN had a global *audience* which the Iraqis wished to reach, an audience that resulted from both CNN's use of *technology* and their long-term *institutional* development. It was further a question of technology, for CNN had a satellite phone which enabled Arnett to file independently without needing to use the damaged Iraqi communications infrastructure. The technological advantage which gave them their night-one scoop arose from *routinisation*, both in the provision of the exclusive telephone line and in the live on-air skills of their staff (Weispfenning, 1993).

CNN's media mogul *owner* Ted Turner (the unlikely case of an hereditary capitalist accused of collusion with Castro and married to 'Hanoi Jane' Fonda) didn't interfere, possibly because of the competitive *commercial* advantage of the CNN exclusive. Ratings went up by 350 per cent and with them advertising rates, with spots that sold for $5000 going up to $20 000 (Weispfenning, 1993, pp. 55–56). As well as selling premium space, CNN in effect received free advertising from other media who commented on their scoop and they cleverly extended this branding by providing their output free to other television services as long as the CNN logo was kept on it.

Was Arnett a maverick running against manufactured consent, providing the only reporting to counter the impression given by the 'smart bomb' footage? He was not the only alternative voice and, later in the war, when harrowing reports, including the horribly burnt bodies of children, emerged from Baghdad, they were shown on NBC, the network owned by a major player in the military industrial complex. Such reporting may be seen to run counter to any theory of dominant ideology or manufactured consent. On the other hand, cameraman Jon Alpert, who had travelled freely inside Iraq, produced material which was offered to two networks who first accepted it and then subsequently decided not to transmit it (Taylor, 1992, pp. 181–3). Even in the case of this material emerging from inside Iraq, commentators who saw the media 'merely serving as a public relations arm for the status quo' (Vincent, 1992, p. 186) would see their theories confirmed while others would draw an opposite conclusion, stating that the coverage of CNN and other organisations from inside Iraq more than countered the military message of 'smart bombs' that did their work without damage to humans.

Conclusions

One theoretical explanation may apply in one case, but not in another. The complex multifaceted world that the news media report admits a number of explanatory theories, none of them definitive. In this matter, as in many, it is wise never to say always. Equally, this study cannot be all things to all people and offer the totality that it says is impossible. This book examines news product as text in several detailed case studies paying particular attention to technology, one area often neglected by academics (Schudson, 1991, pp. 149–50). In order to begin to answer the questions raised above, there is an undoubted need to test theories of news production against the realities of news-workers and their organisations, their wider social and political contexts, but, more importantly, simply to look in a detailed manner at the screen product produced in the brave new world of satellite television and 24-hour rolling news.

|3|

Rhetoric and reality in 24-hour news

Rockets in Whitehall

This is a detailed case study based on transmitted material from a range of television news services as they covered a major breaking news story of undoubted importance, when the British Cabinet and the home of the Prime Minister came under terrorist fire during wartime. The event itself happened at a time of media hyperactivity during a major ongoing story, the Gulf War. It occurred in a part of London, Whitehall, which can be said to be media saturated, with all British news organisations maintaining a permanent presence as part of their domestic political coverage. It was the equivalent of the White House coming under attack (which it has, of course), but with the cameras running. The coverage of the IRA mortar-bomb attack on Number 10 Downing Street on 7 February 1991 is examined, starting with the first reports minutes after the event on two rolling television news channels, and develops as the senior news services on the British terrestrial channels interrupt their normal programming. This material is then compared with the normal run of scheduled fixed-point bulletins transmitted later that day in Britain and America, providing an international multichannel sample. Such a comparative study raises many issues for discussion and shows in detailed, concrete terms how television news has developed and what effect certain of the changes have had. The comparison between the output of the all-news satellite channels CNN and Sky News and the traditional news services on British and American networks highlights a number of crucial issues which must be explored. Changing newsgathering methods and technologies, which make possible near instant reporting, appear to threaten the provision of depth and accuracy. Equally much has changed in the manner in which material, once gathered, is packaged for transmission. But for all the dramatic headline changes in broadcast journalism, certain perennial questions are still crucial, such as access and the day-to-day working relationships between broadcasters, the government information machinery and other sources. All these issues will be discussed, growing out of a close reading of transmitted material.

Sky News were on the air interviewing Liberal Democrat MP David Steel from their then Westminster Studio when the mortar attack occurred (10:08 GMT, 05:08 EST 7 February 1991) only a few hundred yards away. Their studio was sufficiently soundproofed, however, and a dramatic exclusive was missed. Sky's rivals, the senior British news services BBC and ITN, however, were, as we shall see, literally caught in the middle of events. Sky News were first to carry the story at 10:16 GMT, citing unconfirmed reports (no source was given) of an explosion in 'the Horse Guards area of town'. This announcement consisted simply of the newsreader to camera and used no pictures of any kind. At 10:20, after a commercial break, Sky added the detail that the explosion was opposite Horse Guards and reported news from the fire brigade that a car was alight. The second studio anchor, reading from a monitor on the desk, immediately added that 'according to the latest wires we have, a van has exploded outside the Ministry of Defence'. After using and acknowledging these traditional sources, Sky resumed normal programming and continued their phone-in for service wives who were asking Paul Beaver of *Jane's Defence Weekly* about the weapons their husbands were using in the Gulf.

Helicopter journalism

CNN, the senior 24-hour rolling news service and a model for Sky News, reported the story some five minutes after its junior rival (10:21:31) with the studio anchor reading the words: 'Reuters reports an explosion has rocked the Whitehall centre of British government'. Note what appears to be the news agency's cautious use of the general area Whitehall rather than the more specific location mentioned by Sky. The brief to-camera report by the CNN studio anchor gives a general outline of the geography, explaining the relative proximity to Parliament in Westminster and to 10 Downing Street. CNN are clearly depending on the wires as their source while Sky's head start may well have come from their Westminster staff based near to the scene. At 10:24:20 after a short bulletin of non Gulf War news, CNN tells viewers around the world that Whitehall is 'a building, considered the centre of British government', before introducing the first pictures from the general area of the event, with the rider that on this tape of the explosion 'you will be able to hear it, unfortunately you will not be able to see it'. CNN then show (10:24:35) a badly framed shot of the front door of Number 10. Only eight seconds long, the shot, obviously the result of a camera left running in anticipation of Cabinet comings and goings, records four loud explosions all slightly different. The first explosion is followed about half a second later by another which is less loud and seemingly from another location. The third, which in retrospect sounds very like a firework rocket, is quieter than the first two and is followed in turn by a fourth loud report. The picture is badged with a lower third graphic reading 'London Moments Ago' and, after the explosions, shows a policeman moving quickly to the door of Number 10. CNN then run a pre-recorded ENG item on the USSR, which they interrupt after only 18 seconds (10:25:46) to 'go live to London, joining ITN for their coverage of the explosion'. Viewers then see shaky aerial pictures badged 'wtn/ITN'. These helicopter pictures are 'apparently taped just moments ago when the explosion occurred', but at 10:26:38 CNN contradict this assertion and say that they are indeed live. The pictures are very murky and clearly shot from a moving helicopter with some break-up in both sound and vision. Horse Guards Parade can be made out by the knowledgeable viewer, but generally the movement of the helicopter and/or the camera make any orientation virtually impossible. At 10:26:48 the camera actually finds a burning van next to a statue which may have been the site of the explosion. The CNN anchor sees this and comments, but the camera moves off after only 15 seconds, prompting one to ask if the camera operator actually realised what had been seen. Over these searching aerial shots, CNN quote the Press Association to the effect that the explosion was outside the Ministry of Defence and say that Scotland Yard confirm an explosion at Horse Guards. At 10:28:15, the nearly two and a half minutes of helicopter shots end.

Subsequent close inspection of this material reveals two occasions when the burning van was in shot. Early on, as the helicopter hovers over Horse Guards Parade, the camera tilts up to Whitehall near the Banqueting Hall, showing a statue and, just visible beside it, a cloud of black smoke. This shot is held for some time, suggesting perhaps that to the naked eye of the pilot and cameraman it was more visible than to the camera. The helicopter then flies around to film the burning van from another angle, clearly showing a white vehicle with flames coming from the front and back. This shot, however, is only held for 15 seconds as the helicopter and camera move off across the area, returning to Horse Guards and eventually flying off over the Parliament Square area including Westminster Abbey and the Foreign Office. There are no shots of Downing Street itself, though at one point the helicopter appears to be hovering right above it.

Getting permission to film from a helicopter over central London is difficult at any time and it is remarkable that a helicopter was able to fly over such sensitive areas at such short notice, given that the heart of British government was literally under attack in wartime. The quick arrival of the ITN helicopter at the scene was a stroke of luck, as it was already airborne *en route* to another location when first word of the explosion came through. The aerial view thus provided, informed by early knowledge from on the ground, was not necessarily what it might have been. It added a little to the story and provided the first pictures in the form of the brief shots of the burning van, but it did not give the overview that might have been expected from such a bird's-eye view.

Content aside, the communications links involved were considerable and indicate much about the way in which technology has changed the speed with which news can be reported. Live television pictures from the scene were relayed from the helicopter to ITN and then to CNN who put them on-air around the world live within 18 minutes of the event. One news organisation had the technology to get the story, with another having the airtime to report it nearly instantly. In this case ITN provided the news input, CNN the output; a case of cooperation increasingly common between allied news organisations.

While ITN pictures were coming live from the scene and being transmitted on CNN, Sky were using a different technology to speak live to a reporter at the scene. At 10:25:26 they introduce a voice-only link to Whitehall with the comment that according to the wires there have been three loud explosions near the Ministry of Defence and that a van is on fire outside the Banqueting Hall. Sky then go to their Political Editor Adam Boulton, speaking live from the St James's Park (west) side of Horse Guards Parade using a cellphone. As Boulton speaks, the screen shows the stock photograph of him used for such 'phoners' which is shortly replaced by live pictures from the roof of the Queen Elizabeth Conference Centre in Parliament Square, where Sky had their Westminster studio at the time. These pictures simply show traffic in Parliament Square and can hardly be described as informative. This practice of broadcasting live voice from one source and pictures from another is all too common in rolling news. Boulton mentions seeing a cloud of dark black smoke, talks of paratroops in red berets in the area and quotes a policeman as saying 'devices have been found'. As he speaks, his colleague Richard Bestic comes up and tells him there are two unexploded devices and one exploded device. Having gone on-air to report events, Boulton can no longer gather news and clearly has to depend on his colleague for new information. This shift in function to satisfy the relentless demands of rolling news means that reporting live and instantly places limits on the very newsgathering activity meant to be taking place. At 10:27:56 Boulton tells the Sky studio that there has apparently been an explosion inside a building. As he finishes Sky return to the studio to consult their multipurpose expert.

Meanwhile, at 10:27:10 ITN interrupt ITV programmes with a special bulletin. Newsreader Sue Carpenter reports 'a huge explosion in the centre of London. Initial reports say that a van exploded outside the Ministry of Defence in Whitehall, close to Downing Street where a Cabinet meeting is in progress'. This short announcement is accompanied by pictures from the ITN helicopter which are very unclear and which quickly break up. As the pictures degenerate, so does Carpenter's voice track. It is unclear whether the pictures are live or pre-recorded, though the word 'now' is used to describe them. The very first image is a brief shot of the burning van from almost immediately above, but this is lost after only two seconds as the helicopter moves. Interestingly, this exact shot is not in the material transmitted on CNN simultaneously. Clearly one or the other of the two services taking the helicopter pictures had to be using them pre-recorded rather than live (indeed both may have been using recordings). Very often, breaking-story material turns up on-screen, particularly on rolling news programmes, and the anchor is unaware if footage is live or taped. Sometimes it is easy to tell by the nature of the material, while at other times it is virtually impossible and anchors are often heard to ask on-air. Unable to show transmittable pictures from the helicopter, but having accurately reported the story to date and having added the important point that a Cabinet meeting was in progress, at 10:28:03 ITN finishes its special bulletin and the ITV network returns to normal programming.

'Stay with us, we're developing the story, live, on-air'

While the first of the British traditional news services was finishing its preliminary one-minute bulletin, Sky News were developing the reporting of known facts into analysis and speculation when, at 10:28:19, 12 minutes after the first reports, a Sky anchor asks if the attack is the work of the Iraqis or the IRA. So soon after the event, with facts still emerging, rolling news has reported every available scrap of information and has already begun the analysis of happenings, the full extent of which is still not clear.

The BBC, continuing a policy apparent earlier in the Gulf War, did not interrupt normal programming to report the story. At 10:29:47 they ran a special bulletin after the children's television continuity announcements in the normal programme junction. Newsreader Moira Stuart presented four short statements to camera, all of them accurate: there has been an explosion near the Ministry of Defence; a van has blown up; there have been three explosions; the van is outside the Banqueting Hall. BBC pictures are reported as being delayed as a result of their outside broadcast van being under fire and therefore off limits.

While its traditional rivals had provided their viewers with brief details in special short bulletins, Sky News continued its uninterrupted coverage of the event. At 10:33:23 they report 'black smoke coming out of the Ministry of Defence in central Whitehall'. The Sky anchor then asks their audience to stay with them as 'we're developing the story live on-air'. Nowhere could the two cultures of television news be more apparent. While the senior news services of the BBC and ITN, transmitting as part of general television services, can only interrupt briefly with short factual bulletins, the rolling news services have the opposite problem. Given unlimited airtime to fill, they have the ability to broadcast instantly whatever material comes in and, if need be, to pad in the studio in between.

At 10:33 the CNN anchor in Atlanta speaks on the phone to CNN London producer Rob Reynolds who is in his office. He describes telephoning a sergeant at Horse Guards Parade who told him that mortar rounds were fired from a van now on fire. Reynolds mentions speaking to CNN reporter Brian Cabell, who is actually running from Trafalgar Square to Horse Guards. As Reynolds speaks, viewers see the earlier transmitted helicopter pictures of the burning van which are now badged 'ITN Taped Earlier' and which have now clearly been edited. At 10:37 Reynolds corrects the CNN anchor's repeated error, explaining to viewers around the globe that 'Whitehall is a district', not a building.

CNN's coverage does not take the typical form of a reporter live from the scene, but a producer in the office using the old-fashioned wired telephone to contact witnesses and then to phone base. By such orthodox journalism, he gets accurate information quickly and efficiently without actually going to the scene. His newsgathering stops, however, as journalistic input turns to broadcast output and Reynolds has to go on-air to report his findings. Once again, the perceived need to get on-air quickly with any material at all actually prevents further newsgathering.

While CNN were mixing their London reports with continued coverage of other events, Sky News devoted all their airtime to the story in Whitehall. At 10:39 in the Sky studio Paul Cotton, captioned as a 'Defence Expert', says the Public Information Office at the Ministry of Defence has been damaged and that he has just been speaking to 'people down there'. He goes on to say that the explosion is 'almost certainly linked to the Gulf . . . likely to be Iraqis or a group linked to them'. Two minutes later, however, Cotton replies to a question from one of the Sky anchors about the possible culprits: 'who knows at this stage? It could be the IRA, could be the Iraqis'.

Rolling news inevitably includes a certain amount of repetition, with frequent 'recaps'. At 10:44 during such an update the Sky anchor says 'we first saw it on the wires just after ten'. This reference to the source and timing of the story was followed within seconds (10:44:52) by an injunction to the studio team: 'Let's continue the speculation'. Similarly, at 10:46, after 10 minutes of other coverage, CNN recap 'if you've just now joined us . . . '. They begin by showing the shot of the door of Number 10 at the time of the explosion, then continue with a telephone link to London reporter Brian Cabell. During his voice-only report, viewers are shown new material from ground level of the burning van shot from Trafalgar Square. Badged 'ITN taped earlier', this material is actually shot from roughly the same place that the reporter speaks from. These new visuals are intercut with earlier shots of the burning van from the ITN helicopter. Temporally and spatially we have a reporter on the street in London speaking live on a cellphone through the public telephone system to CNN in Atlanta. As he speaks CNN viewers see pre-recorded pictures shot from the same place minutes earlier by a partner news organisation which are being played out either from CNN London or from Atlanta. In this edited picture sequence, shots on the ground are intercut with helicopter shots recorded some time earlier. Technically speaking, the report contains a continuity error, cutting between shots of the van with the fire at different stages. This taped sequence is repeated several times as the reporter speaks. At one point (10:49:07) the live voice report says that no flames can be seen while the recorded on-screen pictures clearly show the van burning.

The event reported happened roughly 40 minutes before and already ITN have produced pictures from two sources and CNN have broadcast live from the scene using the words of a reporter who can see part of the event; a reporter who, it must be said, cautions his audience that the story is only 25–30 minutes old and 'we can't rely on early reports' (10:48:17). In the days before rolling news, very little would have been reported so soon after the event even though pre-transmission newsgathering would have proceeded at the same hectic pace. First output would still have been over two hours away with the additional time enabling a more complete finished product to be presented to viewers.

'Very raw footage'

At 10:49:30, about two minutes after CNN, Sky begin transmitting their first pictures from Downing Street which are described by their anchor as 'very raw footage'. Viewers then see 11 minutes of rushes commented on out of vision by the Sky studio team. The shots start in Downing Street with a recording of other film crews standing around at the moment of explosion. The tape develops as a policeman, speaking into his radio, runs towards an iron gate at the western end of Downing Street. He arrives at the gate just as five men emerge. As they pass the camera, it zooms in to show white smoke appearing from behind the Prime Minister's residence. A security camera is visible on a wall as the camera zooms out again. This sequence is followed by shots out into Whitehall through the barrier at the eastern end of Downing Street. These in turn are followed by short interviews with three of the men who had been seen running towards camera from behind Number 10. The first man interviewed was the last of the five men to run out. His comments are limited, talking of 'yellow-coloured smoke' and hearing two explosions. As he speaks a helicopter can be heard overhead. The next shot consists of a dark-haired man in a red and blue jacket who describes how he was sitting in his outside-broadcast truck when the explosion went off. In response to questioning, he hazards a guess that it was a mortar and states that it hit the green next to the vehicle he was in. This witness was clearly a television technician, though this was not stated in any way. The third interview was with a man in a grey coat, clearly standing in Downing Street, who describes being 'inside the BBC technical vehicle at the back of Number 10 Downing Street' when he heard a tremendous bang and saw a plume of smoke coming up from inside the garden at Number 10. Within 10 seconds another bang followed and he looked around to see a large smoking cylinder lying on the grass by the monument on Horse Guards Parade. As he speaks, once again a helicopter can be heard overhead.

This last interview is followed by a shot out into Whitehall, through the Downing Street barrier. It is just possible to glimpse fire and black smoke on the right-hand edge of the frame, which is partly obscured by the railing in front of the camera. It is not clear if the cameraman sees it clearly, as he pans away when he could clearly have got a better shot. The small black-and-white viewfinder on almost all camcorders can sometimes make it difficult for operators to see clearly all that is being recorded by the camera. This problem might particularly have been the case on a very dull winter's day with flat light and very little contrast. At 10:55 Sky viewers see this tape rewinding in vision and this last shot is replayed so that the studio team can comment on the fact that it does in fact contain the burning van.

In all, this unedited material consists of 27 shots. At the end viewers clearly see a policeman move television crews out of Downing Street into the Foreign Office opposite. A break in the control track indicates that the camera has been turned off before the very last shots on the tape, which are from the end of King Charles Street, showing a deserted Whitehall. Clearly the Sky crew were moved on by police to film in nearby locations before stopping to get the material on-air. This could have been done by returning through the Foreign Office courtyard to their Westminster base just around the corner in the Queen Elizabeth Centre in order to play out the material. There is a feed-point which enables live broadcasting from outside the front door of Number 10 and this could have been used to play recorded material straight out of camera onto air. However, one of the interviewed technicians mentioned that the power had gone off and this may have affected the working of normal links, and it is worth remembering the statement in the BBC bulletin that their van and hence certain linking technology were off limits.

Visual material from the scene was far from the only source of information. At various times in their coverage CNN quote BBC, Sky (both at 10:51) and Reuters (10:54:55). This cross-referencing of other news organisations is both a rhetorical device indicating sophistication and thoroughness, and a pragmatic way of covering one's organisation should mistakes be made. It could also be seen to be symptomatic of sophisticated postmodernist self-awareness; of media transparency, with viewers let in on some of the secrets of the trade. It is certainly a sign of the interrelated nature of the wired world, where television news organisations clearly carefully monitor each other both as a part of cooperative arrangements, institutional alliances and good old-fashioned out and out competition. Shortly after one such quotation of sources (10:54:55) CNN actually go to ITN, taking an entire bulletin already in progress.

Edited packages

ITN's second special bulletin (10:54:49) begins with the same first sentences as their earlier bulletin, with the additional information that staff at the

Ministry of Defence are reported to have been told that there had been a mortar attack on Downing Street and that there was an unexploded device at the scene. Newsreader Sue Carpenter then introduces a taped report saying: 'Robert Hall at ITN has been monitoring the pictures'. This introduction is an indication of an increasingly common practice in television news, where journalists at base voice pictures sent in from a remote source. Often the visuals are from a television picture agency or a stringer and are very often from abroad. Such pictures can be provided with commentary by the newsreader speaking out of vision during the live newscast, but increasingly they are voiced at base by another journalist, creating an edited package. ITN in particular are scrupulous about making this situation clear to viewers in their introductions to such material; other broadcasters, however, are not. Hall's report was 1 minute and 10 seconds in length, beginning with a helicopter shot of the burning van seen from a slightly different angle than that already seen on CNN or ITN. In this material the fire has clearly progressed, indicating that this picture was recorded later than the earlier transmitted versions. A second helicopter shot of a group of people standing in an unspecified open green area follows, before we see ITN's first material from on the ground which consists of general views of police vehicles and traffic being diverted in the Parliament Square–Westminster Bridge area. Hall's voice-over describes how the explosion happened shortly after 10 o'clock and correctly places the van as being at the corner of Horseguards Avenue and Whitehall, 'barely 200 yards from both the Ministry of Defence and from Downing Street where the War Cabinet had been in session'. Early reports are quoted indicating that there have been three explosions, and 'Whitehall sources' are reported to have spoken of a possible mortar attack on 'Downing Street itself'. Hall's piece is followed immediately by a live two-way interview (10:56) with Political Editor Michael Brunson in ITN's Westminster Studio. In response to the oft-used, open-ended question from the studio anchor, 'what can you tell us?', Brunson describes hearing three explosions himself from the Houses of Parliament, which confirms reports of 'three projectiles fired from this van'. He relates how the War Cabinet was actually in session when the explosions went off, quickly moving to another room. Such live two-ways are a stock-in-trade of a Political Editor, though usually they are used more for punditry and analysis than for earwitness reporting of breaking hard news. ITN's second special bulletin ended at 10:58:31, having added some new detail in the form of the report of the War Cabinet which came from a Political Editor near but not at the scene. No indication was given of his source for the information about the Cabinet, though it clearly came as the result of some form of briefing. Interestingly, ITN made no use of their own pictures from the Trafalgar Square end of Whitehall which had been used (and credited) by CNN eight minutes earlier.

At 11:00 the BBC transmitted the first regularly scheduled bulletin to cover the story. Unlike the authoritative minimalism of its earlier short announcement, this bulletin attempted to cover the story more comprehensively. Newsreader Lynnette Lithgow began the bulletin, announcing to camera that there had been an attempted attack on Number 10 Downing Street and that a vehicle had exploded near the Ministry of Defence. Two sources were given to support the statement that missiles were fired from the van and that there had been an attempted mortar attack. A map of the area was used, showing the position of the burning van and its relationship to Downing Street. There were three ENG shots, lasting 23 seconds, showing people leaving the area. These were followed by a voice-only, live two-way, with BBC engineer Charlie Brereton who had been in the BBC van when the missile fell (Sky had interviewed him earlier, transmitted 10:54). This link was followed by a discussion in the studio with Defence Correspondent David Shukman, who cautioned that it was 'much too early to say' if the Iraqis were indeed responsible. Unlike its British competitors ITN and Sky, the BBC had not transmitted pictures of the burning van, nor had it yet shown any material from Downing Street.

At 11:02 Sky transmitted new ENG material which begins with an interview from outside Westminster with eyewitness Dr Andy Ashworth. He is interviewed by an unseen woman reporter and as he speaks Big Ben strikes 11 (indicating therefore that the material was recorded just minutes earlier). He reports being told there were bodies in the van. As this interview finishes, the tape rewinds in vision. More unedited pictures follow from Parliament Square which add nothing to the story. Slightly later Sky provides comment from the scene in the form of MP Paul Flynn on the telephone (11:15:49) who tells viewers that the bombing has 'likely sprung from the diseased mind of Saddam Hussain'.

Shortly after 11:00 CNN feature a second despatch from reporter Brian Cabell in Whitehall. As in his earlier contribution, he speaks on the phone while pictures of the burning van are put on screen. Interestingly, speaking live from the street near the scene, he quotes the latest word from a British news agency, information which had probably been read to him earlier by his London office. This is followed immediately by the CNN anchor in Atlanta reading out to him an Associated Press report stating that smoke had been seen coming from the back of Number 10 Downing Street. Cabell replies that he cannot see that far and therefore cannot confirm the report. He stresses there is no access to the area and that no clear picture has yet emerged, suggesting sensibly that it may be as long as an hour before it will.

Who knows more, an eyewitness reporter at a police barrier with a mobile phone or an anchor back at base with all the incoming information provided by the wires and other media? These sources are used visibly when the CNN anchor (11:16) first reads out a BBC Radio report, then turns to his computer monitor and reads a Reuters report. Clearly, in this case a studio anchor across the ocean in Atlanta has the story so far from the wires and can tell his reporter on the street near the scene.

'We brought it to you first and live'

At 11:20 Sky News reminds its audience that 'We brought it to you first and live', an assertion followed quickly by previously seen recorded material, now edited. The trio of television technicians appear once again, explaining their experiences. They are presented in a different order than they were recorded. There is of course nothing unusual about this temporal rearrangement of news material in the interests of clarity, except in this case viewers had already seen the order of events in recorded order.

Meanwhile, CNN, unlike Sky, were continuing coverage of other events, updating the Whitehall story only at periodic intervals. At 11:31 they returned to Brian Cabell reporting on the phone, still with the helicopter pictures of the burning van used over his voice. He then introduces video-tape of a witness obtained from ITN. Interestingly, when asked 'Did you see the van?' this witness replies 'What van?' This material is an instance of the increasingly frequent practice of location-based reporters introducing video-tape material which is actually played in back at base and which they may never have seen. After the tape Cabell mentions unconfirmed reports of bodies, which were repeated again at 12:00 on CNN.

At 11:35 the BBC transmitted a further special bulletin, including a brief edited ENG package which featured the clearest pictures yet seen of the burning van taken from only about 100 yards away on the pavement opposite Horse Guards Parade. At the time these images were recorded the police clearly had yet to close off the area. These pictures were voiced by reporter Clarence Mitchell, but no indication was given of his location. The reporting of the event had now clearly entered a second phase, with all British news services having run edited packages using pictures from the scene.

Sky's next edited ENG package at 11:51 made extensive use of material from Downing Street, material which was again edited out of recorded order. At one point in this material (11:52:15) the synchronous sound of the videotape is lost and in its place viewers hear a clearly angry voice: 'Control the sound one way or another. It's like my eight year old playing with Nintendo at the moment'. This package was followed by a recap before, at 11:57, Sky News paused for advertisements, their first interval since they broke the story at 10:16. Sky had transmitted over an hour and a half of live television, covering the same breaking story. By any criterion this was a considerable achievement for an organisation only two years old at the time. Nevertheless, this notable accomplishment under great pressure must still be examined critically for this coverage, and the coverage of the other 24-hour rolling news service CNN, was clearly marred by false leads, hurried presentation and plain old-fashioned factual errors. We heard first that a car had exploded, then a van; CNN described Whitehall as a building; Sky reported smoke coming from the Ministry of Defence and this report was later expanded to state that the Public Information Office had been hit. At one point the Iraqis were confidently blamed, an assertion which was repeated by another source. Raw footage of television technicians running around in Downing Street was transmitted, and on Sky a witness told of bodies in the van; CNN also reported bodies. ITN provided live helicopter shots from the air above the scene, but no one saw the back of Number 10 and hence there was no record of the damage actually done. Rolling news and the near instant reporting it makes possible, and even demands, makes it more likely that mistakes will be made and that the confusion, chaos and uncertainty that reigns as any story emerges will be transmitted to the public. It is all too easy to get smug about it and dismiss the johnny-come-latelys of television news as knee-jerk rumour-mongers filling the airwaves with confusion, speculation, rumour and ill-prepared visuals. A senior BBC news manager, who had once astounded a professional forum by telling a conference of his peers in a clear statement of traditional BBC values that he would rather get the story right than get it first, had some interesting comments to make on the subject of rolling news. Such a figure might have been expected to be extremely critical, but he wasn't. In his opinion rolling news can be revisionist; it doesn't need to get it right instantly because it can correct itself quickly enough. In this analysis the viewer is let in on the newsgathering process and sees the story develop on-air. Such television is potentially more exciting, if not more accurate, than traditional fixed-point bulletins. The presentational quality of this kind of broadcasting, however, can be called into question, with tapes rewinding in vision, pictures from one place being voiced from another, anchors making basic factual errors and promising input that never arrives on screen. It needs to be asked if such a style is merely a bad job or has the urgent feel necessary to breaking news. Is it a dynamic and exciting new form of television journalism or is it just television? In instances such as this, rolling news could be characterised as being halfway between the wholesale news of the wire services and the picture agencies and the retail news of fixed-point bulletins on general television services. As time passed and the Downing Street story developed, the news moved from the instant on-air live reporting of the rolling news services into the realm of the fixed-point bulletins, with the journalistic centre of gravity shifting from the 24-hour satellite channels to the traditional network news services.

At 11:53:50 ITN ran their third special bulletin, presented by Sue Carpenter:

> News is coming in all the time on the explosion. Scotland Yard has confirmed there has been a mortar attack on Downing Street. Two or three mortars are believed to have been fired from a van outside the Ministry of Defence building in Whitehall. The attack happened as the Cabinet was meeting. Eyewitnesses have described seeing large lumps of metal flying through the air. The police have said that there are two other suspected devices in the Horse Guards area of Whitehall.

Halfway through this to-camera introduction, a map of the area, with captions superimposed, is put on screen. It is clearly taken from the *A–Z London Street Atlas*, but is an extremely accurate representation of the relative positions of the van, the Ministry of Defence and Downing Street. Pictures from the scene voiced by Carpenter follow and include the door of Number 10 as the explosions occur and the burning van seen both from Trafalgar Square and from the helicopter. In addition there is new ENG material of Lord Waddington, Leader of the House of Lords, remarking: 'whether it is two separate incidents or not I don't know'. Carpenter's voice-over explains that one missile landed in the garden of Number 10, breaking windows, while two more missed and landed on Foreign Office Green. Neil Houghton, the ITN technician previously seen on Sky, then explains, in new footage, how he came under fire. The bulletin ends with Carpenter in the studio confirming that windows were smashed in the Cabinet Room. The main events of the story appear to be emerging clearly an hour and a half after the event.

Fixed-point bulletins

The BBC noon bulletin is usually short and was in no way extended on this occasion. Devoted entirely to the Whitehall story, the report began with the usual studio introduction with the newsreader speaking first to camera and then over a map of the area, which was in turn followed by an ENG package voiced by reporter Jennie Bond which included new visual material from the same picture cluster seen at 11:35. A BBC crew had clearly got quite near to the burning van fairly quickly, as viewers actually see the police moving them on and closing the area. The report contained three eyewitness reports, including both the BBC technician, Charlie Brereton, who was making his third different appearance, and his ITN counterpart, Neil Houghton, in what was his fourth. Both had already been seen earlier on Sky and on their own channels in different variations. The first police spokesman to be seen appears making a brief statement in the street to the effect that the area is sealed and will not be entered for some time. This ENG package was followed by an interview from the BBC Westminster studio with Dr Andy Ashworth who had already been seen in Sky's first ENG an hour earlier. Interestingly, this witness no longer reports the police talking of bodies in the van. The bulletin ends with a live two-way with correspondent Martin Dowle in Westminster who describes speaking with 'officials from Downing Street in the last 10 minutes'. During this report he gives 10:09 as the time of the explosion.

    The ITN News at 12:30 was the first substantial scheduled bulletin to cover the story. Longer than the BBC's five-minute reports at 11:00 and noon, this was the first report on British television to carry other news. The bulletin, presented by John Suchet, used headline shots of the burning van seen from a new angle (behind, on the ground, on Horseguards Avenue, near the main entrance to the Ministry of Defence) and from the ITN helicopter. The shot of the door of Number 10 was followed by shots of the technicians running out from behind Number 10. These had been seen earlier on Sky but were now transmitted for the first time on terrestrial network television. Following these brief headline shots, Suchet reported to camera that windows had been smashed at Number 10 and stated that 'one report says all three [bombs] landed in the garden of Downing Street'. With the announcement that 'these pictures came in a few minutes ago', Suchet began an out-of-vision sequence, with pictures of the burning van fairly early on in the incident and therefore over two hours old. The out-of-vision script continued over a map of the area in the same style as the popular *A–Z London Street Atlas*. Suchet then introduced an ENG package by Robert Hall which reportedly included 'exclusive pictures showing the effect of mortar bombs on the front of Number 10'. This first shot, over which one can just hear an American voice, had already been seen on CNN. Pictures from the ITN helicopter followed which clearly showed the burning van from almost directly above. These are followed by footage shot from the end of Downing Street through the security gates out onto a deserted Whitehall. These shots are virtually identical to those shown on Sky at 10:55 but there are clearly more flames coming from the vehicle indicating that they were shot at a different time. A policeman at the gates is seen to send the cameraman back into Downing Street. This is followed by the shot of the technicians running out from behind Number 10. ITN technician Neil Houghton is then seen in a further new interview; his fifth different sound bite of the morning. A sequence of general views and eyewitness reports leads to the first recorded official comment, a statement in the street from a Metropolitan police civilian press officer, Stewart Goodwin, who clearly states there is a 'lot of damage to the rear of Number 10' (12:36:09). CNN, who had been taking this bulletin since it began, cut away at this point.

Live from the scene

The ITN bulletin continues with a second ENG package by reporter Jo Andrews which shows general views of War Cabinet arrivals before the explosions. This item ends with a piece to camera by Andrews in the Whitehall area which is the first visual appearance of a reporter from near the scene. This recorded appearance is then followed by a live two-way with Michael Brunson from an equally unspecified exterior location, who reports that the bomb landed only 50 yards from the Prime Minister. Brunson recounts being present at a detailed briefing where it was explained that Number 10 was not badly damaged. This, of course, contradicts the message given out by a police spokesman earlier in the same bulletin (which Brunson might not have seen or heard). Brunson cautions that speculation about the cause of the attack is fruitless and remarks that 'we will have to wait and see'.

After a number of other items filling out the story, ITN (13:06) conducts a live two-way with Stewart Goodwin, the Scotland Yard spokesman seen earlier on tape. When asked if the police were watching the van he replies 'I am not prepared to discuss what our activities were' and when pressed further he is equally non-committal. No questions were asked about the existence of video surveillance footage.

This extended ITN lunchtime bulletin had included three ENG packages, one of which was repeated with a slight variation, one of which was background and only one of which featured a reporter in the area. However, it used four live two-ways from the same place in Whitehall, two of them with the same person. There was a studio interview with an expert and other news was covered.

The BBC *One O'Clock News* began with headline shots of the burning van from Whitehall, followed by two totally new shots of the burning tubes lying on the ground in Foreign Office Green. Anchor Martyn Lewis reports (13:00:41) that the anti-terrorist branch are now blaming the IRA for the attack and not pro-Iraqi terrorists. He continues to camera, giving the time of attack as 10:09 and stating that the Prime Minister and the War Cabinet were 'beyond question' the target. The story to date is related 'from what has been pieced together': a van was driven into Whitehall and then abandoned; three mortar bombs were fired through the roof of the van at Number 10; these overshot, landing in the garden of Number 10; two other suspect devices have been found; two men were seen running away from the van. This studio narrative shifts without introduction into an ENG report by the BBC's Chief Political Correspondent, John Sergeant. In this piece the ubiquitous ITN technician Neil Houghton appears again, here captioned as Graham Everitt. Shakey and uninformative general views of Downing Street soon after the explosion are then followed by a BBC technician making his first interview appearance since he was seen running into Downing Street in the first material transmitted on Sky. He is wrongly captioned as being a Scotland Yard spokesman when he would seem to be Graham Everitt, with the BBC seemingly having got one name super ahead of itself. The police spokesman, Goodwin, then appears some time after his name caption. This is the same material seen earlier on ITN (12:35) but from a much better camera angle and with an extra sentence of statement on the end.

This is another example of a 'picture cluster'. In ordinary domestic newsgathering there inevitably arise situations when two or more competing ENG crews are present at the same scene, both recording it from only slightly different positions. Often film crews appear in each other's material as camera operators all crowd round the same detail. This 'hunting in packs' is common at normal times in relatively stress-free domestic newsgathering, sometimes the result of restrictions imposed either by minders, physical circumstances or a combination of both. Such material inevitably has the same content in spite of the marginally different camera angles. In this case there was a more obvious visual difference than usual, but not one which altered the informational content of the pictures. While both the BBC and ITN used this material in edited packages, Sky were to use the same spokesman in the same situation live at 13:13. Clearly, there were at least three crews present at what had become the live feedpoint from Whitehall.

After a brief return to the anchor in the studio at 13:05 to state that a police press conference has confirmed the IRA as being responsible, the BBC run a second ENG piece voiced by Clarence Mitchell. This report uses new pictures taken in Horse Guards Parade which are acknowledged as being from a freelance cameraman. They show two long cylinders, each burning at one end. In one shot a television van is just visible a short distance away from the projectiles. These pictures, taken from some distance using the zoom lens, are supplemented by a wider angle shot briefly showing the relationship between these two unexploded devices, the television outside-broadcast vehicles mentioned so often and the back of Downing Street.

After an attempted live two-way with eyewitness John Kennedy fails for technical reasons, Martyn Lewis conducts a live two-way interview with Nick Buckley, the BBC technician earlier referred to as Charlie Brereton by his employers. He mentions seeing a huge plume of smoke coming from behind Number 10. The BBC are then able to complete the two-way with Kennedy (who was seen earlier on ITN at 12:30) in their Norman Shaw North Studio in Westminster. He describes the event from the Whitehall side and speaks of seeing a van in flames. This eyewitness report is followed immediately by a live two-way with Political Editor John Cole in the BBC's Westminster Studio, who discusses the implications of an attack where the Cabinet were saved only by bomb-proof netting. Additionally, Cole reports that the office of civil servant Murdo Maclean at the back of Number 12 has been badly damaged. There was no indication that Cole had been to Number 10, and all this information was clearly the result of a briefing, although this was not actually stated in any way.

The BBC then shifted from the live report with a man near the scene to an edited ENG package on anti-terrorist security by Defence Correspondent David Shukman, which also reviewed the history of IRA mortar bombs. This piece represents a clear shift from the reporting of actual events to analysis and background. This style of reaction background piece from a specialist correspondent, usually back at base, is a common device very often used by diplomatic correspondents.

BBC live reporting from the scene then continued in the form of a phone link with Polly Toynbee reporting from a press conference at Cannon Row Police Station where reporters were told of a crater in the garden of Number 10, that the back of the building had been scorched and that windows were broken on all floors. This briefing process, supplementing Scotland Yard's earlier statements in the street, ran parallel to the briefings given by the Whitehall information machinery to political correspondents in Westminster but which were markedly less detailed about the extent of the damage.

The BBC main one o'clock bulletin carried five ENG items by four different reporters (the fifth piece, a brief sound bite from Foreign Secretary Douglas Hurd, consisted only of synchronous sound and used no reporter voice-over), including a background piece and an all-party reaction piece. Two reporters worked from Westminster and two were back at base in Television Centre. No less than six live two-ways were used. Three different locations in Westminster were used for these, two of them different BBC studios. These live links also included comment from as far away as Scotland in the form of an academic expert at Aberdeen University.

American morning news

Owing to the five-hour time difference between London and New York, the American network breakfast news programmes were running the story at about the same time as the first British bulletins. NBC transmitted the story first, simply because *News at Sunrise* aired a full hour before the other morning network news programmes. At 6:00 EST, the American coverage of the event began with a short headline read over general views of police in the streets. A van explosion outside the Defence Ministry was reported, as were two unexploded bombs in the back yard of Number 10 Downing Street. This report was repeated at 6:19 without the mention of unexploded devices. By 6:28 NBC had shots of the burning van and explained that mortar bombs had been fired at Number 10 during a Cabinet meeting. ABC *World News this Morning* at 7:00 led with the story, quoting the BBC before doing a live two-way with Barry Dunsmore in their London office. Beginning to camera with the proviso that 'reports are still coming in' the London report then used a map of the area, helicopter shots of the burning van and general views of the police, and explained that a van had fired three projectiles. All the statements were accurate, all were qualified and attributed to 'reports', 'witnesses' and the Press Association. When asked a question by the New York anchor, Dunsmore replied 'Well frankly, it's not entirely clear, but from this report I've just read to you, Mike, it would seem . . .' In response to a second question, Dunsmore mentioned Saddam Hussein's threats of terrorism and pointed out that the IRA could be responsible, before ending with the rider 'but at this point that's pure speculation'. CBS too began with a live two-way with their London office. Using helicopter shots and general views on the ground, Bill Whittaker's report equally quotes 'eyewitnesses' but mentions 'as many as five mortars' being fired from the van outside the Ministry of Defence and appears to regard the Downing Street attack as a separate incident. The report ends by stating 'the van, which is still smouldering, is said to contain a number of unexploded mortars'.

At 7:30 ABC ran a second two-way with London which added the news that a plume of smoke had been seen from the garden of Number 10. As before, ABC scrupulously attributed every statement, either to 'eyewitnesses' or 'sources in the Prime Minster's office'. All network reports up to this time were from their London offices and, unlike CNN and Sky, they had not despatched on-screen talent to the scene with cellphones.

At 8:00 NBC *Today* had a live phono interview with Nick Buckley, the much-seen BBC engineer, here called Charlie Brereton, the possible result of traditional links between NBC and the BBC. He described hearing three explosions and seeing a fourth unexploded bomb. When asked if there was any serious damage, he replied 'apparently there was some structural damage to Number 10'. NBC then linked to Sky's London studio to talk to Paul Beaver who accurately outlined the situation to date.

More than three hours after the event and with literally hours of broadcasting devoted to it, the vast majority of the viewing public had yet to see the news. The attack had been exhaustively covered, with the main outline of events clear, but there was still some confusion about certain details. Nevertheless, the emphasis shifted from newsgathering to presentation, from input to output. Rolling news had had its day, or more accurately its hours. With few new developments, they could now only repeat the story to date. However, having only produced their early editions, the main fixed-point bulletins of the senior news services still lay ahead.

CNN and Sky, of course, continued broadcasting throughout the day, constantly recapping, inevitably engaging in repetition. Rolling news, broadcasting 24 hours a day, always has a certain amount of redundancy. Given the ample airtime there is always an opportunity for the provision of background. This particular afternoon Sky inevitably used a number of live two-ways with experts and politicians, alternating these with links to their own staff and repeated, and at times revised, ENG material. Only at 13:30, after over three hours on the story, did Sky run its first other news since the story broke.

At 14:19 Sky transmitted a live relay of a press conference from outside Cannon Road Police Station. Scotland Yard spokesman Stewart Goodwin was asked about the situation at Number 10: 'What news on getting down there for a facility?' 'Can we all switch off now?', came the reply. Whatever was then said was off the record and not for public consumption. In any case, it did not result in any pictures from the scene, for no facility was granted.

The early evening news

It can hardly have been a leisurely afternoon at the BBC and ITN as they prepared their early evening bulletins. New material continued to emerge, with the Queen commenting on the event in a speech and the House of

Commons debating the issue of security. ITN used both of these elements in the headlines of their 17:30 bulletin, which added several new aspects to the story. An introductory 'three-dimensional' graphics sequence voiced by the studio anchor offered a clear overview of events. Two new eyewitnesses then appeared on tape. The first, a Mr Patel who was the driver of a bus which had been passing along Whitehall, actually describes the rockets going off. His testimony is followed by the previously seen television technicians who then give way to the second new witness, a government information officer who was inside Number 10 overlooking the garden. These witness statements describe the event from three different points of view. A report from a further Scotland Yard press conference adds the fact that the van driver escaped on a motorbike driven by an accomplice. This contradicts earlier reports to the effect that men were seen running away, and no indication is given as to how the police knew this. A graphic sequence is used to explain events in the Cabinet Room. Two ITN reporters appear on the scene, one in a recorded piece, the other in a live two-way. A total of 16 minutes of the bulletin were devoted to the story.

BBC Six O'Clock News

The BBC's main bulletin at 18:00 introduced the story by reminding viewers that the story was now eight hours old. This studio introduction from Anna Ford used a map to explain the order of events. The substantive ENG piece at the top of the programme included the bus driver Mr Patel making his first BBC appearance, with different remarks from those given on ITN minutes earlier. The much seen television technicians followed. New material included the Scotland Yard Press Officer Goodwin describing the crater as being 'some feet across and not very deep'. David Shukman's report finished with a piece to camera in a darkening Whitehall which stated that the mortar round may have hit a tree. John Sergeant's political-reaction piece included footage from the House of Commons. In this, in response to a question from former Home Secretary Merlyn Rees who says that the vehicle was parked for eight minutes before the explosion, the present Home Secretary, Kenneth Baker, denied any breach of security, saying the van 'stopped casually for a few minutes'. No comment was made on this imprecise answer, nor was any explanation offered as to how a former Cabinet minister who would have had regular dealings with the security services might have come by such information.

New pictures were shown from the interior of Downing Street, showing business as usual, with a visitor being greeted in the oft-seen photo opportunity. There were no shots of the Cabinet Room nor of the garden. Testimony direct from the heart of the matter was provided in the form of minister David Mellor who described seeing a tree 'not where it should be'. Like ITN, the BBC used a graphic representation of the Cabinet table and similarly ended their coverage of the story with a live two-way with their Political Editor. Their 21 minutes of coverage included unique pictures of Horse Guards Parade and the only interview until then with Cabinet eye-witness David Mellor, though the BBC did not claim any kind of exclusive. ITN, on the other hand, had rightly claimed an exclusive both for their heli-copter pictures and the shot of the door of Number 10.

In their regular evening bulletins both BBC and ITN had made good use of 'three-dimensional' graphics and considered picture editing to explain the proper order of events, and each gave a detailed overview. ITN particularly made effective use of the available pictures. Here orthodox news was clearly displaying its strengths. Just as serious newspapers have responded to the threat of television news by including more features and having more per-sonality columnists, so too fixed-point bulletins on general programming channels need to respond to the challenge of the rolling news services by doing what they do best.

Nine O'Clock News

The BBC's second major news programme of the evening was to extend the explanation of the event with a new map and an animated 'three-dimen-sional' graphic to visualise events. These were then followed by no less than six ENG pieces, none of them repeated. The lead ENG was by Jennie Bond, which covered the same ground as David Shukman's in the *Six O'Clock News* and which used many of the same pictures, but which was neverthe-less recognisably different, using new eyewitness material. Bond ended her report with a piece to camera in a darkening Whitehall, mentioning that the mortar hit a cherry tree. This was a close copy of the piece to camera in David Shukman's similar piece at 18:00, but was clearly shot much later. The other ENG reports covered events in the Cabinet Room, security in gen-eral and events in the Commons, and there were two background pieces, one on mortar bombs and one on general IRA attacks on the mainland. A live two-way with Political Editor John Cole in Westminster ended the 23 minutes of coverage.

News at Ten

ITN transmitted their main report of the story at 22:00, nearly 12 hours after the event. The headline 'bongs' featured the burning van, the door of Number 10 at the time of the explosion and a shot from their helicopter. The studio introduction was then followed by a detailed graphics sequence, by far the clearest yet seen. The lead ENG item by Norman Rees contained an even more detailed graphic, with animations superimposed on an aerial photo of the area to show the path of the missiles. Such detailed and complex computer graphics would have taken some time to create, as would the pastel drawing of events in the Cabinet Room which followed next in the piece. A speaker exclusive to ITN then appeared in the form of Katherine Coombs, earlier described as a government information officer, but now styled a public affairs consultant. The various visuals seen during the day then appeared in an extremely coherent sequence which had edited the pictures together in such a way as to almost make the voice-over commentary redundant. The television technicians running out into Downing Street were particularly well handled. After the first three ran towards the camera, the piece cut to the last one seen, who then gave his description of events. From this speech it cut seamlessly in mid-sentence to a second technician speaking in vision and finished with his words being used under the pictures of him running away from the explosion. This simple use of the eyewitness's words as a voice-over to the action he was describing was effective picture editing of a kind not usually seen in the news. Almost stereotypically, the BBC did the background of the story in great detail, explaining every possible context, while ITN clearly handled the pictures better and told their story almost without need for words.

Although they devoted 24 minutes to the story, nothing new was added to the reporting of events by *Newsnight* except a live interview with David Mellor repeating his experience. The job this programme would normally do had already been done by the main BBC news bulletins who had themselves devoted over 20 minutes to the story and all its aspects. Equally, *Channel 4 News* did little different from the ITN bulletins on ITV.

The main American network news broadcasts all carried the story, but some way down their running orders. ABC, CBS and NBC all did ENG packages with reporters on the scene but, by then, more than 13 hours after the event, the story was on its way from being news to being history.

With this story there was a level playing field for all British news services and their American network counterparts. Each of the British news services have Westminster premises and all routinely have camera crews outside Downing Street on Cabinet day, while all the American networks have fully staffed London bureaux. No one had any special access denied to others. Sky were first to report the story, while CNN were first with pictures, which were in fact from ITN and which ITN itself hardly used. Bulletins on the senior British services, BBC and ITN, were accurate from the start, developing to illustrate clearly the nature of events. Not needing to turn input instantly into output, these services could piece together the story from a variety of sources, discarding material if necessary rather than rushing to the screen with any tiny bit of new information.

The actual material used to report the story was substantial. Pictures from the scene came from a number of picture clusters, representing a number of different points of view. Both Sky and ITN had filmed the burning van in Whitehall through the railings at the end of Downing Street. ITN's material was from a much better angle and viewers could see the event more clearly; the informational content was greater in one set of pictures than another.

Other picture clusters available included footage from behind the burning
van (ITN, the unspecified American material used on Sky), in Downing
Street (BBC, Sky, ITN), from Trafalgar Square (BBC, ITN) and in
Parliament Square (BBC, Sky, ITN). The BBC had unique footage supplied
by the freelance cameraman in Horse Guards, while ITN had exclusive
material from its helicopter. CNN used this and other ITN material and
voice-links to its London staff. Only at 13:27, over three hours after the
event, did CNN have any form of original pictures when they clearly used
ITN's set-up for a live two-way with a Scotland Yard spokesman, quickly
followed at 13:35 with a link with their reporter Brian Cabell. Previously,
CNN had simply used live voice-links with their London staff over which
they had put a loop of pictures acquired from ITN. Once ITN had finished
its lunchtime bulletin it clearly released its resources for CNN's use, resulting in the face of its reporter first appearing on screen three hours after the
event. Although CNN had reported the story early on and had indeed transmitted the first pictures of the story, provided for them by ITN, they had not
done what they reputedly do best: report live. Reporter Brian Cabell had
actually been in the area from 10:46 when he had phoned in but CNN simply did not have the technology to go live as they were clearly depending on
ITN for links as well as for pictures. The American network morning programmes all reported the story using live links with their London offices,
while by their evening bulletins all had filed edited packages.

The BBC had unique ENG material shot in Whitehall very close to the
burning van and from a freelancer who happened to be in Horse Guards
Parade. From him the BBC had exclusive shots that came very near to the
heart of the matter, though the damage to Number 10 was not visible. ITV
had also shown material from three different physical locations (Downing
Street, Whitehall and from its helicopter), but neither of the senior British
news organisations nor Sky News had any record of the events right at the
heart of the story. Neither the freelance cameraman in Horse Guards Parade
nor the crew in the ITN helicopter had enough information to know where
to look. The helicopter was redirected on the basis of the first news that
Horse Guards was the scene, which it duly filmed. It subsequently found the
burning van near Whitehall and recorded it. The airborne camera was seen
visibly searching but never at any time showed Downing Street. The free-
lancer saw smoke coming from Whitehall and filmed the cylinders burning
on Foreign Office Green, but there was no apparent reason for him to film
over the wall into the garden at the back of Number 10. A significant
amount of material emerged from the scene, considerably more than would
arise in a normal situation, when each news organisation would despatch a
single crew to the scene of a breaking news event which would already have
happened. Equally, the material emerged more quickly given the extensive
broadcasting infrastructure in Westminster and the fact that no crew travel
time was required. In spite of this diversity of material, the central part of
the story was not filmed.

Reporting the story was, like all journalism, a question of access. There was no photo opportunity, no facility was granted to film the garden of Number 10 or the Cabinet Room and when a spokesman was asked on-air for one he replied by asking for the machines to be shut off. For that part of the story journalists had to depend on briefings and there was no way to confirm the official version of events. The government information machinery produced two inside witnesses. David Mellor appeared on both ITN and the BBC, while ITN had the testimony of Katherine Coombs who had originally been described as a government information officer, but who was later styled as a public affairs consultant.

Given the complicated nature of events, no single eyewitness could have told the full story. Indeed, one CNN witness asked about the van replied, 'What van?' Back at base, television news organisations with a diverse range of sources, including each other, could piece together the story over time. No live reporter speaking from the scene could possibly have told anything more than a partial story. Both Sky and CNN had voice from reporters on the scene within minutes of the event, but neither cellphone equipped journalist could do more than speak from the police barricades about what was in his immediate range of vision.

In this case, as in so many, both journalist and viewer alike can only make sense of events further away in time when a pattern has emerged and been literally pieced together from a range of sources. In spite of live rolling news, viewers did not actually see the event nor were they likely to. The accident of the running news cameras outside Number 10 meant that a form of the event was recorded but close examination of the reporting of events, live and nearly instantly, reveals that not everything is known quite so quickly and that time is needed literally to assemble the story and explain it to the viewer. Clearly, the need for understanding is as important in a factual, breaking, hard news story as with more obviously complicated political, social or economic issues.

The actual extent of the damage to the Prime Minister's residence remains unknown to this day and the public may have to await the release of government papers in the year 2021 before knowing the full truth. This in spite of the fact that the whole chain of events was without doubt recorded on videotape. A former Home Secretary, certainly not without senior contacts in the police and security services, stated in the House of Commons that a period of eight minutes elapsed between the van being parked and the missiles being fired. This raises a number of questions. How was this timing arrived at? Did eyewitnesses note the two times carefully or was the event recorded by video surveillance equipment? The motorbike escape of the van driver was announced at the anti-terrorist squad press conference, contradicting earlier reports that a man had been seen running away. All this suggests an authoritative source.

There are numerous security cameras in such a sensitive location as Whitehall. There are six fixed cameras on the outside of the Ministry of

Defence building within 50 yards of where the van was abandoned. Whether these could have seen it depends on how wide-angled their lenses were. However, a large moving camera with an infra-red lamp high on a building across Whitehall could clearly have recorded the van being parked, the attackers fleeing and the missiles firing. The wall separating the garden of Number 10 from Foreign Office Green and Horse Guards Parade is equipped with video cameras and it is hard to imagine that the saturation coverage evident on Whitehall does not extend into the garden outside the Cabinet Room and the Prime Minister's residence, surely a sensitive security area. Should the bombers be prosecuted, no doubt video footage will form part of the evidence against them, as has been the case in many IRA bombing incidents in London. Visual records of the damage done to Number 10 will exist even if the actual event itself was not recorded by surveillance cameras. None of this has been seen on television or in any other form of publication.

Whatever the technology, television news needs access and for the most part this was denied. Live feeds, satellite links, Westminster studios, 24-hour rolling news – all go for nothing if the pictures are of a burly policeman and a piece of plastic tape stopping progress and limiting eyewitness reporting. A major breaking story literally lands in one of the most saturated television environments in the world and, in spite of blanket coverage, events at the very heart of the story are revealed through the traditional briefing process with no certain way of verifying them.

One senior British television journalist has reason to believe there is more to the story than has seen the light of day:

> I'm not even sure now we know the full truth of that thing. I went into Number 10 to interview Major about something completely different about three weeks later. The place was wrecked. The missile had come right into what was called the White Room, which was the one above the Cabinet and they said that the window had been blown in by the blast in the garden by the missile missing. The missile had come in through the roof, straight through the private quarters. There were still ceiling detritus hanging down and the window had been blown out by the thing exiting the room again. Why they took us into that room I don't know, but that's where we were set up and that is where we did our interview. The trouble is that I was really obsessed with the interview. The interview was actually about the end of the Gulf War. I started looking around and thought this is all very odd. This doesn't tie in with what we've got. You know you haven't at that moment got time to start filming and sorting yourself out. But I'm absolutely convinced that we never heard the full story and that in fact they hit the building.

This position is supported by several other possible clues. For a substantial period of time Prime Minister Major was not in fact living at Number 10, but in a flat at Admiralty Arch (*The Independent*, 1992, p. 2; *The Times*, 1992, p. 17). His press spokesman Gus Donohue also moved offices as Downing Street underwent extensive renovation. Early on in the live reporting, mention was made of the fact that an office in Number 12 Downing Street was damaged. This was before the official line emerged and suggests that the damage may have been more than a few broken windows and the sad loss of the cherry tree witnessed by David Mellor. Television news in its most advanced state, operating very much on home territory, had told the story to the best of its ability, but whatever the technology it still could not penetrate to the heart of events and report in the live, eyewitness, 'as-it-happens' style about which we hear so much. The story, as it emerged, came in part in briefings and at press conferences and through witnesses provided by the government information machinery. Access to the garden of Number 10, which had been given before and has been allowed since, was crucially denied on the day. As a result we still don't know the full story.

I doubt that the Chairman of the D Notice Committee sits watching CNN and Sky News 24 hours a day for any sign of possible threats to national security, but should one occur there would be very little the authorities could do about it. Supposing the ITN helicopter, whose output was going out live around the world on CNN, had filmed serious damage to the top floors of Number 10. In such a case it would have been harder to manage the media. As it was the helicopter shots, the reporters on cellphones running down the streets and the numerous film crews notwithstanding, we still had to depend on briefings given to political correspondents in Westminster to tell us what happened at the centre of events.

If the story had happened in, say, 1979 there would have been no CNN or Sky News on the air 24 hours a day able to report instantly, no *Newsnight* to wrap up the day, in fact hardly any morning television in Britain to interrupt. These institutional changes and the effect they have on the news product on our screens is crucial and should be seen as part of the long-term historical evolution of broadcast news.

|4|

The history of television news and its institutions

Today's diverse television news ecology did not spring full born from the mind of a network planner, marketing manager, news doctor or megalomaniac global media mogul. Instead it evolved over a long period of time under the influence of a wide variety of commercial, political and social forces. The inventors of radio, television and the telecommunications satellite could have had no idea of how the technology would be used to create the globally available 24-hours-a-day news services of the late twentieth century. Certainly some examination of the historical development of television news and its institutions is necessary in order to understand fully its present state.

BBC, company and corporation

In the beginning, and for many years after its foundation in 1922, the BBC broadcast a 'news summary' consisting of 'Copyright news from Reuter, Press Association, Exchange Telegraph and Central News First' (Burns, 1977, p. 181). Interestingly enough, the news in the 1920s was considered copyrightable. In the eyes of the law it was constructed, created, unique, not in the public domain, not something objective that anyone could simply 'gather'. These summaries (equally interestingly not the whole of the news) were prepared by the agencies and acknowledged as such (Briggs, 1961, pp. 130–4; Schlesinger, 1987, p. 15). Instead of the vast vertically integrated institution of today, with its army of newsgathering, producing and technical staff, the BBC, in terms of news, was a publisher-broadcaster, putting onto the airwaves a product prepared by someone else, a situation not unlike some arrangements in place today.

The British Broadcasting Company was formed as a commercial company by a consortium of six hardware manufacturers with the express purpose of making programmes for the infant medium. In today's terms the BBC was to be the content provider, producing programme software to drive hardware sales. While a private company, the British Broadcasting Company was subject to strict regulation in return for its monopoly licence from the Post Office, while the consortium gained protection against 'unfair competition' (Hood, 1980, p. 40) from overseas set manufacturers. It was funded not by advertising but by a licence fee paid by the owners of radio receivers. Restrictions unimaginable today were in place, with the BBC unable to broadcast news before 7 pm, the result of intense lobbying from the newspapers and the news agencies who saw their primary business threatened by the new medium. The Sykes Committee (1923, cited in Schlesinger, 1978), the first of a series of committees to report on British broadcasting, acknowledged the potential influence of radio and noted the need for 'uncoloured news' on the BBC. The press lobby made the case that such an ideal could be achieved only if they, the experts, prepared the news for the broadcasters to read (Schlesinger, 1987, pp. 15–16).

As ever, events were to change regulatory frameworks and the BBC began gathering news as a result of the 1926 General Strike: 'One or two BBC employees actually went out collecting the news, a task especially forbidden by the news agencies under normal conditions' (Briggs, 1985, p. 103). The non-appearance of newspapers catapulted the BBC into a new role as the sole source of news, a situation not without considerable political ramifications. Five bulletins a day were broadcast from 10 o'clock in the morning (Cox, 1995, p. 5). Briggs notes that these wireless broadcasts were transcribed by hand and displayed in public places. When the strike ended on 12 May, John Reith, the General Manager, himself read the news, only after 10 Downing Street had confirmed wire service reports. Beginning as it was to continue, the BBC did not rush to air with important news without first checking (Briggs, 1985, p. 105). Already, being accurate with the news was a more important institutional value than being first.

Having conducted itself 'properly' during the General Strike ('they can trust us not to be really impartial' wrote Reith in his diary) (Hood, 1980, p. 45), the BBC, already behaving like a public institution, officially became one. On 1 January 1927 the British Broadcasting Corporation was established by Royal Charter with the newly knighted Reith as its first Director General. Early in 1927 a new agreement was arrived at which allowed the Corporation to broadcast the news from the agencies at 6:30 and additionally gave it the right to broadcast 400 eyewitness reports annually. By 1930 the news watershed had changed to 6 pm, the original staff of two sub-editors had doubled and these four people who constituted BBC News were allowed to receive the news agency wires directly (Schlesinger, 1987, pp. 20–21). Radio was predominantly a live studio-bound medium, although cumbersome technology did exist for 'news observers' to record location-based 'actuality'. The telephone could be used to relay eyewitness reports, as it was to broadcast the fire at Crystal Palace in south London in 1936 (Schlesinger, 1987, p. 22). The reporter was a young man named Richard Dimbleby.

'More by fluke than design'

While British broadcasting had evolved through a series of agreements, public committee reports and regulatory legislation, in America commercial radio news developed 'more by fluke than design' (Smith, 1990, p. 159). While the first radio news was read as early as 1909 (Smith, 1973, p. 48), the evolution of broadcast journalism was slow. The 1928 presidential election results were reported on CBS by a sportscaster speaking in the intervals of a live concert. Stationed in the offices of a New York newspaper, Ted Husing added up the totals himself, declared the final result and scooped the newspapers by hours (Mayer, 1987, p. 159). In spite of its 1931 slogan 'Columbia the news network', CBS employed no editors or reporters, but instead used half a dozen public relations men to rewrite wire copy to be read by announcers whose only qualification was their voice. Real journalism was done elsewhere and, as in Britain, the new medium was predominantly a passive relayer of agency material. This source of news, however, was withdrawn in 1933 when the American Newspaper Publishers Association brought pressure to bear and Associated Press, United Press and International News were denied the networks under any terms. Consequently, CBS and NBC had to start their own newsgathering operations. A. A. Schecter, who had joined NBC to write publicity copy, became a one-man news department, while CBS established a network of stringers (p. 167). Schecter clipped London newspapers for (hardly topical) material for announcers to read and used the telephone for domestic newsgathering (p. 158). This ad hoc solution was not without problems and by December 1933 the Biltmore Programme was agreed, whereby CBS and NBC were allowed agency copy under certain strict conditions. The networks could transmit two five-minute bulletins at set times with no single item to exceed 30 words in length (10 seconds in broadcasting terms), with listeners to be referred to the evening papers for further details (Barnouw, 1968, pp. 19–20). However, within a year, two of the agencies had bowed to the inevitable and supplied wire copy to broadcasters, with Associated Press holding out until 1945 when legal action forced it to comply (Mayer, 1987, pp. 168–9).

Two emblematic news events in the 1930s were to indicate the power and immediacy of the new broadcasting technology to relay the actuality of dramatic, even historic, events in a way the print media could not. In May 1937, NBC sent announcer Herbert Morrison and an engineer to cover the arrival of the airship Hindenburg at Lakehurst, New Jersey. The recording of this routine event was intended to produce sound effects for the library. When the Hindenburg spectacularly exploded the radio microphone was open and the newsreel cameras were running. These new media had seen and heard a dramatic, unexpected news event, and a breaking story had been recorded for the whole world to see and hear. Federal regulations against using recorded material were swept aside and NBC transmitted the scoop that evening (Fielding, 1972, pp. 215–19; Mayer, 1987, p. 156).

The bias towards the live was not entirely the result of regulation. As late as 1939, CBS President William Paley effectively banned the use of recording on the network. His reasons were entirely commercial, protecting the networks from losing their entertainment stars. He feared that performers such as Bing Crosby, if they could record their own programmes, could sell them directly to local stations, cutting the network out of the profitable equation. When the compact and flexible reel-to-reel tape recorder we know today was developed in the 1940s much of the finance required was to come from the said Bing Crobsy, who was clearly motivated by more than a desire to hear his own voice. Correspondents Ed Murrow and William Shirer vainly tried to convince Paley that recording equipment was needed to cover the events that were to lead eventually to the outbreak of war. Recorded pieces could be assembled throughout the day as events unfolded and played to listeners in evening programming. If the diplomatic crisis led inexorably to war, live radio might be left behind, feared Shirer:

> in order to broadcast live, we had to have a telephone line leading from our mike to a shortwave transmitter. You could not follow an advancing or retreating army dragging a telephone line with you. . . . With a compact little recorder you could get into the thick of it and capture the awesome sounds of war (Smith, 1990, pp. 174–5).

Paley was not convinced by the logic of the argument and remained adamant that broadcasting had to be live.

Prime Minister Neville Chamberlain's return to Britain from Munich in 1938 was an early example of live location newsgathering. His arrival at Heston aerodrome was covered by the BBC on radio and, on *television*, to a maximum possible audience of 100 000 viewers (Short, 1989, p. 11). This planned, set piece event, enabled by the deployment of substantial outside broadcast resources, was symbolic, for the momentous events that followed inevitably were to transform both broadcast news and the world it reported. Not surprisingly, in time of accelerating dramatic events, the public turned to radio news, and during the Munich Crisis the BBC was allowed to broadcast bulletins in daytime hours. When war broke out in September 1939 the news came in a noon bulletin and all restrictions were consigned to history. Reporting from London, CBS correspondent Ed Murrow told listeners that the crowd that had gathered outside Number 10 Downing Street had in fact heard the news on the radio of a car parked nearby (Mayer, 1987, p. 168).

Reporters

It is possible to chart the birth and early evolution of broadcast news in terms of two larger than life figures, Ed Murrow of CBS and the BBC's

Richard Dimbleby. As depression turned into war, the news was still agency copy read by anonymous announcers, but correspondents with characteristic voices and, in time, faces, were to change broadcast news forever.

Edward (né Egbert) R. Murrow, who, unlike many radio pioneers, had never worked in newspapers, was sent by CBS to London, as European Director, primarily to organise material for talks programmes. As Europe slid into war, Murrow quickly moved from buying schools programmes into organising and broadcasting reaction to the advance of Nazism. In a pioneering transmission on 13 March 1938, which was in fact his first on-air appearance, Murrow, speaking from Vienna with Hitler's arrival imminent, linked together correspondents in Berlin, Paris and London using short-wave radio (Mayer, 1987, pp. 164, 176–7). The 'round-up', had been invented and was used a further 14 times that year to cover the Munich Crisis. In the words of one contemporary commentator, 'a new dimension has been added to politics and diplomacy. For the first time, history has been made in the hearing of its pawns' (quoted in Barnouw, 1968, p. 83). Both the technologically enabled broadcasting convention and its reputed political effect had been identified over 40 years before CNN was to market such news values aggressively. Like CNN, routine planning and technological foresight were as important as the ability to extemporise for long periods on-air. When Murrow dramatically described storm troopers entering Vienna, his voice was relayed via a short-wave transmitter in Berlin. Obviously such a link could not be relied on. CBS engineers helped the Czechoslovakian government to develop a short-wave installation so direct communication with New York would be possible when the inevitable happened. 'It was all very deliberate, like wiring a parade route' (Barnouw, 1970, p. 79). One commentator is perhaps guilty of exaggeration when he states that 'together with Edward Murrow, CBS invented network news' (Auletta, 1991, p. 59), but it is clear that he was the right man in the right place at the right time. Murrow's correspondence from London was to have substantial political and professional resonance:

> The turning point came when Edward R. Murrow's broadcasts from Blitz-ravaged London filled America's living room and helped to bring the nation out of its isolationist mood. Murrow not only reinforced the journalistic principles that had been laid down in fits and starts at CBS since the early 1930s, he came to symbolise the integrity and independence of the news division (Smith, 1990, p. 160).

Beginning rather dramatically with 'This ... is London', Murrow followed his characteristic long pause with a unique style of reporting (Cox, 1995, p. 11). He captured the actuality of the Blitz by placing microphones at the feet of Londoners entering air-raid shelters and with his voice could both evoke moods and analyse incisively. His most famous broadcast came from a rooftop in London during a German air raid:

The strongest impression one gets of these bombings is a sense of unreality. Often the planes are so high that in even a cloudless sky you can't see them. I've stood on a hill watching an aerodrome being bombed two miles away. It looked and sounded like farmers blasting stumps in western Washington. . . . Even when the dive bombers come down looking like a duck with both wings broken and you hear the hollow grunt of their bombs it doesn't seem to have much meaning (Smith, 1990, p. 175).

Four decades later, when CNN broadcast live from Baghdad as the bombs and missiles fell, the spirit of Ed Murrow lived on, although he would no doubt have winced at how the language had suffered in the meantime, with television journalists seeming to have lost the classic word-painting skills of the great radio correspondents.

If Ed Murrow was the right man in the right place to take American radio news forward a quantum leap, in Britain Richard Dimbleby was one of the first to see the opportunities offered by the new medium. A third-generation print journalist, the 23-year-old Dimbleby wrote to the head of the infant News Department with a list of proposals which included the unheard of practice of reporters recording interviews with eyewitnesses (quoted in Scannell and Cardiff, 1991, pp. 122–3). Rewarded with employment for his suggestions, he quickly developed his role as Topical Talks Assistant to that of what we would describe today as a reporter. Dimbleby covered the 1936 fire at Crystal Palace live from a public telephone booth, beating the newspapers by hours, while his pioneering coverage of the Fenland Floods in 1937 involved recording actuality sound on location, with the discs despatched to London in the custody of a railway guard (Miall, 1994, p. 54).

Sound recording of this kind came no more easily to British broadcasting than it did to American radio. 'Bottled recording' had been discussed as early as 1927 and by 1931 the BBC had a 'Blatterphone' recording machine which was used experimentally. It was hardly perfect, and editing the steel tape was difficult and dangerous. The Watts disc, recording onto a lacquer or acetate-coated surface, like making a gramophone record, came into use in 1933. Even when the technology existed there was a disdain for the use of recorded material, 'almost on moral grounds' (Briggs, 1979, pp. 120–1). David Howarth, Dimbleby's producer, tells of the tribulations they had trying to get the BBC to allow them to make and use location recordings:

We even plotted to have the recording gear made in secret and put in the back of my car and broadcast its discs without telling anyone how we made them but that fell through because neither of us could afford it. It sometimes seemed hopeless to move the BBC and at one time we tried to sell ourselves and our ideas to Ed Murrow whom Richard greatly admired (Smith, 1973, pp. 86–7).

In early 1939 Dimbleby went abroad to Spain, reporting on the retreat of the defeated Spanish Republican Army into France, speaking live into a 10 o'clock bulletin 'with one foot in France and one in Spain' (Scannell and Cardiff, 1991, p. 132). Dimbleby was one of only two reporters at the BBC when war broke out in 1939 (Cox, 1995, p. 6). He had gone to Paris one week before the war was declared, in an ordinary car with 'cumbersome' recording gear in the back seat and two cans of camouflage paint (Briggs, 1979, p. 182). The war enabled Dimbleby to develop as a reporter. After the frustrations of the phoney war, he travelled to the Middle East, covering events in over a dozen countries, before returning to Britain in 1943. It is said the BBC's first radio reporter was also its best (Cox, 1995, p. 7), but by the middle of the war Dimbleby was not alone in practising the new craft of radio war correspondent. From the deserts of Northern Africa and from the Italian peninsula reporters of the War Reporting Unit covered the war, producing *War Report,* a special nightly news programme which attracted huge audiences. Dimbleby himself reported from bombers over Germany, described the crossing of the Rhine and broadcast from the ruins of Hitler's study (Miall, 1994, pp. 55–6). His moving description of entering the concentration camp at Belsen was radio journalism at its very best, which was itself to become part of history, recording both the horrors of the war and its end. It was also to be the end of an era in broadcast news.

The war accelerated many developments already in progress. Not surprisingly, technology was one area where growth was exponential. Before the war, sound could be recorded on phonograph records, steel tape or, alongside pictures, on film. None of these processes was lightweight and when the BBC went to war in 1939 a car with recording apparatus in the back seat was considered a major advance (Schlesinger, 1987, p. 22). War correspondents eventually had a relatively compact disc-recorder before first wire and then flexible tape replaced steel as the medium for the magnetic recording of sound. Lightweight film cameras, some developed by the Germans for use in aircraft, enabled military and newsreel cameramen to work in dangerous situations unthinkable earlier. The rudimentary computers developed to crack codes were hardly seen as the newsgathering and production technology they were to become, and advances in electronics made for defence reasons were to facilitate the post-war development of television. More important than technology, however, the methods of broadcast journalism evolved equally quickly. The eyewitness reporting of hard news stories on location and the use of these recorded pieces in live studio bulletins set a pattern still in use in the television news of today (Briggs, 1970, p. 49).

The birth of television

Television transmissions had started in 1936 in Britain in 1935 in Germany, and, in 1939, at the New York World's Fair, Franklin Roosevelt became the first American President to appear on television (Barnouw, 1968, p. 126). In July 1941, when CBS broadcast its first programmes to a single New York City station, 15 minutes of news were included (Tracey, 1995, p. 120). Subsequently this grew to half an hour of output. When the Japanese bombing of Pearl Harbour brought America into the war in December of that year, 'television returned to the laboratory' (Abramson, 1995, p. 31) but not before CBS in New York ran a nine-hour live special. WCBW came on-air an hour early and broadcast non-stop without any film, explaining events to its small audience of New York City viewers (Cox, 1995, p. 12). Television news had gone on its first 'roll' to cover a major breaking story for as long as was necessary.

Whereas the Germans continued broadcasting throughout the war, including television news (Smith, 1995, p. 64), BBC television was closed down to prevent *Luftwaffe* bombers from using the transmitters as homing beacons. On the morning of 1 September 1939, 'Black Friday', the day the Second World War broke out, Barkinshaw, the engineer in charge of BBC television transmissions at Alexandra Palace, received a message at 10 o'clock ordering that the station should be closed by noon. The last item to be transmitted to visitors at Radiolympia was a Mickey Mouse cartoon (Briggs, 1965, p. 622). On 7 June 1946, the day after the great victory parade in London, BBC Television Service was resumed. 'In order to emphasise the continuity, the first day's programme included the interrupted Mickey Mouse cartoon of 1939' (Briggs, 1985, p. 243).

Newsreel pictures and radio words

Post-war British television news was hardly dynamic. Radio news division produced a 10 minute bulletin which was read by an out-of-vision newsreader over a shot of a clock (Cox, 1995, p. 13). While there had been no pre-war television news, as in America, Movietone and Gaumont–British newsreels had been shown on television twice weekly. This practice did not continue after the war, as the film suppliers feared the competition and, rather than joining forces with the new medium, tried to beat them by refusing to cooperate.

The then Director General, Sir William Haley, a distinguished former newspaperman, was deeply suspicious of the newsreels, seeing them as entertainment. To use the medium of film for proper news would, in his view, 'subordinate the primary functions of the news to the needs of visual presentation' (Goldie, 1977, p. 41). As Brian Winston has pointed out, newsreels were hardly high-quality journalism, in fact 'they were something less than journalism, period' (Winston, 1993, p. 183), exhibiting certain clear values, with an emphasis on certain hard news stories such as train crashes and human interest. It could be argued that such picture-led stories are exactly what filmed news does best and that the film-makers of the newsreels, unencumbered by any print-derived journalistic values, actually used their visual medium appropriately. It has been remarked more than once that television news was the bastard child of the cinema newsreel and radio news, and in the immediate post-war period this was clear in certain institutional arrangements. Before the war early American news transmissions had included both Pathé and 'especially made' newsreels (Winston, 1993, p. 184) and, when normal service resumed, the networks looked to these film operations either for staff or product.

NBC pursued the former path, hiring Paul Alley from Hearst MGM News of the Day to produce news telecasts. An $8000 Mitchell camera arrived from the Office of War Information, equipment which was to service NBC newsgathering for two years. By 1947 the network had contracted Jerry Fairbanks Productions to provide film reports, switching a year later to Fox Movietone, before eventually deciding to produce their own films (Barnouw, 1970, p. 41). CBS were more inclined to the radio pattern, according to veteran broadcaster Reuven Frank. In his view, their television news exhibited 'the same structure for writers and editors, the same standards, purposes and emphasis on words' as radio. After several failed in-house attempts, CBS hired Telenews, a subsidiary of Hearst–MGM, to produce film footage for their broadcasts (Frank, 1991, p. 31).

In February 1948 NBC took over *Camel Newsreel Theatre* which had been produced by its tobacco company sponsor in cooperation with Twentieth Century Fox's newsreel operation. Within a year, the programme had grown to a quarter of an hour in length and, as *Camel News Caravan*, was to run with the same presenter until 1957. CBS equally bedded down their news output, and, in August 1948, *CBS News with Douglas Edwards* began a run which was to end in the 1960s with the appearance of Walter Cronkite.

Thus, before 1950, American television news was an established feature on the broadcasting map, produced, for the most part, by in-house network news divisions. In 1950 CBS–TV News had 14 full-time staffers, a number which grew to 376 by 1956 (Smith, 1990, p. 361). These institutional arrangements produced what was already a distinct form of output. This characteristic mixture of live studio 'reads' (from radio) and recorded location film reports (newsreels) was arranged in a running order progressing from the most important and serious items to the light-hearted. In this respect bulletins were like the newsreels before them, once described as 'a series of catastrophes, ended by a fashion show' (Fielding, 1972, p. 228). Brian Winston (1993, pp. 185–6, and 207, note 3) documents the various output permutations tried by the networks and skilfully analyses the earliest surviving television newscast from 1949, outlining the television news grammar that informs broadcasting today. As on radio, the news was read and, in television, in-vision newscasters became authoritative and much respected figures. In this respect, there is every reason to believe that CBS Television News will span half a century having used only three main news anchors: Douglas Edwards, Walter Cronkite and Dan Rather. This continuity is apparent in other aspects of the screen product.

Reuven Frank describes the early days: 'at NBC, the term "Newsreel" was not a figure of speech but an accurate description of a fact of life'. Cameramen recruited from the newsreels used hand-held clockwork cameras which, although lightweight, were capable of recording only 70 seconds of mute film without reloading. They filmed 'ice-cream eating competitions and press agents' schemes'. Only in Washington could NBC record pictures with sound (Frank, 1991, p. 32). The newsreel legacy had a significant effect on journalistic practice:

> the camera as arbiter of news value, had introduced a drastic curtailment of the scope of news. The notion that a picture was worth a thousand words meant, in practice that footage of Atlantic City beauty winners, shot at some expense, was considered more valuable than a thousand words from Eric Sevareid on the mounting tensions of Southeast Asia. Analysis, a staple of radio news in its finest days and the basis for the fame of Swing, Murrow, Kaltenborn, Shirer, and others, was being pushed aside as non-visual (Barnouw, 1970, pp. 42–3).

Generally speaking, the technology used to make early television can be simply described as large and cumbersome. Fred Friendly, Ed Murrow's Producer and eventually President of CBS News, compared television reporting to writing a news story using a two-ton pencil (Mayer, 1987, p. 202) and even today the pencil still weighs about 500 pounds. When Murrow and Friendly flew out to cover the Korean war for CBS they took a 'single-system' camera, enabling the synchronous recording of sound and picture. Their operation was hardly flexible and lightweight, with 20 CBS staff accompanying them, bearing witness to the long-running, and still current, network tendency single-handedly to inflate airline profits (p. 152).

News had made the transition to the small screen and taken its part in the life of the nation, but in some views it was hardly without its problems: 'Television news at the start of 1953 was an unpromising child, it was the schizophrenic offspring of the theater newsreel and the radio newscast, and was confused as to its role and future course' (Barnouw, 1970, p. 40). The faces that were to frequent American living rooms throughout the Eisenhower era were dismissed as 'out-of-work actors with suitably mature faces or advertising readers who failed to measure up to the task' (Smith, 1973, p. 80). Those that saw television as the wrong place for serious journalism were confirmed in their judgement when NBC started the *Today* programme. Breakfast television with news bulletins every half hour proved less than popular until the arrival of one J. Fred Muggs, a chimpanzee who became the first, but not the last, animal to rescue such early morning programming. Whether meant to be a presenter, guest politician or typical viewer, his role was understandably downplayed by an NBC executive looking back. Frank explains the rebirth of the programme: 'they went back to presenting news as they always had, with a slight bias to what was heard over what was seen, like a radio program, because people do not watch as much at that hour as they listen' (Frank, 1991, p. 48). Television news had been born but it had yet to develop much beyond the cradle:

> The idea of the reporter using an instrument of broadcasting whether with sound or picture or both as a reporter uses his pencil and notebook, was not present in the mind of early broadcasters or executives. So long as news remained in bulletin form, a recital of 'facts' told by the news agencies and read straight into the microphone or camera with little or no background coverage, news failed to take off in either broadcasting media (Smith, 1973, p. 77).

The charges levelled against much of early television could hardly be aimed at Ed Murrow who, after a period as an executive, arrived from radio, bringing with him a concept for a new kind of programme. *See it now* imported the formula that had made *Hear it now* legendary in sound broadcasting. American radio had always had a tradition of news commentary, with CBS at one time employing 'some thirty or forty news analysts who have nationwide audiences' (Mayer, 1987, p. 170). Certainly, there had always been more to radio journalism than just the transmission of wire service material in brief bulletins. *See it now* was conceived as 'a sort of *Life* magazine for the airwaves that would capture significant stories in documentary style' (Smith, 1990, p. 160). Murrow was suspicious of television news, seeing it as lacking the depth of commentary possible on radio: 'most news is made up of what happens in men's minds, as reflected in what comes out of their mouths. And how do you put that in pictures?' (Mayer, 1987, p. 182). The first programme of *See it now,* however, was notable not for its hard-hitting journalism but for a hi-tech extravagance involving the leasing of a video landline to San Francisco, enabling viewers to see both the Golden Gate Bridge and the Brooklyn Bridge on a split screen. As was often the case, the pioneers of television 'felt awed by their new medium and needed to spend time exclaiming the wonder of it' (Barnouw, 1970, p. 45). This was the same era as the much hyped outside broadcast in Chicago that Lang and Lang had based their research upon.

It is pretty much a commonplace that the elaborate outside broadcast coverage of the 1953 Coronation of Elizabeth II was a crucial event in the development of British television. Some 56 per cent of the population tuned in, in a country where there were only two million domestic sets. Sales of domestic receivers rose dramatically as a result (Briggs, 1985, p. 74) and a network of cable links in central London was installed which is still in use today. The event was a major one for the American networks who rushed to beat each other in getting film of the Coronation on-air. At the time, film would have had to have been processed and then flown by piston aircraft across the Atlantic. CBS set up telerecording equipment at Heathrow airport which would transfer the live television pictures transmitted from central London onto film. A large aircraft had been chartered and film-processing and editing equipment installed on board. As the *Constellation* flew across to Boston the film was developed, edited and given an Ed Murrow commentary. NBC conducted a similar operation but both were beaten by the BBC and a new technology that was to change television newsgathering more than any development in electronics. Commercial jetliners did not yet cross the Atlantic, so the BBC enlisted air force support to jet its film-recorded version to Newfoundland, where a Canadian fighter took it on to Montreal and from there it was sent by landline to New York to be used by ABC, the new third network (Barnouw, 1970, p. 45). Without the advantage of the jet, CBS were beaten by 15 minutes, but they still had the added value of Ed Murrow (Cox, 1995, p. 31).

Gifted as he was as a live broadcaster, Murrow's most important contribution was in the context of the filmed report. He and Friendly brought documentary and journalistic skills of an 'investigatory' kind to television (Smith, 1973, p. 210), producing a series of films that helped to bring down Senator McCarthy: 'The sequence of *See it now* programmes on McCarthyism 1953–55 had an extraordinary impact. They placed Murrow in the forefront of the documentary film movement; he was hailed as its television pioneer' (Barnouw, 1970, p. 54). Murrow became 'the most highly respected broadcast journalist of the time' (Frank, 1991, p. 46), with new correspondents described as 'Murrow's Boys' developing in what has been called the Golden Age at CBS (Auletta, 1991, p. 142). Radio talks and commentary had grown into a form of television journalism distinct from the news. It did not, however, flourish as Murrow and Friendly had hoped. By 1960 Murrow had left CBS and television, while Friendly, then President of CBS News, stayed until 1965 when 'the commercial pressures encircled and strangled Friendly's movement' (Smith, 1973, p. 210). When the network decided to show *I Love Lucy* reruns rather than live coverage of the Senate Foreign Relations Committee on the Vietnam war, an era had ended (Auletta, 1991, p. 333).

'Here is an illustrated summary of the news'

In Britain, the news form was slower to evolve. BBC television had no competition except from factors inside the corporation, with many believing to this day that the powers that be in Broadcasting House in central London were less than enthusiastic about the infant television service based at Alexandra Palace in the northern suburbs. When the cinema newsreel producers refused to provide television with any product after the war, the BBC decided to make its own, beginning in January 1948. True to their roots, these newsreels were not made by the journalists of News Division, but by part of the Television Film Department. Their agenda was visual and dramatic, with cameramen, not reporters, being the key figures. In Britain, the bastard child that emerged in America had not yet been born, and when the Korean war broke out it was covered separately for the BBC by Rene Cutforth reporting to radio and by television newsreel cameramen Ronnie Noble and Cyril Page. These figures had a role perhaps unique in television news, working for the most part alone. Noble's work, in particular, has been described as being 'remarkably imaginative' (Smith, 1988, p. 235). In addition to the newsreel, television still broadcast its 10 minute sound-only bulletin at close-down, read 'over' variously 'a darkened screen' (Paulu, 1961, p. 88), the BBC logo (Schlesinger, 1987, p. 37), a shot of a clock (Cox, 1995, p. 13) or a still of Big Ben (Burns, 1977, p. 183).

The marriage of the news and the television newsreel eventually took place in July 1954 when News Division took over its visual rival out at Alexandra Palace. The result, imaginatively entitled *Television News and Newsreel*, began with the sombre announcement: 'Here is an illustrated summary of the news. It will be followed by the latest film of events and happenings from home and abroad' (source: Simpson, 1993). The continued separation of 'read', agency-based material and filmed reports was clear. The birth of the new hybrid prompted *The Listener* to write:

> Now the illustrated news service and television, entitled *News and Newsreel*, will have a more immediate purpose. The hard news will be presented with the aid of still photographs, or film shots where available, maps and charts. The service will include also the latest moving pictures from at home and abroad and, on suitable occasions, live reports or interviews. Ultimately films may be obtainable from across the world almost as swiftly as telegrams can be received. Meanwhile this television – which must be flexible to begin with – will not and perhaps cannot replace the frequent bulletins of sound broadcasting (*The Listener*, 1954, p. 8).

Even these humble hopes for the new service, expressed in what after all was a BBC publication, were not to be realised. The tone has been likened to 'a foreign office communiqué' (quoted in Schlesinger, 1987, p. 37). The news values were serious, with the running order decided by Radio News at Broadcasting House. Audience response, according to research at the time, was lukewarm, comparing the *News and Newsreel* to 'an old-fashioned lantern show' (BBC Audience Research, 1954, quoted in Schlesinger, 1987, p. 38) or, according to *The Star*, 'about as impressive visually as the fat stock prices' (Briggs, 1985, p. 293). Only a month after its preview of the new service, *The Listener* published a damning review by Reginald Pound which made a telling transatlantic comparison: 'as for the sharp edged awareness which makes American television news, at its worst as well as its best, that does not exist' (1954, p. 186). The in-vision newscaster, already well-established in America, was literally nowhere to be seen. It was only during the emergency conditions of the war that BBC radio announcers were identified by name, and it was to take a further, if not quite so dramatic, external event before BBC Television News was to have a human face.

Much of the blame for the sorry state of BBC Television News has been laid at the door of its Head for many years, Tahu Hole, about whom no commentator appears to have written a single favourable word. Former BBC Director General Alasdair Milne (1989) states simply that 'everybody thought BBC Television News, under Tahu Hole's guidance, pathetic' (p. 31), 'the news was a joke' (p. 8). A New Zealander by birth, Hole had come to Britain before the war to be the London correspondent of the *Sydney Morning Herald*. Reporting the outbreak of war to the southern hemisphere from Broadcasting House he soon became BBC staff. After the war, he rose up the news management ladder until a colleague's illness led to his promotion 'into a post that was well beyond his capabilities' (Miall, 1994, p. 125). Given his exotic name, one might imagine him to have been a flamboyant, exotic figure, a Maori or half-Maori war correspondent roaming the world from big story to big story much as his fellow country-man Peter Arnett would do in the 1960s. Instead, as Head of News Division, Hole exhibited a degree of caution remarkable even in the BBC of the day. Not only did he have a news service untroubled by on-air human personality, Hole also had little room for such journalistic fripperies as scoops. All stories had to have a second confirming source. Exclusives were not to be used. This led to the exercise of a great deal of ingenuity on the part of foreign correspondents:

> I learnt that if I got an exclusive story the only way to get it on the air was to give a carbon copy to my competitor from Reuters, even at the expense of being thought soft in the head by him (quoted in Miall, 1994, p. 126).

Admittedly this was the television news environment where until 1957 there was a rule preventing the discussion of parliamentary issues for a fortnight before any vote and where elections were not properly covered until 1959. In August 1955, just over a month before the launch of the BBC's first competition, Tahu Hole articulated his view of the news:

> A news service without principles and standards is like a man without character. . . . When a listener tunes into the BBC for news, he knows he will be told the sober truth. The growing television public must be told and shown just that (1955, p. xxi).

Faced with competition, the inadequacies of BBC television news became all the more apparent, and Hole lost control of what had become known as 'the Kremlin of the BBC' (Greene, 1969, p. 123). After a move sideways into administration, Tahu Hole took early retirement from the BBC at the age of 51, a rather more rare event than it is today, and one, at the time, taken as a clear sign of failure.

Independent Television News

Into this stuffy world of 'sober truth', where legend has it radio news announcers wore dinner jackets to speak in an anonymous corporate voice, came a fascinating mixture of visual imagination and journalistic flair when, on 22 September 1955, the BBC had its first real rival in over 30 years of broadcasting. Independent Television News was a unique service dedicated to producing news only; it was not a division of a network or larger broadcasting organisation as such. It was the contracted supplier of news bulletins to the federal ITV commercial television system and was owned by its customers who funded it from their advertising revenues. In this way the new commercial television system could have a reliable news service which was for the most part insulated from possible proprietorial interference.

The day before the new service started, its Editor, Aidan Crawley, told a press conference that ITN would allow its 'newscasters' to 'inject their personalities' (*The Times*, 1955, p. 4) into stories. Given that the BBC had only revealed the faces of its newsreaders some weeks before, without being so radical as actually to name them, ITN was making a quantum leap forward in its use of 'newscasters' with journalistic credentials (one of whom was a woman). An initial staff of 170, recruited from the dying newsreels, Fleet Street and the BBC, had been producing pilot bulletins for several weeks. The format for the 10 pm newscast was a 13½ minute programme using the now standard pattern of interwoven spoken and visual material, with the final five minutes in newsreel form. Overseas visuals were to come from CBS (Cox, 1995, p. 44). The London *Evening Standard* reviewed the first night's transmissions: 'snippets of information personalised with a few jokes cannot compare with the full factual résumé of the BBC' (publicity material, ITN, 1995). Only two stories were actually different from the BBC running order. One was the marriage of a 15 year old Italian princess; the other the first ever pre-verdict coverage of an Old Bailey trial (Cox, 1995, p. 46).

In January 1956, after the launch of what one of the first newscasters, Robin Day, was to call 'the most important new national organ of news since the war' (1990, p. 84), Aidan Crawley resigned owing to stress in the relationship between ITN and its parent ITV companies, which led to a dramatic cut in funding and a shift in scheduling to a later slot. Although the new commercial television system had a statutory obligation to carry news, it was not perceived as being enough of an audience puller to justify the 10 pm slot it had at first occupied. Crawley was succeeded as Editor of ITN in March 1956 by Geoffrey Cox, then a Fleet Street assistant editor who had a range of broadcasting experience. Cox quickly perceived the shortage of filmed material available, not just to cash-strapped ITN but to all broadcasters in general. It took anywhere from 24–48 hours for material to arrive from abroad, a far cry from today when some say there is too much material. Even at home, limited resources meant that 'one of the key decisions of the day was how to best deploy the cameramen' (Cox, 1995, p. 67).

In May of that year CBS produced a report from Nicosia in Cyprus of a riot which was reported with synchronous natural sound, i.e. location-recorded. Cox was very impressed and saw in this kind of coverage the future of newsgathering. Within two months a similarly dramatic story had been filmed in Britain with full location sound (p. 71). The event, a clash between strikers and police outside a factory, pointed towards more than just the arrival of a technology, but also towards a problematic area of reporting that was to be a subject of concern for the next 20 years.

The dispute, at the British Motor Corporation works at Longbridge near Birmingham, was the first major strike in the auto industry since the war. Both ITN and the BBC covered the story and their output was compared by a third party:

> The BBC treated the subject with scrupulous fairness. A few brief newsreel shots were supplemented by long carefully modified verbal reports of what people involved had said, and what the management and unions were going to do. Factual, but to the great majority of people dull. The ITN version consisted largely of lively, gripping film shots of the picket line outside the factories (the part which, let's face it, had the greatest appeal for the mass of the public) backed by a simple lucid commentary giving the main facts (*TV Mirror,* 8 September 1965, quoted in Briggs, 1995, p. 154).

The arrival of ITN offered the BBC competition and the viewer a different kind of news.

In the opinion of one of its founders, ITN in its first years 'went on to revolutionise TV journalism, and knocked the BBC for six in the process' (Day, 1990, p. 84). It might be easy to overstate the impact of ITN simply by comparison with the lacklustre BBC television news of the time. Certainly, the new service stood in sharp contrast to the staid BBC, on which it was clearly having an effect:

> the most emphatic change has been in the BBC's response to controversial topics. Impartiality can only be maintained with difficulty on television. It can closely resemble bad manners. This has been fully recognised by Independent Television News, whose newscasters demonstrate that informality is quite compatible with balanced opinion. Although BBC newscasters preserve characterless anonymity, the service is now admitting reports that do not merely oscillate between the official and the harmless (*The Times,* 1956, RTS Supplement, p. iii).

A year later another commentator was to write comparing the output of ITN favourably with the BBC:

The limitations of the BBC in this field seem to be due to the fact that its news is more or less an illustrated version of its long established methods of presenting news in sound. It is mainly a pictorial edition of sound, pre-occupied with accuracy and balance to the exclusion of elements of drama and immediacy which do not necessarily inhibit the truthful imparting of facts. The BBC television news is too docile and obedient to the precepts of its distinguished sire in sound; it would be all the better for running away from home and following the example of its more adventurous cousin (or half brother) who uses news as a drum to beat up an attentive audience, not as an album or as a scrapbook (*The Times*, 1957, p. iii).

ITN proved 'that TV news could be dramatic and vivid and amusing, without being sensational or biased or trivial' (Day, 1990, p. 90); it could, in its own words, 'combine the verve of Fleet Street with the authority of the BBC' (ITN, 1995). The news no longer emerged *ex cathedra* from the august portals of Broadcasting House read by anonymous voices over static visuals. The news had grown in Britain and new variations had evolved.

Certainly BBC television news had a long way to go before it lived up to the standards set both by its independent television rival and by the output of other parts of its own organisation. News had always been seen as a serious endeavour, its editors saw themselves 'as supplying (in sound) the equivalent of *The Times* or *Daily Telegraph;* to use pictures was to descend to the level of the popular press' (Hood, 1967, p. 106). Such an environment gradually changed and by 1958 Tahu Hole became Head of Administration. Hugh Greene, the new Director of News and Current Affairs, commissioned a report on his sad legacy. Three *television* producers were consulted and these wise men 'saw with stark clarity that as long as people who had little or no first-hand experience of working in television news continued to control the output (with Tahu Hole very much in mind) then most of the obvious faults would continue' (Milne, 1989, p. 32). Greene took their advice and 'restored freedom' to News Division (Greene, 1969, p. 123), bringing in staff from the much respected World Service news at Bush House. Stuart Hood, the new Deputy Editor, arrived with the intention of making television news 'as good as the *Daily Mirror*' (Briggs, 1995, p. 156). To achieve this aim of quality populism he wrote to his new staff, outlining production values unheard of at Alexandra Palace: 'What we want to achieve in a television bulletin is, first of all, professional gloss and secondly, pace' (p. 156). Gloss! Pace! At last BBC television news was beginning to escape from its radio legacy and from the culture of corporate caution embodied by Tahu Hole. Meanwhile, exciting developments were happening elsewhere.

News versus current affairs

Both Ed Murrow and Richard Dimbleby had left hard news behind after the war for another form of television journalism. Emerging from the talks tradition in British radio and its American cousin, the commentary, current affairs or public-affairs broadcasting was the news feature pages of the television newspaper, working in a way hard news bulletins could not. Murrow and Friendly had shown with *See it now* what television could do journalistically if given free rein. Stuart Hood, for a time Head of BBC News and later an academic, has remarked on their achievement:

> What marked these programmes was their power and impact. They were technically exciting, both in terms of camera-work and editing. They were courageous. They chose for their themes the great social and political issues facing the American nations. They contrived to be at once highly personal and yet balanced. Beside them much of British television's output looked pale and restrained (1967, p. 119).

Nature abhors a vacuum and what Tahu Hole and News Division would not, or could not, do was to be done by BBC Current Affairs, which grew out of the talks tradition imported from radio. As early as 1949 Grace Wyndham Goldie originated a series called *Foreign Correspondent* using mute pictures voiced in London. From such beginnings, what was to become BBC Current Affairs went on to develop new forms of pictorial journalism as diverse as the weekly flagship programme *Panorama* (presented by Richard Dimbleby), *Viewfinder* (presented by Aidan Crawley) and the daily magazine *Tonight*. BBC correspondent Martin Bell describes the state of BBC journalism when he joined the corporation in 1962:

> Current Affairs was definitely the senior service. It enjoyed enviable viewing figures, prime-time prominence and lavish budgets. All the excitement and creativity lay across London in the Television Centre and Lime Grove. News remained in exile atop its old headquarters at Alexandra Palace where television began. Thus marooned in the museum of the medium, it was restricted in the schedule to twelve-minute bulletins, delivered in a style not so very different from that of the old cinema newsreels (1995, pp. 115–16).

Television has always had golden ages where the memory of lost glories shines brightly in comparison with the grey dullness of the present. One of these ages was Hugh Greene's BBC, but, tellingly, any list of BBC accomplishments in the 1960s and 1970s makes no mention of the news. Nevertheless, when the Pilkington Committee reported in 1962, it gave a clean bill of health to both varieties of British television news:

> Our general conclusion is that the country is well served by the national news bulletins of the BBC and ITN. The selection and presentation of

both services is fair and objective. For the television news services, a particular but important part of television broadcasting, competition has worked well. Each of the two services is good in itself; each is different from the other in style and approach. Hence they offer the viewer a worthwhile choice, and stimulate one another (quoted in Cox, 1995, p. 179).

Although slower in developing than American network news, the British variants showed a greater difference between themselves, offering viewers a choice of distinct kinds of news rather than a nearly identical product differentiated for the most part only by the use of high-profile personality presenters.

In 1969 BBC TV News moved from Alexandra Palace to Television Centre and joined the rest of the television world. Not much further forward than CBS had been 20 years earlier, the BBC's much deserved reputation in other areas of broadcasting, including radio news and the World Service had yet to filter through into television news.

News at Ten

In July 1967 ITN started *News at Ten* as a 12-week experiment (Potter, 1990, p. 107). There was initial reluctance amongst the ITV companies to screen a half-hour news programme in such a prominent place in the schedule, but the newscast was extended on condition that the *Roving Report* and *Date Line* news features be dropped and that there would be a commercial break half way through. The first edition ended with Alistair Burnett explaining the new mission:

> Our aim is to bring you every weekday evening a half-hour news in depth at a peak viewing hour, a new venture in British television. For television itself is now better equipped to cover the world's news than it was when the old, short news bulletin was devised. We know it means asking you to develop a new viewing habit at 10 o'clock every evening but we mean to make it worth your while (Cox, 1995, p. 191).

In only its second week of broadcasting, Dame Margot Fonteyn and Rudolph Nureyev were arrested in San Francisco following a drugs raid. ITN booked a 10 minute unilateral satellite feed to bring in the pictures at an estimated cost of £7000. According to one commentator,

> they created a sensation editorially as well as financially. . . . By the end of the decade satellites had begun to girdle the earth and represented the beginning of a twentieth century version of the penny postage revolution. Television news was no longer a scarce resource (Potter, 1990, p. 109).

Even in the 1970s, however, for the vast volume of foreign news, it was still possible for the print media to beat broadcasters for speed (Potter, 1990, p. 115). Filing stories by satellite was still an expensive business, limited to transatlantic use. ITN's coverage of the 1967 Six Day War was a source of pride within the organisation as viewers were able to see pictures in the evening of events they had read about in that morning's paper. This was at the time revolutionary. Film from the Middle East was flown to Rome, where it was developed and then sent on the Eurovision landline to Brussels and then from there on to London (Potter, 1990, p. 116).

Stuart Hood, writing in 1967, outlines the problems news editors had in using pictures:

> It has become something of an art in the writing of television bulletins to marry pictures which are up to twenty four hours out of date with the latest information on the same story, which has come straight off the news agency tapes. For in spite of the developments in telecommunications one of the main problems of television news remains the difficulty of procuring pictures in time ... film can still take a day to arrive from the other side of the world and satellites have so far proved disappointing (p. 116).

The scale of newsgathering in the late 1960s can be seen by the fact that in 1968 ITN's operating budget was only £2 million. They employed 19 reporters and 12 film crews and had only two staff correspondents based overseas, one in Washington and one in Rome (Potter, 1990, p. 128). Only in the event of a very important story would a correspondent be sent abroad, owing to the expense. Union regulations required all crews to be flown first class and ITN correspondents could sometimes work with UPITN crews already stationed abroad, whereas the BBC did not follow such a policy and use Visnews agency crews.

'The whole world is watching'

Having established itself as a recognisable form as early as 1949, American television did not stand still throughout the 1950s. In 1956 NBC launched *Huntley–Brinkley Report*. This team had been used earlier in the year to cover the American political conventions and was to have a tremendous effect. 'In memory, pairing Chet Huntley and David Brinkley would be seen as the one act that catapulted NBC to the top of whatever heap network news had become' (Frank, 1991, p. 110). The first transmission of the new programme was on 29 October 1956, the day Israeli troops attacked the Suez Canal and Russian tanks entered Hungary. Neither event was reported with location film, which was not unusual at the time. When pictures of events were available, every attempt was made by figures such as producer Reuven Frank to use them appropriately:

> NBC News was beginning to accommodate itself to our way of seeing pictures, to our proposition that television news was, above all, seeing things happen. Cameramen were enthusiastic, reporters and bureau chiefs less so. Our system was to have cameramen film news events, to edit their film into a narrative, then, as the last step, to write a script that included the description of the event and its news relevance. We did not use reporters on the scene, who would speak a script to which pictures would be matched – risking the danger of throwing away the best pictures because they had not been scripted for. So although we had some good reporters, we used them very little, far less than CBS did and perhaps more than we should have (p. 118).

The Quiz Show scandals of 1959 helped news to become the acceptable, responsible face of television, as did the fact that it was cheap compared with other forms of programming. As the network news divisions flourished so too did local news, growing dynamically across the country, most notably at KNXT, a CBS-owned station in Los Angeles. Robert D. Wood, the station General Manager, created *The Big News*, a 45 minute programme utilising specialist reporters linked by a studio 'anchor man'. By 1968, 228 local stations were broadcasting 30 minute daily news programmes (Smith, 1973, p. 84). In September 1963, first CBS and then NBC extended the network evening news to 30 minutes. Walter Cronkite, already a familiar face on network television, who had taken over anchoring CBS News just over a year before, interviewed President Kennedy to mark the occasion (Frank, 1991, p. 183).

The Kennedy years were good for the medium, aided by a telegenic young President who loved televised press conferences. Hardly surprisingly, the tragic end to Camelot was a major event in the development of television news. CBS's young Dallas reporter, Dan Rather, beat the other networks by 17 minutes with the news of Kennedy's death (Boyer, 1988, p. 230) when a phone line he was using to confirm a doctor's report was accidentally open to a CBS Radio editor in New York (Mayer, 1987, p. 193). In Britain, the BBC scooped ITN, reporting the President's death before the official White House statement and before Reuters. The beat came from the Monitoring Unit at Caversham who picked up a Voice of America radio report. The inbred caution of the sound era had gone, with the corporation employing its vast resources to advantage. *Tonight* was on-air live and broke the news to Britons (Cox, 1995, p. 168). On both sides of the ocean television went on a roll through the long weekend until the funeral. On Sunday NBC were relaying events at police headquarters as part of their rolling coverage, as Lee Harvey Oswald was brought down from the cells. Reporter Tom Pettitt watched as Jack Ruby shot the man who reputedly had shot the President. Later he was to tell *Newsweek* that the words went from his eyes to his mouth without passing through the brain (Frank, 1991, p. 189). Television had recorded a live murder for the first time. Some 96 per cent of America's televisions were tuned to the coverage of events through the weekend, with viewers watching an average of 32 of the 82 hours of coverage as Cronkite and the other network anchors reassured the mourning nation (Mayer, 1987, p. 194). As one academic commentator has remarked: 'television journalism grew up in Dallas, for never before had it faced such a story with so much responsibility for telling it' (Schramm, 1965, p. 11).

The withdrawal of Lyndon Johnson from the presidential race; the assassination of Martin Luther King and the riots that followed; the hope of the Prague spring; a second, unthinkable, Kennedy assassination; the troubled Democratic convention in Chicago where demonstrators chanted 'the whole world is watching' before the cameras as the Chicago police ran riot; the invasion of Prague by Soviet bloc troops – all these events made 1968 a monumental year for television news and the world it broadcast to. But this veritable cascade of major news events was subsumed by the one big story that ran throughout the most written about year in US history (Frank, 1991, p. 250).

Vietnam

On 30 January 1968 the Vietcong and the North Vietnamese army launched the Tet offensive, taking advantage of the Vietnamese New Year (Tet), normally a time of ceasefire. With enterprise and daring they attacked urban targets throughout South Vietnam, even penetrating into the US Embassy compound in Saigon. Crucially, this event was recorded for Americans to see in their living rooms and it was not the only memorable event to happen in sight of the cameras.

On 1 February, during the third day of chaos in Saigon, South Vietnamese police chief Brigadier General Nguyen Ngoc Loan pulled his revolver from its holster, held it to the temple of a Vietcong suspect and summarily executed him in full view of both Associated Press photographer Eddie Adams and South Vietnamese cameraman Vo Suu who worked for NBC (Arnett, 1994, p. 251). The still image was seen first by the world, as it could be transmitted quicker. The NBC film was sent to Tokyo for processing, where it was edited before being sent by satellite to NBC in New York where it was twice further cut before transmission, for reasons of taste (Frank, 1991, pp. 252–3). How much of the horror of the event viewers were to see was clearly crucial, though in Saigon the event seemed less remarkable to one observer. 'General Loan does that all the time. That's not news' said a Vietnamese employee of *Time* magazine, explaining why he hadn't bothered to report the event at all (*Vietnam stories: the camera at work*, BBC2, 27 March 1995). In the space of a few days the American public saw both that the war was not progressing as they had been told and that young Americans were dying in support of a violent and corrupt regime. 'I thought we were supposed to be winning this goddam war' remarked Walter

Cronkite when he saw CBS's first pictures of the Tet (Cox, 1995, p. 4). He thought as many Americans must have thought, and, after a visit to Vietnam, Cronkite tempered his language somewhat before pronouncing in a special report on 27 February 1968:

> To say that we are closer to victory today is to believe, in the face of the evidence, the optimists who have been wrong in the past. To suggest we are on the edge of defeat is to yield to unreasonable pessimism. To say that we are mired in stalemate seems the only realistic, yet satisfactory conclusion (quoted in Hallin, 1986, p. 170).

According to one commentator it was the first time a television anchor had declared a war to be over (Halberstam, 1979, p. 514) and certainly US President Lyndon Johnson was not happy to see that he had lost Cronkite (Hallin, 1986, p. 170).

It has often been remarked that the Tet offensive was a propaganda victory but not a military victory, and certainly it was to be a further seven years, on 30 April 1975, before Saigon fell. As communist forces closed in on the southern capital some journalists left, filming their dramatic evacuation from the US Embassy (Michael Nicholson, ITN; Ed Bradley, CBS), while others remained. The BBC's Brian Barron filed the historic news by telex as North Vietnamese tanks arrived in the streets, while Australian cameraman Neil Davis was waiting at the Presidential Palace as the tanks burst through the ornamental wrought iron gates and a Vietcong flag was triumphantly displayed for him to film (Arnett, 1994, p. 304). The network bulletins that night had to use pictures of the evacuation from the day before. The first television news pictures of the fall of Saigon on Wednesday 30 April did not appear on NBC until Friday 2 May, when all the networks led with American unemployment. Only NBC had pictures from Saigon, the other two networks carrying the story of Smokey the Bear 'retiring' as the US Forest Service symbol. When ITN's Sandy Gall, who had stayed behind in Saigon, returned to Britain, his material had to wait six days before transmission because of an ITV technicians' strike. What had been the biggest story in the world was over.

Vietnam was supposed to be television's first war (Hallin, 1986, p. 6), notwithstanding Korea, but pictures still took days to reach the screen, long after events had been reported using still images and wire copy. It certainly wasn't the zenith of technological development, but the American war in southeast Asia resonates because of the continuing assumption that television news had more effect than ever before, or since, simply because the Pentagon did not understand the potential power of the medium. Never again would reporters wander war zones at will. The perception that the American media caused the war to be lost, however wrong-headed, certainly led to much closer military control of journalists in subsequent conflicts. Pictures from the Falklands took up to 23 days to arrive on British screens (Harris, 1983, p. 56) when it might have been technically possible for them to arrive significantly sooner by satellite had the authorities been inclined to help (Morrison and Tumber, 1988, pp. 166–8). Journalists were 'pooled' for the Grenada and Panama adventures, as they were to be in the Gulf. In that sense Vietnam marked the end of an era of innocence in foreign war reporting, if the word innocence can ever be attributed to such an activity.

Vietnam and Watergate were two overlapping and long-running news stories which confirmed the news media in their reputed role as the Fourth Estate, ensuring the proper functioning of democracy, and protecting citizens with their ceaseless harrying of the irresponsible and the powerful. The fall of Saigon and the resignation of a two-term President were seen by some as evidence of a healthy functioning media debating foreign policy misjudgments and exposing foolish and corrupt politicians. However, what was to one point of view responsible behaviour in a democratic society was to another unwarranted power in the hands of an unelected elite. In November 1969, Vice-President Spiro Agnew attacked the media, outlining a 'credibility gap . . . not in the offices of the government in Washington but in the studios of the networks in New York'. Speaking from Des Moines, Iowa, and thus requiring the networks to engage in technical contortions not required had he been speaking from New York or Boston, the soon-to-be-disgraced Vice-President, in a speech written by Pat Buchanan, claimed 'a narrow and distorted picture of America often emerges from the televised news' (Epstein, 1973, p. 6; Frank, 1991, p. 293). Agnew and Buchanan were not alone in holding this view, nor was it confined to their particular section of the political spectrum.

State and media, politicians and producers

A thorough examination of the constantly shifting relationship between the media and state, between politicians and producers, between government and broadcasting institutions, is beyond the scope of this study. Suffice it to say, as Richard Collins has, that it is not possible to theorise satisfactorily the relationship between these antagonists which is the result of a constant process of renegotiation (Collins, 1990, pp. 234–5). Certainly, even a brief mention of empirical examples in Britain shows a diversity of relationships that seems to preclude any definitive positioning of the news media as either harriers or supporters of the *status quo*. If the BBC were onside in the case of the 1926 General Strike, Suez represented a contrary aspect to the relationship between the state and the media. If certain academic accounts are accepted, the news media were inevitably biased against labour in all of the long-running industrial disputes in the 1970s, while the reporting of the American bombing of Libya incurred the public wrath of Conservative Party Chairman Norman Tebbit (Barnett and Curry, 1994, p. 41; Corner, 1995b, 68 ff.). A long list of such contrasting examples could be presented.

It would be simplistic, however, to assume that for every clear instance of the media supporting the *status quo* there are equal instances of clear opposition. Hallin (1986) in his thorough study of the media coverage of Vietnam concludes that very often media opposition to government policy is a reflection of divisions within the policy-making elite itself rather than the result of independent journalistic action. Once opposition to the Vietnam War developed inside the State Department, the Pentagon and Congress, the media reflected this shift towards a new consensus, rather than creating it by their reporting. Even this model does not appear to be subtle enough, as policy-makers themselves are media consumers, and a television record of American soldiers setting fire to a Vietnamese village is as likely to have an effect on them as it is on voters.

Media opposition to government policy is often credited to what I call the Denis Thatcher syndrome, which consists in the simplistic assumption that all broadcasting organisations, particularly the BBC, are full of 'reds' (Barnett and Curry, 1994, p. 39; Harris, 1983, p. 84). Personal factors and *ad hominem* criticisms invariably surface. *Newsnight* anchor Peter Snow was severely criticised during the Falklands conflict when he exercised due professional scepticism and remarked of one official report: 'if we believe the British, and I have already pointed out that we have good reason to . . . ' (Milne, 1988, p. 17). This 'unacceptably even-handed' behaviour led to tabloid outrage and questions in the House, and the Chairman and Director General of the BBC were summoned before the Tory Media Committee to what one MP present was to describe as 'the ugliest meeting I have ever attended in my years as an MP' (Harris, 1983, p. 85).

Interestingly, Snow, a former Defence Correspondent, was later to be accused of being too gung-ho in his coverage of the Gulf War: 'Peter Snow's enthusiasm for toy tanks is not just a harmless obsession but an affliction bordering on derangement' (Naughton, 1991, p. 76), while his BBC colleagues Jeremy Paxman and David Dimbleby were attacked as being 'television grandees' who 'betrayed their responsibilities to a contemptible degree' (Keegan, 1991, p. 11) simply because they did not agree optimistically with every word spoken to them by retired military men. Journalist John Pilger was later to attack Dimbleby, interpreting the very same situation entirely differently: 'There sat David Dimbleby and Sir Michael Armitage, former head of defence intelligence, as if they were in their club' (1992, p. 144). Predictably, such a variety of attacks from the political left and right alike leads to the obvious response from journalists: 'We must be doing something right'. Clearly there is tension between cultures which is exacerbated at times of emergency and crisis when long-contested areas of debate inevitably come out into the open. Cases such as the Falklands War and the Gulf War graphically demonstrate the fault lines that exist in relations between the media and officialdom. As Robert Harris concludes in his excellent study of the media issues raised by the Falklands conflict:

The instinctive secrecy of the military and the Civil Service; the prostitution and hysteria of sections of the press; the lies, the misinformation, the manipulation of public opinion by the authorities; the political intimidation of broadcasters; the ready contrivance of the media at their own distortion . . . all these occur as much in normal peace time in Britain as in war (1983, p. 151).

As if that weren't already complicated enough, into this complex dynamic comes an additional factor when one profession that thinks of itself as simply doing its job under great pressures constantly finds itself under what appears to be unjustified attack by ideologically motivated commentators who know nothing of their world.

Bad news

Conflicts and misunderstandings occur not just between the media and politicians, and television journalists are often scrutinised themselves with the same rigour that they would apply to politicians. There is a rich academic tradition of comment and criticism going back to the founding of broadcasting. Seen from broadcasters' point of view, much of this work is very often puritanical, with an anti-television predisposition, and some is from a recognisably left-of-centre political viewpoint. Very little has any effect at all on broadcasting practice. This conflict of cultures is nearly as old as the broadcasting media themselves (Lazarsfeld, 1948), with sparring usually limited to spirited discussion at those conferences where media academics and television journalists all too rarely meet (Schudson, 1991, p. 141).

This divergence is best illustrated by the furore created by the work of the Glasgow University Media Group (GUMG). Their research, beginning with *Bad news* in 1976, suggested that British television news was guilty of bias in its coverage of industrial affairs. Since ITN took its sound camera to Longbridge in 1956, relations between management and labour in British industry had taken a significant place high up the British domestic news agenda, and by choosing such a subject the research was bound to prove controversial. The GUMG nailed their colours firmly to the mast in the first sentences of *Bad news*:

Contrary to the claims, conventions, and culture of television journalism, the news is not a neutral product. For television news is a cultural artifact; it is a sequence of socially manufactured messages, which carry many of the culturally dominant assumptions of our society. From the accents of the newscasters to the vocabulary of camera angles; from who gets on and what questions they are asked, via selection of stories to presentation of bulletins, the news is a highly mediated product (GUMG, p. 1).

Such notions were hardly novel in academic circles but the GUMG analysis met with a violent reaction, with news professionals stoutly defending their profession from such charges. Journalists, after all, were 'telling it like it is', working hard under great pressure, and they were not pleased to be told by a group of sociologists, probably of a left-wing tint, that they were not doing their job properly. In defending themselves by claiming they were being objective about the events they were reporting, media professionals were confirming an academic analysis, behaving just as one academic observer (Tuchman, 1972) said they would, by evoking objectivity as a 'strategic ritual'.

The Glasgow findings were discussed at the highest level in the BBC, with the Director General himself leading the discussion with the view that

> there would be no sense in attacking *Bad News* in detail . . . Desmond Wilcox felt it would be dangerous to launch a widespread attack on the discipline of sociology, which included some perfectly responsible practitioners. . . . DG agreed that the BBC could examine the aims and politics of sociology (quoted in GUMG, 1995, p. 380).

Such internal BBC comments have a ring of truth to anyone who has ever had access to Directorate News Current Affairs (DNCA) minutes. As a young contract researcher in the late 1970s I was able regularly to read the DNCA minutes and was always amazed by the often self-critical nature of the debate recorded. It was no surprise that these widely distributed papers were regularly leaked, but what was revealing was the selective way in which they were quoted in the alternate press.

The GUMG timed their work in order to report to the Annan Committee on Broadcasting and, as a result, the *Bad news* issue generated a great deal of wider media coverage. A form of dialogue did take place, with the Glasgow academics being invited to the Edinburgh Television Festival and being treated to a private visit by the BBC Chairman. The Glasgow findings were not universally accepted inside the academic world and the group were accused of presenting, in certain parts of their work, 'yellow press pastiche as sound sociology' (Schlesinger, 1987, pp. xxxviii and 47). ITN cooperated with an academic response (Harrison, 1985) which acknowledged faults in the television coverage of industrial issues while attacking the Glasgow Group's work as being 'far stronger on assertion than on sound scholarly demonstration'. In this view, their findings 'are at best exaggerated and fre-quently they are flatly innaccurate . . . . while facts are massaged out of all recognition' (pp. 69 and 120).

Clearly the GUMG work had some effect (Harrison, 1985, pp. 9–10). In fact, one senior journalist spoken to for this study told me that 'ITN got quite paranoid about it', while another claimed that it had an effect pre-cisely because it was, in his words, 'over the top'. 'Everyone has a copy in their locker', he said. Like the confrontational industrial disputes which were the subject of the first GUMG studies, a vigorous claim by one side promotes a strong response by the other and a dialectic of sorts leads to some development that might not otherwise have emerged had a more cosy relationship existed between certain academics and broadcasters. In this analysis there was something of a pragmatic outcome. Whether the GUMG theories were right or not is not an issue, curiously enough, and for this reason their work is discussed here in the history of news institutions and not in the overview of academic theory. This is a testament to the Group's political astuteness, if not their theoretical sophistication. As an academic social construction, in its own way as manufactured as the news, their work had an effect. I give them the last word by way of summary:

> we suggest that news is a selective combination of ritual, rhetoric, factual claims and statements, informed (sometimes misinformed) speculations and interpretative comment. We find it difficult, indeed unhelpful, to assign labels like 'objective', 'impartial' or 'neutral' to such a manufactured product. The beginning of wisdom is to recognise news for what it is and not what it claims for itself (1985, p. 237; 1995, pp. 17–18).

Bias against understanding

About the same time as the original GUMG remarks, a series of articles appeared in *The Times* which severely criticised television news. These articles were by two media professionals, neither of whom worked in news. One was a man who was to go on to become head of BBC journalism and eventually its Director General, the other was eventually to be the Economic Editor of BBC News. John Birt, then the Head of Current Affairs at London Weekend Television, and Peter Jay, the presenter of its flagship current affairs programme *Weekend World* and Economic Editor of *The Times*, accused the news of 'a bias against understanding' (Birt, 1975, p. 14). Instead of explaining the economic problems of the nation in a wider context, the daily reporting of events led to a flood of unexplained facts:

> The news, devoting two minutes on successive nights to the latest unemployment figures or the state of the stock market, with no time to put the story in context, gives the viewer no sense of how any of these problems relate to each other (p. 14).

Effective news analysis could come about only as a result of radical reforms:

> We should redesign television news programmes so that they devote much more time than they presently do to the main stories of the day; and so that these stories are put in the fullest possible context in the time available (p. 14).

The distinctions between news and current affairs should be abolished in favour of 'an integrated operation' producing an hour-long daily 'flagship' programme backed up by weekly and monthly news analysis slots. This output would be produced by a unified news and current affairs staff 'organised into subject teams headed by subject editors, such as a political editor, a foreign editor, an industrial editor and so on'. These reforms could best be carried out in the context of the BBC rather than the fragmented ITV sector: 'the BBC, being capable in principle of a strategic command decision, is on the face of things better able to undertake a radical change which will offend many entrenched interests' (Birt and Jay, 1975b, p. 14).

Reactions to these suggestions were diverse. The BBC Chairman, Sir Michael Swann, publicly endorsed the argument, distributed copies of the articles amongst staff and in time invited the authors to Broadcasting House, where 'the governors came quite close to the proposition that maybe we should bring these lads in and have them do their number on news and current affairs' (Barnett and Curry, 1994, p. 79). In opposition, the then Director General, Charles Curran, responded with a paper which convinced the good and the great that the theory in question was in fact more to do with the sociology of management than with the news. For the time being the mission to explain remained a theory.

As theory it did not impress media academics. 'Their views were far from radical, merely popularising a critique which had been familiar for many years' (Golding and Elliott, 1979, p. 218), wrote one team, while another media scholar remarked tellingly 'there is little which is original or novel in this *potpourri*. But the impact . . . has been considerable, which is more than one can say for the efforts of most media sociologists' (Schlesinger, 1987, pp. 244–5). This commentator saw their work as naive in its inability to look beyond the world of television news and warned, somewhat prophetically:

> The organisation of broadcast journalism is not so independent a variable as Birt and Jay would like to believe, and radical change is likely to meet resistance. . . . A news organisation wedded to a policy of corporate caution, which directly derives from the consensualist political constraints facing the BBC, is unlikely to initiate travel along such a potentially dangerous path (p. 245).

Annan

The Committee on the Future of Broadcasting chaired by Lord Annan considered the views of 750 organisations and individuals, including the GUMG and Birt and Jay. Annan pronounced on a variety of issues, not the least was the vexed issue of impartiality: 'the notion of impartiality is under siege. It is attacked by sociologists who point out that no-one can be perfectly impartial' (1977, para. 17.8). Accordingly, the Committee systematically discussed impartiality with regard to Northern Ireland, party politics and industrial affairs, concluding that 'broadcasters were not guilty of deliberate and calculated bias' (para. 17.17) but found that they 'do not represent adequately the industrial and commercial life of the country' (para. 17.19). They declared that 'news cannot be some sort of objectively established entity' (para. 17.29) and applauded 'the variety of news outlets and of editorial judgements, both in broadcasting and in the press, which is maintained in the nation' (para. 17.30).

Both the BBC and ITN took the occasion to reply to the Birt–Jay thesis. ITN feared the suggested approach ran the risk of alienating the audience by 'boring them to death', while the BBC attacked the proposals as 'a bias against unadorned fact' (para. 17.50). Annan recommended the appointment of specialist correspondents (para. 17.51) but suggested news and current affairs programming remain distinct. News was not seen favourably by the Committee. It was too stereotyped and unvaried, lacking in explanation, especially at the BBC where

> news is particularly singled out by many experienced foreign observers as the one weak spot in an output for which otherwise they have the highest praise. The broadcasting organisations should concentrate more on strengthening and varying their television news programmes (para. 17.53).

BBC News was hardly given a clean bill of health, with Annan *et al.* coyly evoking unnamed foreign observers as the authorities for such a judgement. Objective notions of the news were rejected, and more variety of output was called for. While Annan had no direct power to implement such changes, pressure was building on the traditional news services.

Significant changes were nearer than many expected. Already by 1980 the debates about the nature of the news occasioned by *Bad news* and by Birt and Jay appeared to have had some effect with the creation of *Newsnight,* launched with joint news and current affairs staff. This daily 45 minute programme on BBC2 was designed to be issue-driven rather than event-driven and would have the opportunity to cover stories in depth and at greater length than the shorter traditional bulletins. This pattern of main bulletins followed by late-night analysis had actually existed before in the commercial sector when ITN had, for a time, a 'two-tiered bulletin' with the main 9.25 programme supplemented by 10 minutes of analysis on *Dateline* at 11 pm, but the system went in the compromise which led to the creation of *News at Ten* (Cox, 1995, p. 157). Equally, the BBC had had programmes such as *24 Hours* and the late-night *Tonight* which ran from 1975 to 1979. When the newly created Channel 4 began transmitting in 1982, ITN provided the daily news service to the channel, whose founders made the bold decision to place their nearly hour-long news in prime time at 7 pm. British television had another variant on the news, one which consciously sought 'to blend news narrative with analysis' (ITN, 1995, p. 18). In the short space of two years the news map had altered considerably. With the new additions, British television had four channels, each with recognisably different types of news programming, with both *Channel 4 News* and *Newsnight* universally acknowledged as being successful in moving beyond the 'unadorned fact' of 1970s television news.

Very much like the GUMG, Birt and Jay seem to have had an effect. It could be said that their ideas were very much in the air, with the polemic activity both of the Glasgow academics and of Birt and Jay crystallising views that were widely held inside parts of the profession. The evolution of broadcast news away from the mere relaying of agency reports was continuing, with growth, as ever, a balance between the forces of conservatism and caution and those of innovation.

Troubles

When the BBC Chairman testified to the Annan Committee he was of the opinion that 'BBC current affairs programmes lacked ideas because they tried too hard to keep out of trouble' (Annan, 1977, para. 17.59). He had underestimated his programme-makers. Even before the election of Margaret Thatcher, the BBC was under considerable political pressure. In 1978 Labour Secretary of State for Northern Ireland, Roy Mason, took the corporation to task for becoming a mouthpiece for IRA propaganda and reminded them that the charter was due for renewal. The Labour government considered imposing boards of management to give greater control over the day-to-day running of the corporation, which figures such as Tony Benn saw as being irredeemably right wing. Events continued after Margaret Thatcher's election, many of them tied to the vexed question of Ulster, mostly arising from current affairs programming rather than news. A *Tonight* interview with Irish National Liberation Army figures; a *Panorama* team filming an IRA display of strength at Carrickmore; the Falklands incidents mentioned above; *Real lives*, a controversial Northern Irish documentary; *Secret society: Zircon* when police actually raided BBC Scotland to seize material; the news coverage of the American bombing of Libya – all these events put the BBC under great political pressure as its charter came up for renewal.

Director General Alasdair Milne eventually went, to be replaced by Michael Checkland, a compromise candidate who was an accountant with no experience of journalism. Thus it came about that John Birt came into the BBC at the level of Deputy Director General, from LWT, hired partly on the basis of his published views on news. Birt was put in charge of BBC's journalism with the mission to put its house in order.

Birt, bias and bi-media

It is perhaps appropriate to begin discussion of the Birt regime with the words of a reforming Director General himself on the state of the BBC journalism he inherited:

> news was news and current affairs were current affairs and never the twain should meet. They had been living in water-tight compartments for many years in an atmosphere of mutual distrust and even contempt. My job as I saw it was to weld together the news and current affairs elements in radio and television so that they could carry out their respective functions against a background of shared policy and journalistic assumption. I had to create an atmosphere in which journalistic enterprise and talent could flourish without any loss of reliability (Greene, 1969, p. 127).

This comes not from John Birt's secret autobiography but from the pen of Hugh Greene, writing about events nearly 20 years before Birt's arrival at Broadcasting House. It was as accurate of the BBC in 1987 as it had been of the BBC in 1959. Since its arrival from Alexandra Palace, television news had existed in splendid isolation in 'the Spur', an extension to Television Centre, while current affairs inhabited the Lime Grove studios some way away physically and a considerable distance apart culturally. Although there was some semblance of bureaucratic unity at the very top of the organisation, for all intents and purposes the two empires were as independent as they had been in the days of Tahu Hole. It was not impossible, and indeed not uncommon, for the BBC to be represented at an event by film crews from News, *Nationwide, Newsnight* and even *Panorama*, with a radio reporter or two also in attendance. Current affairs teams would often fly into a foreign location, such as South Africa, where news had a permanent presence, and create a reaction that made the resident correspondent's life difficult and, while the viewer might have been served by the resulting programme, nothing was done for the cause of corporate harmony and the long-term reporting of events.

Some current affairs programming had a reputation for being somewhat newspaper driven, originating very little of its own material. One daily programme morning meeting inevitably consisted of staff discussing the papers almost exclusively. I was told by one now senior producer that the secret of success in such a context lay in obtaining a local newspaper that no one else had. She also related how the programme in question was very nearly taken off the air when strike action broke the flow of cuttings from Fleet Street. Researchers worked on the phone, with a finger in their ear to shut out the noise around them, one eye on the clock, cutting in hand, mouth in overdrive and brain in neutral, with the result being a skateboarding vicar or the like. Another current affairs producer told me of his own early experience on a local newspaper where journalists refused to accept calls from researchers at what they jokingly called the British Bubblegum Company, telling them that they should do their own work.

Specialist correspondents did exist in news, some of whom reported both to radio and television, economics specialist Dominick Harrod being one example of this early form of what is now called a bi-media worker. In fact it was only in 1972 that television and radio reporters had been formed into media-specific teams (Schlesinger, 1987, p. 75), prior to that reporters had rotated between Television Centre and Broadcasting House in a form of 'bi-mediality' experienced by some reporters active today (Bell, 1995, p. 117). Neither news nor current affairs were above reform, but neither were they irredeemably lost. Almost in spite of itself, the lively, and at times badly organised, collection of baronies and production villages that constituted the pre-Birt BBC was capable of producing some of the best television in the world. What was at issue was whether to get in the decorators or the demolition squad.

At London Weekend Television John Birt and his colleagues had used a method of working that was an anathema to the flexible, organic methods used at the BBC. On *Weekend World* Birt's teams had worked from scripts prepared after extensive research before filming even began. Fear ran through the BBC that such methods would be imposed on them. 'Scriptoids', as one foreign correspondent called them, did not arrive as standard BBC practice, but a wide range of reorganisations did take place. Consultants were consulted and charts flowed. News and current affairs were joined under one common management, specialist bi-media teams were formed and substantial resources were poured into the new News and Current Affairs empire. Dissent rumbled through the ranks and at times emerged in public with 'old soldiers' such as India correspondent Mark Tully putting their heads above the parapet to lament the way things had changed for the worse (Snoddy, 1993a, p. 9).

Dissent was not universal, however, and one distinguished foreign correspondent in his mid-50s, who engagingly described himself as a 'hack' when he was anything but, told me that the Birtian reforms had given him wonderful new opportunities both to do longer current affairs programmes and to report to radio. At a time when he might be expected to be winding down his career, he was having a fresh lease of life and new outlets for his work.

Interventionist in a way no BBC Deputy or Director General has ever been, Birt's directives have permeated news and current affairs practice. Many television professionals see the Birt reforms as producing a bias away from pictures and traditional news values (Gallagher, 1996). The combination of the mission to explain and bi-media working have led to a return to a culture of words where television pictures have once again become wallpaper laid over 200 words of broadsheet journalism. The clear distinction between the news values of the BBC and ITN has been maintained and indeed widened.

Revolutions, the fall of ageing empires giving way to a new world order, the technological change of a new information age and a new economic accountability made the late 1980s a time of unparalleled change. The world outside the BBC was also changing in its normally untidy and fractious way. Early in 1991, a new combination of broadcasting letters sprang to the lips of people who hadn't even seen the news service in question and who probably couldn't see it. Developments already well in progress over a decade, the significance of which were suddenly to become clear, intruded from the unlikely source of a room in a Baghdad hotel.

CNN

On 1 June 1980 at 6 o'clock in the evening Ted Turner sent the first edition of Cable Network News up to the satellite. The mixture of technologies seems perhaps strange to millions around the world who think of CNN as a satellite service, but the original intention was to provide a news service to cable stations which was distributed to their 'cable heads' by satellite, then predominantly a wholesale distribution medium. At the end of the first hour's broadcasting, Louis Hart, one of CNN's debut anchors, told viewers: 'Stay with us, we are going to have all kinds of news, views and special features, from now on and forever' (Mayer, 1987, p. 213). Turner was disparaged as a 'lunatic' for setting up CNN, according to sources at NBC (Auletta, 1991, p. 33). CNN ran a different kind of operation from the networks. Turner had avoided unionisation and therefore had more flexible working procedures and fewer staff. CNN anchors and reporters were paid considerably less than their network equivalents and as a result CNN was able to produce round-the-clock news coverage for one third of the budget required by the network news programmes. Much of their coverage consisted of live links rather than polished, edited ENG pieces and they had no reservations about using pictures from outside sources. Their rolling news format actually consists of a fairly conventional half-hour bulletin repeated every hour, 'at the top of the hour', with the second half of the hour devoted either to feature programming or discussion, with the possibility of extending the main bulletin and going on a 'roll', covering the same story almost exclusively.

'Chicken Noodle News'

Originally dubbed Chicken Noodle News by the network competition, many in traditional broadcasting do not think very highly of CNN. One anonymous network correspondent has said 'I say let CNN send out the kids to gather the news – vacuum it all up and disgorge it without any picking and choosing and then let the networks explain what it is all about' (Kimball, 1994, p. 120). CNN's innovative activities were not confined to the journalistic and the technological. A million dollars in legal fees went on suing the White House to get CNN into the 'pool' (MacArthur, 1990, p. 21). They also did good deals. The upstart news service reputedly has the best press facilities in the Pentagon simply because Ted Turner donated a satellite dish capable of receiving CNN signals to the Department of Defence (Kimball, 1994, p. 128), although it is a bit hard to imagine the American military really needing help to receive signals from a satellite. Called 'the mouth from the south' by his network competitors (MacArthur, 1990, p. 21), Turner claimed his motto to be 'early to bed, early to rise, work like hell and advertise' (Source: *The Tycoon,* Channel 4, 23 March 1994) and, certainly, self-advertisement is a conspicuous feature of CNN's broadcasting.

When President Reagan was shot in 1981, less than a year after its launch, CNN beat the networks with the story by four minutes, going on a roll for 29 hours to cover events (MacArthur, 1990, p. 21). The *Challenger* space shuttle disaster in 1986 was broadcast live by CNN alone, who proved themselves more than capable of competing with the networks. What doubts remained were removed by the Gulf War, although one BBC news executive spoken to for this study referred to CNN coverage as being 'a mile wide and an inch deep', a view he apparently altered when he crossed the Atlantic and joined CNN.

By 1992, CNN had 1800 full-time employees, half of them based in their Atlanta headquarters. Of those, 170 are on-camera talent anchors and reporters. When it began in 1980 CNN was available in 1.5 million homes via cable, by 1986 that figure had risen to 35 million. In 1992 60 million households around the world were able to receive CNN (Mayer, 1987, p. 216). By 1995 CNN boasted it was distributed on 14 different satellites reaching 200 nations and territories around the world, with 21 international, nine domestic bureaux and 600 affiliated stations, of which 400 were in the USA (press Release CNN, 1995). Their signal was reputedly within reach of 98 per cent of the world's population (Flournoy, 1992, p. 2). Losses of $77 million in the first five years were reversed to a $339 million profit in the five years to 1990. CNN International, launched in October 1985, lost money for five years before breaking even (Culf, 1996, p. 16). CNN Interactive is a 10 000 page Internet presence.

Downsizing the networks

Almost as if they were intentionally playing into Turner's hands, the networks took their eye off the proverbial ball. During 1986 all three networks changed ownership, becoming part of larger corporate concerns. News had always had to fight its corner even before the takeovers, and forces that drove Murrow and Friendly away from television were even more in evidence by 1986. Network news had been a money loser and the new corporate masters of the networks didn't see any reason why that sad state of financial affairs should continue. The network operations that together employed nearly 2000 staff in Washington and 600 in London (Mayer, 1987, p. 205) were seen as extravagant. Cuts ensued and by 1996 the three networks combined had fewer overseas bureaux than CNN alone (Culf, 1996, p. 17). CNN's public relations triumph in the Gulf War did little to raise the network news divisions in the esteem of their new owners, who saw themselves paying enormous sums for something that was being done better elsewhere. *Newsweek* even went so far as to state that CNN's first-night scoop from Baghdad was 'the night the networks died' (Alter, 1991, p. 41).

Real world events, however, wait for no one. Broadcasting executives may downsize, shift focus and redefine strategies while management consultants reorganise corporate structures, de-layer and create cost centres, but the world goes on producing the exceptional events that constitute the news. And news organisations go on reporting them. CNN's success spawned imitation. In February 1989 Sky News's 24-hour service went on the air as part of Rupert Murdoch's package of British satellite channels. This first challenge to CNN went practically unnoticed, prompting very much the same response from the BBC and ITN as the American networks had reserved for CNN (attack in public but watch in the newsroom). In his first appearance as Prime Minister, John Major strode out of Number 10 Downing Street to address the assembled cameras. Whether by accident or design, he went straight to the Sky television position to speak and left the BBC and ITN with nasty profile shots. The next day Sky ran full-page advertisements in the papers noting their triumph. In spite of losing £20 million a year, Murdoch soldiers on, both for the prestige Sky News offers as the acceptable face of satellite television and perhaps, as he sees it, as the first part of a global network of ASkyB, BSkyB, linking his American, Australian and British interests. Murdoch has said CNN is too liberal and accused Turner of 'brown-nosing dictators'. Hardly surprisingly, Turner has responded by comparing his Australian-born rival both to an insect and to Hitler (Culf, 1996, p. 16). But Citizen Turner, 'the mouth from the south', and Citizen Murdoch, the 'dirty digger', are not the only players now on the global stage.

The BBC, a much respected force in international broadcasting since the 1930s, has sought to capitalise on its 'brand name', creating World Service Television. After the success of 'Scud FM', the rolling radio news it ran during the Gulf War, the BBC sought various ways of getting into the 24-hour business (Hall, 1992, p. 15). The result, BBC *World*, is now received in 43 million homes in 111 countries, delivered in conjunction with a number of partners. At one time its mixture of news and other factual programming was carried on Hong Kong based Star TV's southern beam, resulting in Madhur Jaffrey's Indian cooking classes and *The Late Show*, a stylish contemporary arts programme, being available to potentially half a billion viewers in village India, a situation one might describe as vaguely postmodern and certainly very global. When Rupert Murdoch took over the lossmaking Star service in 1993 he removed the BBC from the northern beam that broadcasts to China in order not to displease the Chinese who were less than happy about the BBC's coverage of human rights issues. Eventually he reclaimed the southern beam in April 1996, denying the BBC a large-scale outlet in Asia.

MSNBC, the result of a partnership between Microsoft and NBC, uniting the world of 'Mr Gates' and Bill Gates, was launched on 15 July 1996, creating what will turn out to be either the wondrous hybrid new media of the future or a brave experiment doomed to failure.

A host of competitors are now chasing Turner, once the upstart but now the challenged *status quo*. No longer is CNN the only 24-hour news service and, while still pre-eminent as a global channel potentially used for telediplomacy, it is now just one of many services. We shall now examine a case when CNN and its traditional rivals covered an historic event with significant implications.

5

International television coverage of the bombing of the Baghdad 'bunker'

On the morning of 13 February 1991, day 28 of the Gulf War, three journalists thrown together by circumstances, who did not even know each other's names, came away from a smoking, smouldering building in a Baghdad suburb where clearly large numbers of people had died. One, a German photographer, turned to the other two and remarked 'we've just seen history'. The event they had been to cover was a central one in the air campaign waged against the Iraqi capital and a pivotal one in the media coverage of the Gulf War. This chapter examines the way in which 12 different television news services in five countries reported the bombing of the al-Amariya installation as the news broke through the following day. Although journalists, Peter Arnett among them, had been in Hanoi during the Vietnam War, for the first time in history journalists were reporting live from an enemy capital under fire and, equally uniquely, their reports and much of the raw material from which they were made has been recorded for analysis. What does this unique archive tell us about events which are already contemporary history?

The powerful images from the Middle East that filled television screens around the world from January to March of 1991 live in collective memory. It is incumbent upon those who study the electronic media to make the all too obvious assertion that these memorable images were not the war itself, but television's coverage of the war. That is not to dismiss the media record, which became not just contemporary comment on events but in some way a part of those events. This was a war where weapons produced images; where 'smart bomb' footage was played back on global television to reassure the domestic audience and intimidate the enemy. In a world where weapons produce videotape recordings, such recordings perforce become *part* of history. Media scholars now have the opportunity to examine not only the media product but also the process whereby it comes into being. Journalists who have reported on historic events can be interviewed about those events and their versions of them.

BBC television reporter Jeremy Bowen, his BBC radio colleague Alan Little, ITN cameramen Phil Bye and Jim Dutton and ITN producer Angela Frier were all involved in reporting the event from Baghdad and all were interviewed for this research. ITN's Baghdad reporter Brent Sadler, now with CNN, answered questions on the telephone from his foreign posting. Senior executives in both the BBC and ITN and the editors of individual bulletins were also interviewed. Peter Arnett (1994) went into purdah and granted no interviews until his own book was out. A brief interview with him was obtained for this chapter after the British publication of his book. Other journalists who reported from Baghdad have written books about their experience. CNN producer Robert Wiener (1992) recounts his experience behind the scenes of CNN's operation and offers a different perspective from Arnett's. The BBC's John Simpson (1991) was not in Baghdad at the time of the bombing of al-Amariya. His book provides useful background, however, given Simpson's time in the Iraqi capital before and during the first days of the war. Alfonso Rojo, of the Spanish newspaper *El Mundo*, remained in Baghdad throughout the war, including the period when CNN's Arnett was supposedly the only Western journalist present. His despatches which were printed in *The Guardian* are arguably the best journalism of the war. Rojo's book (1991) is both insightful and humorous and, unlike many memoirs, tells us much about other journalists. These accounts, the interviews and the extensive videotape record constitute a substantial body of information upon which to base a study of a crucial incident of location-based television reporting.

The bombing

At around 4:45 Baghdad time on that morning of 13 February 1991 two GBU-27 2000 pound electro-optical 'smart bombs' dropped by two separate F-117 Stealth fighters from Tactical Fighter Group smashed through the 10–15 foot thick steel reinforced roof of a large concrete building in the middle-class suburb of al-Amariya. The building, identified by the Allied military as the Al Firdos *bunker,* was being used as a bomb *shelter* by a large number of women and children (Atkinson, 1994, pp. 275 and 285). By about 11 am local time (8:00 GMT), up to seven hours after the event, Western reporters and film crews were taken to the scene. The wired media world went into overdrive reporting what might have resulted in the single most important story of the air war.

The bombing of the installation and how it was reported on the television screens of the world offers a paradigm of whole media war. It involves the unprecedented issue of large numbers of reporters working from an enemy capital under fire, filing reports that the said enemy might attempt to use for propaganda purposes to reach over the heads of governments and their persuasion machines and speak directly to Western public opinion. The reporting of the story involves censorship and indeed, as we shall see, self-censorship. The bombing showed what 'smart bombs', the precision ordinance that seemed to wage war with uncanny accuracy, actually did when they hit their targets. It also involved the issue of how such material was released by the Allied military. There were no security or intelligence reasons for not adding to the stock of 'precision ordinance' footage already shown, yet the pictures were not released in spite of a press conference request to see them. But whereas the Allied military were careful not to allow the release of any footage that showed evidence of 'collateral damage' or worse, the Iraqis, hardly surprisingly, were not.

Scholars monitoring the satellite traffic out of the Middle East that morning were among the first to see some powerful pictures transmitted from Jordan. They were a shot fired in the Iraqi propaganda counter-offensive, their answer to the 'smart bombs' of the Allies. These Iraqi VNRs (video news releases) had been sent overland from Baghdad to Amman as part of the Iraqi government's attempt to influence world opinion. They showed civilian bomb damage, including wounded children crying, but they were not to be needed on this occasion as reports straight from Baghdad, filed by Western television reporters, eclipsed them.

The breaking story: 'the makings of a major tragedy'

The first report of the bombing to reach the television screens of the world was from CNN's Peter Arnett who reported voice-only (the screen showed a frequently used still photo of him seated by the dish of his satellite phone in the garden of the Al-Rashid Hotel) at 10:01 GMT, speaking about 'the makings of a major tragedy' and referring to the building as a 'civilian bomb shelter'. The by then standard CNN graphic which read 'cleared by Iraqi censors' was on the screen throughout the report. Arnett described being taken inside the 'shelter' and spoke of seeing bodies 'charred almost beyond recognition' both at the scene and at nearby Yarmuk Hospital. He ended his report saying 'this is the worst of the civilian incidents we have seen in Baghdad so far'. The CNN anchor then asked Arnett if the incident was collateral damage related to any military target in the vicinity. Arnett replied that he thought not and described the area and the shelter, concluding, 'from what we could see there was no immediate military target within miles of this place'. The live two-way conversation continued with Arnett describing the previous night's heavy bombardment. He said that a building he was not allowed to mention had been hit, but then suddenly, in mid-sentence, he said he could 'say it now', and told the audience that the Conference Centre near his hotel had been hit. Arnett had clearly been given the go-ahead by his listening minder to give details of the strikes. He then described how journalists had been told of the al-Amariya incident earlier that morning and had gone to the scene where they found firemen and both the Iraqi Minister of Information and the Baghdad Chief of Police. It is worth stressing the long delay of up to seven hours before journalists were taken to the scene. This has been used by the military to suggest that the Iraqis used this time to demilitarise the bunker for presentation to the Western media. This scenario seems unlikely since when they did arrive reporters found a smouldering ruin which was only just being entered by rescuers. Arnett reported Iraqi assertions that the building was a shelter and that there were no military targets in the area. He finished by relating the experiences of an eyewitness who had spoken to him at the Yarmuk Hospital.

Arnett told me of his feelings before going on-air with such an important story. He said 'my eyeballs were popping out' and he had to 'struggle to contain' himself because of the danger of 'emoting on air'. This was as much because of the excitement of getting the story first as from his response to the horrors he had seen. He said he was aware that live television reporting could be dramatic but that it had its pitfalls, the worst of which was: 'learning to speak before you think'. Arnett pointed out that the long hours of CNN transmission enable his network to provide both the first impressions of the instant live report and more reflective background analysis in the hours and days following a breaking story (interview with Arnett, March 1994). In his book Arnett (1994, p. 410 ff.) relates how Atlanta told him 'just cool down' as he filed this first report.

This first report of the event on CNN contained neither location pictures from the scene nor visuals of any kind from Baghdad. Arnett was reporting using the satellite telephone he had used for most of his sojourn in the Iraqi capital. However, he was no longer alone and now had competitors from the traditional news services in Europe and North America. His organisation alone of those in Baghdad transmitted news 24 hours a day and could put his reports on the air virtually instantly without needing to interrupt regular programming. This technical possibility meant that CNN journalists such as Arnett could report live to a global audience, scooping the opposition regularly. Such accessibility to the airwaves coupled with the competitive drive of all journalists can have a considerable effect. The ability to report instantly means that most often such a facility will be used. In such a situation there is little time for reflection or corroboration and what gets said can become a factor in the unfolding events themselves. Arnett's report of the event was the first of a wave of reports from Baghdad that day which would themselves become part of the war of words.

'I believe you do have pictures'

Sky News reported the story first on British screens (10:24 GMT) using neither pictures nor location voice report, with the studio presenter simply quoting and crediting CNN, and using the word 'shelter' to describe the target. By 10:30 GMT CNN, however, were using pictures from ITN which at first were simply put on-screen while the studio newscaster was reading an item about a separate bombing incident in eastern Iraq. Arnett was then introduced and spoke live from Baghdad, still voice-only. He began by saying 'I believe you do have pictures' which indeed were rerun as he spoke. They were credited to ITN and consisted of three shots on the roof of the building showing firemen with hoses directing water into a large hole. There then followed shots of rescue workers inside the building. Arnett again spoke of the possibility of 'a major tragedy'. He explained that a dozen crews had been taken there that morning and stressed it was a shelter and made it clear that bodies were being removed.

Some of this material was used by ITN at 10:54 GMT when the first pictures of the event were shown on British TV. The item was introduced in the studio as follows: 'Iraq says Allied bombers have destroyed an air-raid shelter in the centre of Baghdad'. There then followed the same ITN pictures used by CNN earlier, with Arnett's same voice-over. BBC1 reported the story in their 11:00 GMT scheduled bulletin, maintaining their policy, that seemed to have developed after the first days of the war, of waiting until such regular fixed-point bulletins to report breaking stories rather than interrupting regular programmes. In this bulletin BBC Radio's Alan Little reported voice-only, describing the chaos of the rescue operation and stating that 'everyone inside died'. The phrase 'air-raid shelter' was used both in the report and in the studio introduction, which also contained the standard BBC disclaimer that reports from Baghdad were compiled under 'Iraqi restrictions'.

Peter Arnett reported, now live to camera, apparently from the garden of the Al-Rashid Hotel, in the 11:00 GMT CNN bulletin. During his piece to camera and subsequent interview with the CNN anchor, pictures from al-Amariya were shown, often with very little correlation between them and what Arnett was saying, suggesting that he may not have been able to see them. He described how journalists were taken to the scene three hours earlier. There were new shots from ground level, showing the smoking building and uniformed men outside it, including in the foreground one shot of a helmeted soldier with a rifle. A third shot showed firefighters in breathing apparatus entering the building. There was also a shot of a sign in English and Arabic clearly reading 'shelter'. Other new visual material consisted of various wide shots of the building and immediate area and different angles showing firemen hosing the bomb entry holes on the roof. Earlier pictures of this same scene were repeated. The voice-over summarised developments as they were known to date. Viewers then saw their first view of Yarmuk Hospital – three wide shots of blanket-covered bodies lying outside on the ground. At this point Arnett's live voice-over was closely related to the pictures on-screen. He explained that the Iraqi Health Minister had been present at the hospital and had given a small press conference for the 20 correspondents covering the story. Also present, but rather less forthcoming, was the Iraqi Minister of Information. Clearly the Iraqis regarded this as a major media event not to be left just to the usual minders. More new shots from both outside and inside the building were shown as Arnett talked. In response to questioning from Atlanta, Arnett described the covered bodies at the hospital as one of 'the most grisly scenes I have ever seen'. As he spoke, the not terribly detailed pictures outside the hospital were replayed. In response to another question Arnett explained that journalists had been told 'we could speak as we will'. He went on to outline the conditions under which he had been working since the first night of the war and stated categorically that this was the first time that there were no restrictions whatsoever placed on his reporting. Nevertheless, after his piece ended the CNN anchor said Arnett's transmissions were 'under Iraqi government control'.

Picture clusters

A similar disclaimer, worded as 'Iraqi restrictions', was still in use when BBC TV showed the first material from their Baghdad reporter Jeremy Bowen at noon London time. The studio introduction used the word 'shelter' three times to describe the building. Bowen's report was the first complete ENG package out of Baghdad reporting the incident. Unlike Arnett's live commentary to ITN pictures, this was a proper, fully edited, location report. It was short, only 62 seconds long, containing five shots, one of which was a piece to camera by Bowen. Although marginally different from visual material seen earlier from the scene, the shots in the BBC piece were basically of the same events taken from different angles. These shots included the view from the roof of the building and firemen hosing the bomb entry holes.

This is a clear example of what I have chosen to call a picture cluster, where the same event or object is seen from only a marginally different point of view as several crews film alongside each other, capturing the same details with only minor variations in framing and camera moves. Firemen pointing hoses into the bomb entry holes on the roof of the building, for example, were shot from several different positions. This material appeared in nearly every report from the scene with the same informational result. This picture cluster was the first of many to emerge from the events of al-Amariya. Other general views from the scene included shots of the immediate area from the roof, showing both the neighbourhood and the rescue operations. These were the shots used in the BBC piece, with Bowen's piece to camera being shot on the roof near the bomb entry holes.

Changes in videotape editing equipment have made it almost the norm to take edit suites abroad and to assemble complete stories *in situ* for transmission by satellite. At one time reporters would have sent 'rushes' and 'track', unedited visual material and voice-over, back for editing at base.

Instances of this traditional way of working were observed during the Gulf War. At the time of the bombing the BBC had editing equipment in Baghdad, but the Iraqis had only given them enough visas for television reporter Jeremy Bowen, his radio colleague Alan Little and freelance cameraman Rory Peck. Peck and Bowen performed basic editing, cutting out unneeded material, but the bulk of their footage was sent unedited with a voice track, and the story was assembled in London (interview with Jeremy Bowen, July 1992).

This pattern of returning to base to assemble material, record voice tracks and/or report live by satellite phone or visual link is best illustrated by Peter Arnett's movements on the day. The CNN man appears fleetingly in one of the BBC's shots of the bomb entry holes on the roof of the building, most probably shot some time after 8 am GMT when Western journalists first arrived at the scene. Seemingly these were among the first pictures filmed by all crews present as they formed the basis for the first reports from the scene. It should be remembered that Arnett's first report roughly two hours later at 10:01 GMT was voice-only and seemed to be from the Al-Rashid Hotel. As pictures emerged by 10:30 GMT they were from this cluster, shot on the roof. These were followed by the first shots of the interior of the building and then by general views on the ground. The commonsense viewer might be tempted to speculate that crews were taken to the scene, they filmed from and on the roof, were then allowed into the shelter briefly, before being taken to Yarmuk Hospital (Arnett in his live piece, CNN, 11:07 GMT, mentions filming at the Yarmuk Hospital 'an hour later' than the filming inside the building, i.e. roughly 9:00–9:30). Reporters such as Arnett would then have returned to the hotel to file their stories by satellite link, with the camera crews returning to al-Amariya to film the unfolding civil defence operation. However, order of transmission clearly does not necessarily equate to order of acquisition. A crew and reporter arriving at the scene of what was clearly a major event would unfailingly go right to the heart of the matter. This would have been the interior of the shelter. Only afterwards would general shots of the areas be obtained; wide shots used to establish the story for viewers. These shots would perform a certain narrative function and, to do this job of setting up the reporting of the event, they would almost certainly be used at the beginning of edited pieces.

Rushes

A set of unedited rushes of the event sent from Baghdad indicate something of the order in which journalists encountered the events. This material, sent by the French channel Antennae 2, was recorded in the following order:

1 Exterior building, bodies in truck.

2 Interior building, looking up stairs.
3 Interior building, reporter piece to camera on stairs.
4 Interior building, debris.
5 Interior building, badly burnt body.
6 Exterior building, interview with Iraqi in orange hard hat.
7 Exterior general views.
8 Exterior from roof.
9 Exterior bomb holes on roof.
10 Exterior bomb holes on roof (piece to camera).
11 General views on ground.
12 Shelter sign (in Arabic and English).
13 Interview with woman wearing traditional clothes (in English).
14 Exterior Yarmuk Hospital, bodies in yard.

Packaging

Although now emerging from Baghdad, pictures of the event were not to be used in Sky News' noon GMT bulletin. This report began with a studio introduction which spoke of two *missiles*, mentioned 400 dead and referred to the building as a 'shelter'. There then followed a voiced-over report which used earlier pictures of civilian damage which were not from the al-Amariya area, other Baghdad general views (women in traditional robes walking down the street) and which speculated that bridges might have been the real target. The piece included a previously filmed statement of British Defence Secretary Tom King on the question of civilian damage. Sky News finished the piece using a section from the Iraqi VNR transmitted that morning from Amman. This use of Iraqi-originated material was clearly acknowledged. This piece was packaged from already existing footage, none of it fresh from the scene, none of it original. Whether viewers seeing only this version were short changed is an open question. Certainly the impact was nowhere near as great as that provided by picture clusters soon to emerge.

At 12:30 Sky News transmitted, as per normal, the *Today* programme from the American network NBC, who used the BBC's Alan Little's voice-over with new pictures of grieving Iraqis outside the shelter. This picture cluster formed the bulk of the NBC item which also included earlier seen pictures from the scene of the bombing and from Yarmuk Hospital. Little's voice-over was not delivered, but was clearly part of a two-way telephone conversation, with the US-based questioner being edited out. The grieving relatives had not been filmed before, nor had they been mentioned in earlier reports. Little made it clear the grief did not appear to have been stage-managed: 'what was particularly striking about it were the men outside . . . one man was quite inconsolable with grief'.

The NBC studio framing of the piece made it clear that reporters had been taken to the scene and said the material from Baghdad had been 'cleared by

Iraqi censors'. It is interesting to note the difference between that wording and CNN's 'under Iraqi government control' and the BBC's 'Iraqi restrictions'. 'Clearing' material for transmission has almost a positive connotation and the word was often used during the war in conjunction with Allied information policy. 'Cleared by military authorities' has a different ring to it from phrases using the words 'control', 'censorship' or 'restrictions'.

Lunchtime bulletins in Britain

As time passed the reporting of the story changed, with events being progressively revealed and with newsrooms having time to prepare more substantial pieces. A second wave of reporting could be seen in the scheduled lunchtime news bulletins in Britain. The ITN 12:30 GMT bulletin was the first major news broadcast to deal with the story. The programme headlines referred to a 'shelter' and showed pictures from the scene and from Yarmuk Hospital. John Suchet's studio introduction spoke of 'two missiles' hitting the building. There followed a short series of pictures voiced by Suchet. Some were new, but they clearly seemed to be variants on previously seen material, i.e. they were from the same picture clusters already transmitted. In his introduction to a film report by Robert Hall, Suchet used the alliterative phrase 'Baghdad bunker', the first time that television reports had referred to the building as anything other than a shelter. This same introduction also questioned the accuracy of 'smart bombs'. Hall's piece on civilian bomb damage set the background for the breaking story from Baghdad, using previously released pictures. ITN then repeated Peter Arnett's first voice-only transmission, including the phrase 'makings of a major tragedy'. They developed the story further with a short filmed interview with the frequently seen expert Colonel Mike Dewar speaking of the risk of 'the propaganda war turning against us'. This led quickly into a live interview from a Saudi rooftop with British military spokesman Niall Irving. Group Captain Irving's was the first Allied public response and he said if reports were true it was 'not an intended target'. He made it clear that the British were not involved as Baghdad was not being bombed by the RAF. He also stated that precision munitions were being used in all Baghdad attacks. When pressed, Irving said either reports were propaganda or 'a terrible tragedy' had taken place. He was then told by John Suchet that pictures coming in to ITN clearly indicated that women and children had been killed. Irving hesitated and then said, 'in that case something did go wrong'. The interview ended with him saying that if reports were true, there was 'every likelihood there was a mistake'. It was to be a long while before such candour on the subject was to be spoken on the record by military spokesmen.

At 12:47, interrupting another live interview, ITN ran a filmed report from their Baghdad correspondent Brent Sadler which they said was subject to Iraqi censorship. Clearly the item had only just arrived. The piece began with new pictures of grieving Iraqis outside the shelter. Sadler's voice-over spoke of a 'grotesque procession of incinerated people' and said the building was 'undeniably used by civilians'. He described 'harrowing scenes of human agony', spoke of 'victims' and stated that 'no one has survived'. There were two shots of badly burnt bodies; one a close up of bodies in the back of an open truck, the other a wide shot outside Yarmuk Hospital. They were more horrific than any seen previously. The pictures included general views around the building seen earlier plus the new shots of grieving hysterical relatives. Sadler did a piece to camera inside the building, standing on an open staircase, dressed in a blue blazer, white shirt and tie. He referred to rescue operations taking place behind him, i.e. up the stairs. As he spoke a bearded Iraqi, standing next to him, stared at him unbelievingly. This piece to camera and the two new picture clusters of grieving relatives and bodies being carried out in blankets added another dimension to the story. Viewers could not see all the grim details, but Sadler's voice-over description of one body being carried from the smouldering interior, 'I think it was a woman', was perhaps more powerful. The story now had pictures of victims and it had their grieving relatives. It had become a story about people, not a building.

Interviews with the ITN Baghdad team reveal a complex pattern of newsgathering that day. ITN reporter Brent Sadler and cameraman Phil Bye had obtained an exclusive facility with the Mayor of Baghdad and had left the hotel early that morning without their competitors knowing. When the rumours of a serious civilian incident began to circulate in the hotel a mini convoy of vehicles made its way to the scene. WTN cameraman Mohammed Ali al Asad was working under ITN direction. He attended the scene along with other journalists then returned with his pictures, which were those first seen on CNN at 10:30 GMT. Realising a major story had broken, ITN producer Angela Frier awoke cameraman Jim Dutton who had been up all night filming the bombing. He went to al-Amariya, filmed additional material and returned to the hotel where Frier began to edit the story. Meanwhile the ITN team with the Mayor had arrived at the scene, gaining additional access because of the Mayor's authority. Sadler returned to the Al-Rashid Hotel just in time to voice-over the 12:47 package and provide the piece to camera. After transmission Frier and cameraman Jim Dutton returned to the scene to film more material and take stills. After hearing from London that the Americans were claiming the building was a command and control centre, Frier returned for a second time alone to inspect for such a possibility. ITN also filmed there the next day, as did the BBC.

The BBC's 13:00 bulletin referred to the said building as a 'shelter', still mentioned Iraqi government restrictions and warned viewers of 'scenes which you may find distressing'. Viewers heard and saw the first ordinary Iraqi to speak from the scene. This silver-haired middle-aged man spoke in clear but emotional English:

I don't know . . . why do they hit children and old ladies? Is that fair? I lose my wife and my children. Is that fair? Nobody say something to stop this massacre. They should not . . . I can't say anything more [he breaks down and cries].

The filmed report from Baghdad ended with the first appearance of a man who was to become a familiar and articulate figure on the screens around the world before the long day was out. Dr Paul Boghossian, Head of Surgery at Yarmuk Hospital, was not new to television, having appeared on ITN some 12 days earlier (Taylor, 1992, p. 179). He spoke in clear English: 'This is the most vicious and cruel attack that I have ever witnessed'. Neither of these two grey-haired men fit the visual stereotype of an Iraqi male: neither was dark, neither had a moustache. Dr Boghossian was in fact not even Iraqi, but an Armenian, though this was not mentioned at this time. After the item finished, anchor Michael Buerk in the studio stated 'Many of the pictures coming from Baghdad of burnt civilian bodies are considered too dreadful to show you'. There followed a recorded, voice-only, interview with Jeremy Bowen in Baghdad. Buerk asked 'if it was a shelter'. Bowen replied that he was as 'certain as I can be it was a shelter'.

CNN's 13:00 GMT bulletin had the first American response, quoting an unnamed Pentagon official who said there was no way to say if the building was a shelter or if the casualties were civilian or military. He added that it was not in the American tradition to hit civilian targets. Peter Arnett's latest report from Baghdad followed, which consisted of a live link followed by an edited location report including statements by the Baghdad Chief of Police and the Iraqi Minister of Health. In the same bulletin Arnett referred twice to the 'multinational' bombing of Baghdad. Dr Boghossian made his second appearance, this time saying that the main problem was identifying the badly burnt bodies, including a one-month-old baby.

Live press conference: the military response

The Allied military clearly had a media management problem. Instead of being able to release information as they saw fit, when they were sure of what they knew and of what they were going to make public, they were faced with a situation where journalists in Baghdad were doing their bomb damage assessment for them and indeed telling them things they didn't know themselves, including the fact that they had quite possibly made a terrible mistake. Brigadier General Richard Neal would have gone into the daily afternoon briefing (15:00 GMT), carried live by Sky News and CNN, aware that he would encounter some tough questioning. Well rehearsed as usual, he carried out the standard update, pointedly referring to oil well fires started by the Iraqis. At 15:20 GMT he began to speak of 'the bunker strike'. At 15:22, during Neal's response, CNN split the screen, showing pictures of the press conference and exterior shots from al-Amariya at the same time. Viewers saw the aftermath of the event and heard the explanation. The screen contained at once the civilian damage in Baghdad and the military justification from Saudi Arabia. They were in effect invited to make up their own minds, to compare the explanation with the result. Neal used the word 'regret' twice, but still countered questioning aggressively. Interestingly, his language appeared to become more natural, containing less military jargon and fewer acronyms than had been the case in his regular briefings earlier in the war. He 'umm'ed' considerably. At 15:30, in defence of the Allied bombing campaign to date, he said 'you've seen the film and photography of the past three to four weeks'. This evocation of precision munitions was to prompt the obvious question from a reporter. Would the military 'make video of the strike available?' Neal replied 'I can check on that' and asked an off-screen assistant to make a note of the request. Importantly, he did not deny the existence of the 'smart bomb' footage of the al-Amariya attack.

A few minutes later, on CNN (15:50 GMT), their military analyst James Blackwell discussed the possibility of the video being made available. This was quickly followed by a live interview with Gene Randall at the Pentagon. When the CNN anchor asked him about the release of the footage Randall was eloquent with his body language, shaking his head negatively before saying 'that remains to be seen'. Clearly there were two levels of communication going on here, one the truth of the matter (for the professionals?), the second the official, slightly more diplomatic, line (for the viewer?).

At 15:55 GMT CNN had Peter Arnett reporting again, with new footage including an interview from a hospital bed with a badly burnt 17-year-old boy who was said to be a survivor. His comments were translated by Dr Boghossian. Arnett was adamant that there were 'no restrictions' on his reports. There was clearly tension between him and Reid Collins, the CNN anchor. At one point Arnett simply did not answer a question about the 'bunker'. This tension was to continue for some time and up to a week later Collins appeared to be distancing himself at CNN from the views of their Baghdad reporter. At times there seemed to be a fear that their exclusive, on-the-spot reporter might go native. At one point CNN anchor Reid Collins closed a two-way conversation with Arnett in Baghdad with the remark that '*Mr* Arnett's transmissions are subject to Iraqi government *control*' (CNN, 15:05, 20 February 1991). Arnett later wrote of his feeling 'that even my own news organization was doubtful about my ability to assess the facts' (1994, p. 390).

All the journalists interviewed for this study stated that no Iraqi censorship of any kind took place that day. Both Arnett and the BBC's Jeremy Bowen told me that in their view the key to the genuineness of the story was the Iraqi reaction. Not only was censorship lifted totally, but the reaction of the Ministry of Information minders was totally different from that shown in any previous incident of civilian bomb damage. Whereas previously the minders would denounce the 'perfidious Bush' in overblown rhetoric while remaining calm, in this case all Iraqi officials were themselves visibly disturbed.

The allied military response was escalating. The British military's evening briefing was carried live as usual by both CNN and Sky News. Niall Irving said 'I'm totally convinced from pictures I've seen so far that this bunker looked like a military structure'. He didn't explain whether these pictures were of military or journalistic origin, nor was he asked about their source. They were not shown. Irving was clearly better prepared to take the official line than he had been hours earlier when interviewed by ITN.

British early evening news bulletins

Television reports were now to reflect the official response. What had earlier been unhesitatingly referred to as a 'shelter' by both the BBC and ITN now came to be described in a variety of ways. *Newsround,* a 17:00 BBC1 bulletin aimed at children, spoke of 'a building in Baghdad' in its headlines and told of civilians 'sheltering in an air-raid bunker'. This carefully balanced use of terms was repeated during the voiced-over location report, with both the word 'shelter' and the Allied claim that it was a bunker being mentioned. The pictures used in this report were views from the roof of the building showing fire engines and the much used shots of firemen hosing the bomb entry holes on the roof of the building. This report was followed by an item which used (and acknowledged) Iraqi television pictures of civilian bomb damage.

Newsround's precise use of language was to be continued throughout all the bulletins that evening as the vast majority of viewers were to see their first reports of the incident. ITN's News at 17:30 referred to 'a reinforced building in Baghdad' in Fiona Armstrong's studio introduction and reported both the Iraqi claim that it was a shelter and the American insistence that it was a bunker. She introduced the location material saying, 'Brent Sadler's reports are subject to Iraqi censorship'. Sadler's report from Baghdad began using the term 'shelter', then employed the word 'bunker', but after this even-handed opening both his voice-over and his piece to camera inside the building used the words 'shelter' or 'sheltering' a further four times. His language can only be described as strong. Sadler used words and phrases such as 'horror', 'a giant smoked-filled furnace incinerating its victims', 'a grotesque procession of human remains', 'harrowing', 'disturbing scenes of trauma', 'carnage', 'remains which may never be identified'. His piece to camera was different from that transmitted at 12:47, though it was clearly shot in the same place, at nearly the same time, with the same bearded Iraqi staring at him in disbelief. The report contained one very unspecific wide shot of blanket-covered bodies outside the Yarmuk Hospital. This carried a CNN graphic and replaced two much more detailed shots of burnt bodies that had been used in the ITN lunchtime bulletin. Clearly a decision had been taken to remove material from the earlier transmitted version. There were four shots of grieving Iraqis interspersed through the piece. One such shot was voiced over with the words 'distraught hysterical people'.

The BBC *Six O'Clock News* was careful in the language of its studio introduction. Anchor Peter Sissons referred to 'a hardened concrete structure which the Iraqis say was a civilian air-raid shelter and the Americans insist was a military command bunker and a legitimate target'. Sissons introduced Jeremy Bowen's Baghdad report with three qualifications: he was taken to the scene, the report 'was compiled under Iraqi government restrictions' and viewers were warned 'you may find some scenes in it distressing'.

Bowen's language was more measured than that of his ITN counterpart, but the piece seemed nevertheless to have a stronger emotional tone, imparted perhaps by the comments of Iraqis at the scene, perhaps by the tone of Bowen's delivery. The strongest word Bowen used himself was 'dreadful', an understatement in the circumstances, and which was used not to describe the bombing itself but the scenes of grief outside. This grief was prominent in the piece. The silver-haired man appeared as before with his tearful plea to end the 'massacre'. Bowen reported Iraqis at the scene as saying 'the British and Americans were savages, animals and criminals'. There was a brief and unspecific wide shot of the blanket-covered bodies outside Yarmuk Hospital which was from the same picture cluster as ITN's. Neither of these shots showed the horrific detail that was there. There were shots of burnt survivors (children) which were credited to NHK by means of a lower third graphic. The piece included an extended statement by Dr Boghossian, Head of Surgery at Yarmuk Hospital where the survivors and bodies had been taken. The doctor's statement was one of *six different* remarks of his that were to be used in various packages sent from Baghdad that day. He said, 'This is the most vicious and cruel attack that I have ever witnessed and I can only hope that those that are responsible for this can be forgiven by God'. This statement with its religious evocation was a fuller version of that used by the BBC at 13:00.

Over a year later Bowen was to reflect on the tone of the story:

> I thought well you've got to just play it very straight. I wouldn't anyway use language like 'carnage' and 'inferno' and 'the horror erupted', because I think that's clichéd . . . with TV reporting and there's a big story with powerful pictures, you don't need to hype up the script, pictures say what's happening, and as long as I feel that it's necessary to give some pointers. At one point I say something like, 'these are genuine emotions', this wasn't rehearsed or whatever, which I felt was the right thing to say, because the pictures were showing them screaming (interview with author, July 1992).

After the edited location report from Baghdad and the reporting of the responses to the event, Jeremy Bowen was interviewed from London, as he had been at 13:00 and would be later both in the *Nine O'Clock News* and on *Newsnight*. Two-ways were used frequently during the war and there were times when location reporters working under varying degrees of restriction and censorship were questioned quite aggressively by studio anchors. Here Bowen was asked questions which he had in effect answered in his piece. It is difficult to say whether the authority of reporters in such circumstances is increased or diminished. Bowen himself claims he saw no objection to this practice and did not in the least feel threatened or that the value of his filmed report was being called into question. John Pilger (1992, p. 113), however, wrote of 'the interrogation by satellite that the BBC's man in Baghdad, Jeremy Bowen, had to endure following his harrowing and personally courageous report'.

ITN's *Channel 4 News* at 19:00 GMT used the word 'bunker' in its headlines, and spoke of the 'horror of war' and 'gruesome images of death' in its studio introduction, with Jon Snow using both of the opposing descriptions of the building: 'air-raid shelter' and 'bunker' (twice). Viewers were told: 'Western reporters have seen dozens of charred bodies brought out of the bunker'. There was no statement about whether such scenes had been filmed. The by now standard 'health warning' that reports from Baghdad 'were subject to Iraqi censorship' was extended to include two further comments: 'Correspondents in Iraq are restricted to areas approved by the Iraqi authorities' and 'the report does contain pictures of some casualties'. This remark, though clearly a warning, was much more neutral than the BBC's earlier admonition which had used the word 'distressing'. *Channel 4 News* used Brent Sadler's ITN material from Baghdad, but this version was longer than that transmitted on ITV at 17:30, with a new beginning and with the more detailed shots of badly burnt bodies that had been used at lunchtime restored.

At 20:07 GMT CNN broadcast what was the last new material of the day from Baghdad. Peter Arnett began with a live link then ran a taped report which included an interview with the Baghdad Chief of Police and the shelter manager. A badly burnt 17 year old boy survivor was translated by Dr Boghossian, who also appeared, saying the main problem was identifying the bodies. The doctor told the cameras that there was the body of a baby only one month old. The shelter manager said that the Allies were so upset about an oil slick and asked if Bush really cared more about dead birds than humans.

British evening bulletins

The BBC *Nine O'Clock News* had slight variations from the version transmitted at 18:00. There was only a two-part warning in the studio introduction, mentioning 'Iraqi government restrictions' and the fact that some of the scenes might be found distressing. Viewers were no longer told that

Bowen had been taken to the scene. (Bowen had himself stated this in his earlier piece and would do so in this one.) This version contained some different shots of the exterior of the building and the crowds outside, including a close up of a child looking through a wire fence. There was a new statement from an Iraqi official in an orange hard hat who said simply 'Totally civilian area'. The grieving grey-haired man appeared as before, as did the articulate Dr Boghossian. The doctor's was a new statement, however, equally as strong as his earlier remark. Instead of evoking the Almighty, he went right to the core of the matter: 'Was it necessary? . . . all this, was it necessary to shoot a shelter? Would it help to liberate Kuwait as they say that what we are doing this to liberate Kuwait. I am not a politician, but I just can't understand. What has this to do with the liberation of Kuwait?'

This sort of change in reports between early and mid-evening bulletins is common in normal circumstances. This may be because new material is available or it may be the result of a conscious decision by a programme editor to give the viewer a different package, perhaps of a different length or with different emphasis from that transmitted in an earlier bulletin. As the doctor's two sound bites appear to have been recorded at the same time, one can surmise that the change was made on editorial grounds. The impact of the piece is, if anything, stronger for the change. Instead of hoping that those responsible would be forgiven by God, the doctor's new statement is more rational and aims itself straight at the heart of the matter – the liberation of Kuwait. He even uses the rhetoric of the White House, echoing Marlin Fitzwater's statement of 16 January: 'the liberation of Kuwait has begun'. This juxtaposition of the task the world has accepted as necessary with the horror before their eyes is remarkably powerful. The change of statement did not diminish the piece in any way; however, had the doctor been removed altogether it might have been a different matter.

Back in the studio Michael Buerk framed the piece saying, 'You should know that many of the pictures from Baghdad of the burnt bodies of the victims were considered too grim to show you'. This was only the second overt admission of self-censorship (both made by Buerk and both worded almost identically), although clearly something of the sort had been happening all day on all channels. The implication was clearly that the decision not to use the pictures in question had been taken in London. Although some Baghdad-based reporters were able to edit their material on location, modern videotape standards would allow a quick re-edit without discernible loss of quality. A WTN news agency picture package transmitted from Baghdad at 14:30 GMT would have been available to anyone who chose to use it. It contained detailed close-ups of uncovered burnt bodies both at Yarmuk Hospital and inside the shelter. At one point on that tape a voice (almost certainly the cameraman's) is heard to say, 'they won't use this'. A second faint voice says, 'shoot it anyway'. The judgement of the first voice was right.

ITN's *News at Ten* began with a long overview by Alastair Burnet in the studio, including quotations of various responses to the bombing. He stated that 'Western correspondents reported seeing more than 200 bodies, including women and children'. This figure was a clear increase from the dozen mentioned similarly in *Channel 4 News* at 19:00. Correspondents had seen these bodies, but would viewers? The report from Baghdad was then introduced by newsreader Julia Somerville. The word 'shelter' was used twice in this introduction, while the term 'bunker' was not. There was a two-part warning: 'Our correspondent Brent Sadler's reports are subject to Iraqi censorship though the Iraqis didn't cut or alter anything in tonight's. Some of the pictures are distressing' (note the use of the same actual word as the BBC).

Brent Sadler's report was different again from the versions transmitted at 12:47, 17:30 and 19:00. The phrase 'horror of what happened' was removed, and the word 'victims' replaced by 'those inside'. There was an addition to the voice-over: 'Washington claimed the shelter was an active command and control bunker'. This addition seems an unusual remark for a Baghdad-based reporter to make and one wonders how he would have come by such information. The Mayor of Baghdad appeared, speaking in English: 'I can't tell you what's my reaction. Nobody can comment on that [*sic*] pictures'. Note he says pictures, clearly understanding that television pictures of what he could see were indeed being flashed around the world. The phrase 'grotesque procession of human remains' was removed as was the word 'harrowing', but the phrases 'dismembered corpses' and 'human debris' remained. 'Remains which may never be identified' at 17:30 changed to simply 'remains' in this version. The piece to camera was the same as earlier.

Stewart Purvis, then Editor in Chief of ITN, told me:

> I did some re-editing myself on the *News at Ten* version that night. . . . I was actually proud that it managed to convey the horror without elongating the shock effect. Other countries were transmitting material that we wouldn't have conceived of showing. There were one or two things we showed earlier in the day which in retrospect, considering the transmission times, probably shouldn't have been used, but in general there is this balance between trying to convey what it's like to be there and not over egging the pudding.

After the piece had run, ITN now too acknowledged not showing all the available pictures: 'Well, as we said, the Iraqis didn't censor any part of Brent Sadler's report, but we at ITN did edit out some scenes because we regarded them as too distressing to broadcast' (note the same word again). ITN here followed the BBC in admitting to what might be called self-censorship, with the decision to edit out scenes apparently made on grounds of taste and decency. Neither channel presented any other reason for not showing the pictures and in so doing treated them as any other news event where horrific details of human death and injury were available, the crucial difference, of course, being that normally viewers would not be told of pictures, say of a train crash, that were available but not being used. Every day of every year pictures are left out of bulletins for all manner of reasons, but as a matter of course viewers are not told that or given reasons for such exclusions.

Sadler's language had clearly changed since the report transmitted at 17:30. The alterations were in his voice-over commentary and seemed to be more in terms of shifts of tone rather than representing any new informational content. Had he had second thoughts or had word come back from London to tone down some of his language? Reporters, no matter how consciously unbiased and professional, cannot help but be affected by what they see and to identify subtly and unconsciously with those around them who share perhaps the same fate as possible victims of bombardment. This might particularly be the case when working *in extremis*, and one can hardly imagine a more extreme circumstance than being under the heaviest aerial attacks in history. I call this the chameleon effect, and it applies clearly in the Gulf War, where uniformed reporters with the troops, using phrases such as 'our mission', were as much an example of it as reporters working behind enemy lines. Had Ed Murrow or Richard Dimbleby crawled out of a shelter in Dresden on that morning after, ironically exactly 46 years to the day before, what would their responses have been and how would history have seen them?

What model does a reporter have for the tone of such a piece? The natural disaster in the third world, the famine report with its concern and compassion, the matter of fact reporting of an automobile crash? What do you tell the world when you've seen the horrors of war at their worst and when the live satellite link is waiting and will brook no delay? What are the military, diplomatic and domestic political consequences of what is said, possibly live, possibly ad libbed? Can history be written in minutes? Considered that way, and from the perspective of a point later in time, the journalists working under such pressure did a remarkable job. Behind enemy lines, well out of the reach of the Allied military spin doctors, they could report one side of the things – the view from the ground. Their reports could be altered back at base, they could be put under pressure from London to make modifications, but the essential tone of what they were reporting could not be changed except by total removal. For ITN's Brent Sadler, the Baghdad experience was an echo of the American bombing of Tripoli which he had also covered. While the BBC and their reporter Kate Adie came under attack from Conservative Party Central Office, ITN and Sadler did not (Corner, 1995b, p. 68).

The possibly controversial use of a Baghdad-based reporter was simply not an issue for Sky News. They had no reporter there and had to package other people's material as they had done earlier in the day. In their 22:00 programme *Sky World News Tonight*, they began with headlines which balanced 'Baghdad's evidence' with 'Washington's evidence'. In a studio piece to camera Sky News' presenter referred to 'a building in Baghdad' and reported the American claim that it was a bunker. Their edited package used NHK pictures (acknowledged in a lower third graphic) and was voiced by London-based reporter John Cookson. Like the picture clusters seen earlier, there were scenes both inside and outside the building and at Yarmuk Hospital, but these were different in detail. A shot from the roof of the building zoomed in on a burnt body in the back of an open truck and a different wide shot of the scene outside Yarmuk Hospital both gave more detail of burnt bodies than any material transmitted earlier in Britain. There were also different shots of grieving Iraqis and another statement from the Iraqi Health Minister clearly made at the same time as the more frequently used 'It could not have been a mistake' comment used by both of the other British news services. This new remark by the Minister referred not only to the incident in question but also to the general bombing of Iraqi targets, including churches and mosques.

After this, Sky News did something no other television service had done. Making use of library pictures, they showed a Stealth bomber taking off into a sunset. This was followed by 'video game' footage (six different black-and-white shots of smart bombs hitting targets, with a voice-over clearly stating they were from earlier action), but then they did not do the obvious and cut to shots from on the ground at al-Amariya. (It was to be nearly a year before anyone did this simple edit and transmit it on television and nearly five before the actual 'smart bomb' footage was shown in a 1996 BBC series on the Gulf War.) The use of library footage is frequent in television news programmes and increasingly, but not universally, this is signalled to the viewer by the use of a lower third graphic. Doubtless we see more of this type of footage than we think and there are good professional reasons to justify its use, particularly when it is acknowledged. The opportunity existed for the telling of a brutal truth in two or three shots, two or three shots that in effect summed up the whole air war. However, this emblematic piece of videotape was not transmitted.

At 10:45 GMT, BBC2's daily news and current affairs magazine programme *Newsnight* ended British television's reporting of the story. Presenter Jeremy Paxman clearly had no compulsion to beat about the bush. In the programme's headlines he spoke of the 'end of illusions about the Gulf War', with 'women and children and old people killed by Allied warplanes in our name'. These comments were followed by two shots from Baghdad – a badly burnt boy in a hospital bed and a wide shot of the body-filled courtyard outside Yarmuk Hospital. The voice-over ended by asking: 'At what point does a justifiable war become unjust?'

The programme's substantive report began with Paxman speaking to camera. He went straight to the heart of the matter:

Until today it had seemed such an uncannily sanitised war – clever bombs that wrecked real estate, but somehow appeared to leave people unscathed. Now the first mass civilian deaths, unintended though they may have been, present the Allies with a potential public opinion and diplomatic nightmare.

He continued, discussing the situation both at the United Nations and amongst moderate Arabs. Viewers then saw pictures from Baghdad with Paxman's pre-recorded voice-over. 'This was the first time we have seen what smart bombs do to human beings', he said over the same wide shot used in the headlines. This shot, of hospital staff pulling blankets over badly burnt bodies, was on screen for 15 seconds. Three shots inside the target building followed, including one in which CNN's Peter Arnett could be seen. These shots had already been seen on the BBC. There followed four shots of grieving Iraqis at the scene which again were not new in themselves, but the order in which they were edited and Paxman's voice-over was. This grief was immediately followed by the Allied military explanation in the form of press-conference footage of Brigadier General Neal explaining that the target was a command and control centre. Paxman's voice-over continued, using the word 'shelter' rather than 'bunker'. The grieving silver-haired Iraqi made another appearance, his statement somewhat shorter this time. His plea 'nobody say [*sic*] something to stop this massacre' and his subsequent breaking down in tears were removed. Abd As-Salem Muhammad Saeed, the Iraqi Health Minister, made his previously seen statement, claiming there was no chance that the strike was a mistake. This statement was balanced by another by General Neal who said that militarily nothing had gone wrong.

  Newsnight's coverage was clearly different. There was no use of a Baghdad reporter. They had the same pictures from the same clusters as were available to earlier BBC bulletins and only one or two new ones were used, with no substantive addition to the content either in terms of informational content or emotional tone. The crucial difference was that the pictures were newly edited and the piece voiced-over with commentary written in London. The Allied military response was included in the same edited package, giving perspective not possible from Baghdad. There was no self-censorship admission as there had been in two BBC bulletins, both presented by Michael Buerk, and in ITN's *News at Ten*. As *Newsnight* effectively ended the day on British television, the story began to take shape on American screens.

The American networks

The early evening bulletins American viewers saw on network television were transmitted nearly 24 hours after the actual bombing. The simple reporting of the event was evolving with time into the reporting of the various reactions to it. Each of the three major American network news services reported the story in a fundamentally different way. These differences were determined not so much by editorial considerations as by logistics. ABC had a reporter in Baghdad, CBS did not, while NBC continued a long-standing relationship and used BBC material.

ABC's coverage began with studio anchor Peter Jennings speaking of 'what all agree is a tragic loss of civilian life'. The shelter versus bunker choice of words was not a problem for Jennings. He said: 'the US describes the target as an air-raid shelter in a civilian neighbourhood which had been converted to a command and control centre'. Bill Blakemore's filmed report from Baghdad was introduced as being 'cleared by the Iraqis' and had a lower third graphic over the first shot which read 'The Target'. ABC's pictures were related to but different in detail from those used on British television. There were grieving Iraqis, including three shots of a man seen earlier on the BBC, who was quoted here indirectly: 'the man said to us, "this is the product of your democracy"'. The shelter supervisor, a 12-year-old survivor, 'men waiting outside for news of their wives', and 'rescuers' ('One said he'd take revenge even if it takes ten generations') were all quoted similarly. Rather than rely on finding English-speaking Iraqis at the scene, this method of indirect quotation enabled a wider range of statements to be reported, but it is interesting to note that the Iraqi Health Minister who spoke in English in earlier bulletins was here only quoted indirectly over a shot of him. Jeremy Bowen's BBC reports used much more direct quotation of Iraqis, but also used such indirect quotations as 'People told us that the British and the Americans were savages, criminals and animals'.

The only person to speak directly in the piece was Dr Boghossian, who asked: 'Is this in conformity with international regulations? Just have a look won't you [pointing to bodies]. Would you call this mercy and justice? This is the most horrible, the most cruel thing I have ever witnessed'. Blakemore used the word 'shelter' throughout his voice-over and described the event as a 'tragedy'. He ended saying:

> there were no restrictions on journalists as we covered this story today. We were able to talk with anyone we wanted to in and around the shelter and the hospital. Iraqi officials called it a great crime and said otherwise the event speaks for itself.

Neither he nor the ABC anchor made any comment on the horrific pictures which were not being shown. Following the Baghdad report on 'The Target', Bob Zelnick's report from the Pentagon began with a lower third graphic 'The Explanation'. ABC were clearly chaptering their coverage, balancing the report from the event with the American military response.

CBS's *Evening News* balanced the terms 'bunker' and 'shelter' in Dan Rather's studio introduction and warned viewers 'Pictures of the Baghdad bombing include some graphic scenes of the reality of war. We caution you that some may not be suitable for children'. They did not admit to any kind of self-censorship. Though himself in Amman, Jordan, Doug Tunnell began his piece with pictures from the Baghdad scene and used the word 'bunker' at first, before twice calling it a 'shelter'. Dr Boghossian appeared, his sound bite again asking a question: 'I was shocked it was in a place like this. How would anybody think of striking a place like this?' Like ABC, the CBS piece contained reported speech of 'Iraqi officials' and 'a grief-stricken man' (the same one seen on ABC). After this opening, Tunnell appeared in a piece to camera in Amman and the report shifted considerably to begin reporting the response to the event in the Arab world. While clearly able to add a voice-over to pictures from Baghdad, CBS's Jordan-based reporter shifted the balance of his piece onto his own ground, including an interview remark by an Arab commentator who stated 'I think the United States people running this war are either liars or very stupid people. They may have smart bombs, but they don't have very smart minds'. This change of emphasis clearly had editorial validity, but may have arisen simply because of where the reporter was. Had this reporter not been present in Amman, this opinion would not have been reported quite so soon or in such detail.

NBC's coverage was clearly influenced by its long-standing relationship with the BBC. As in their morning programme, they simply used BBC material from Baghdad. Jeremy Bowen's report for NBC had some new voice-over, but basically it was a version of his earlier BBC reports, edited in a different order. The new material consisted of an up-to-date introduction beginning 'this evening' and a short piece of reported speech which was a quotation from the head of Baghdad civil defence. The grieving silver-haired man and Dr Boghossian appeared as in the BBC *Six O'Clock News*. The doctor's remark, 'I only hope that those who were responsible for this can be forgiven by God', which had been replaced in the BBC's *Nine O'Clock* bulletin, was restored.

There would seem clearly to be an American tendency to use reported speech even when the material is available and in clear English. This practice is called 'goldfishing' in the industry. It occurs when a person is seen on-screen, with their lips moving, apparently speaking, but the sound of their voice has been removed and replaced with either a paraphrase, voiced by the reporter, or by commentary. Two possible reasons for this spring to mind. First, the use of reported speech enables closer control of item length as reporters can adjust the number of words in their paraphrase as needed. This would enable the content of what a witness said to be used even in a brief piece. Obviously the impact of such a mediated statement would be significantly less than if the person were to speak themselves. This would be particularly so with an incident such as this. The powerful statement of the crying man pleading 'stop this massacre' would be reduced significantly if transposed into indirect speech as 'a grieving man who said he had lost his wife and family pleaded for an end to the massacre'. Similarly, the indirect quotation attributed to one rescuer in the ABC report, 'One said he'd take revenge, even if it takes ten generations', would have had a significantly different impact had we seen and heard the words spoken first-hand. The direct impression made by the crying man and by Dr Boghossian, the two grey-haired direct speakers, comes as a totality which would have been lost had any elements, either verbal or visual, been excised.

As the day progressed and by the time the story was nearly 24 hours old the emphasis had shifted from reporting the event to the reactions and explanation; the centre of gravity moved from Baghdad to Washington. This was reflected in Sky News at 22:00 GMT, which included comment by Neal, Kelly, Fitzwater and Cheney. Equally, all the American evening bulletins reported the American response, often clearly chaptering their reports into two sections with graphics and/or words. While the networks clearly felt it necessary to report the military response, European news services were to present yet another perspective.

French, German and Italian reports

The French channel TF1 ran the story as the first item in their main evening news bulletin. Their studio introduction is worth quoting in full (my translation):

> Good evening ladies and gentlemen. The horrors of war. That which everyone has feared has come to pass this evening. Hundreds of civilians, without doubt many families and many children, have been killed in a terrible bombardment in Baghdad. They were grouped in a shelter and thought they were safe. The images that we have received from Baghdad are for certain unbearable. We have of course decided to take out the sequences that are the most atrocious, as we have already done and will continue so during this war. What you are about to see says a lot about the sorrow and grief of those close to the victims.

The taped location report from Baghdad was shorter than the British versions (1 minute 15 seconds compared with 3 minutes 30 seconds–3 minutes 45 seconds) and contained no shots of grieving Iraqis and no direct speech. The voice-over was very straightforward and factual, providing details of the structure, what appeared to have happened and the number of people possibly involved. There was no analysis as such, only the posing of a question: 'Was it a deliberate bombardment or was it a tragic mistake? No journalist can yet judge. This evening Iraq can only send these pictures of its martyrs' (my translation). The pictures sent were not dissimilar to those seen on British and American television, with only a marginal difference in the shots of the burnt bodies outside Yarmuk Hospital. These French shots were closer, but hardly dwelt on the horrific details. The reporter, Jean Francois Boyer, appeared to camera in the report's final shot, where he speculated that the bombing was a possible prelude to the beginning of the land war.

TG1, the main evening news bulletin from the Italian service RAI Uno (broadcast at 20:00 Rome time, 19:00 GMT) ran the story first both in its headlines and in its running order. The headlines consisted of pictures from the scene with banner headlines superimposed. These words were read as voice-over. The word 'massacre' was used to describe the event. Italian viewers thus both saw and heard that word in the bulletin headlines.

As with the French, it is worth quoting the studio introduction in full (translated by a research assistant):

> This technological war with its intelligent bombs and surgical inter-ventions on strategic objectives, tonight sends us from Baghdad images of a massacre. Thousands of people, maybe a thousand, burnt and killed in the refuge, tonight struck in the centre of the city. The Americans say that the struck objective had not been a refuge for years and was an active communications centre. In there it appears there were up to a 1000 people. Now you'll see the pictures, you won't see the worst which we've cut in respect for the poor dead. Men, women and burnt children: which an American General called the collateral effects of war.

The Italian coverage was remarkably like that of the French, with a strongly worded, rhetorical studio introduction being followed by a much more neu-trally worded film report which nevertheless contained more horrific pic-tures than did the British and American reports. The RAI piece was voiced in Rome using CNN pictures, though this source was not acknowledged. This material was from some of the same picture clusters as other reports, but did include some new visual material. The only strong language in a fun-damentally factual voice-over was the use of the word 'disaster' and the phrases 'horrifically burnt and mutilated' and 'painful images, often desper-ate' (translated by my research assistant). There was reported speech quot-ing the Iraqi Health Minister and, unlike the French, shots of grieving relatives were included.

The German service recorded in the Leeds study, the Bavarian station BR3, reported the incident as part of a single, three-part, Gulf War item run-ning only after extensive coverage of domestic politics. Only 20 seconds were devoted to the bombing, with the studio-recorded voice-over being very neutral in tone, with perhaps a hint of regret just apparent. The build-ing was described as a bunker rather than as an air-raid shelter (*Luftschutzkeller*). The brief pictures (CNN origin) used showed more hor-rific details of bodies than were shown on English or American screens. The bulletin itself ended with a silent shot of a bombed church in Dresden.

Conclusions

The al-Amariya incident, when seen from the points of view of 12 different television services in five countries, can tell us much about the reporting of the war and about location-based crisis reporting in general. It reveals much about news values and styles and more importantly about underlying editorial practices in different broadcasting cultures.

Of all the services discussed, the main British services, ITN and the BBC, devoted more time to the story and, seemingly as a matter of course, produced much richer, denser audio-visual texts. The words of ITN's Brent Sadler imparted a particular quality to his pieces, while the presence of grieving Iraqis in the BBC pieces created a different emotional impact. Analysis of the American coverage of the event points out significant differences in reporting conventions which could most clearly be seen in the case of a British reporter altering his material in line with these conventions when reporting for an American network. Logistical considerations are certainly a determining factor in the nature of coverage and this is nowhere more clearly indicated than in the differences between the three American networks who reported the event direct from Baghdad, from Amman, and by the use of a reporter and material from a sister news organisation. Similarly, European coverage ranged from the location report of the French network to the voicing of pictures from another source as witnessed by the Italian and German networks and by Sky News. This packaging of material provided by an agency or another news service is common at all times, most often with smaller, less-well-resourced news organisations. It is becoming more common with all services, owing to increased financial pressures. The particular access problems of reporting from an enemy capital during a time of war may have rendered this case atypical, but nevertheless the variety of methods used to report the event, ranging from the live two-way links of CNN to the back-at-base packaging of RAI Uno, BR3 and Sky News represents the full spectrum of news practice. The 24-hour-a-day news flow of CNN offered a different product from that of the ostensibly similar Sky News. CNN's commitment to live location reporting stood in stark contrast to its British rival's packaging of other services' material.

All news organisations in this sample had the possibility of using more horrific pictures than they did. Both the BBC and ITN (seemingly following the BBC's lead) admitted to not showing such footage, as did the French and the Italian services. Nevertheless both of these channels and the German channel did show more detailed and gruesome footage than did the English-language services in Britain and America. This is clear evidence of different national standards in questions of taste and decency in the reporting of death and injury in factual programming.

The studio framing of the various pieces also indicated national differences. Both the French and Italian studio introductions were more rhetorical and clearly more strongly worded, while, surprisingly, their actual film reports, whether using location-based reporters or studio-voiced reports, were much more neutral in tone. The sense of regret that came from the Allied, but non-combatant, Germans was also present in the French and Italian coverage, but to a lesser degree. Only the German network, of all the services analysed, did not lead with the story at the top of their bulletin.

For all the subtle differences between the various reports, in the final analysis there is a greater commonality between them. All are presented in various national dialects, but basically in the same language of contemporary television news. As a record of an historical event none provides such a radically different version of events that it calls into question the testimony of any other version. Like the images from what I have called the same picture cluster, the reports discussed above are literally different angles on the same story. There are superficially as many stories as reporters, but to admit that is not to surrender to a kind of free-floating postmodernist relativism. The fundamental story told by the various reports has a deeply bedded narrative coherence which underlies all the reports. From the first voice-only reports onwards through the day each further despatch added detail, but none contradicted the first flash. Until American military records reveal the background to the attack, confirming the intelligence on which it was based, very little can be added to the historical context of that story.

From the time of the event various rumours circulated about the nature of the intelligence on which the attack was based. Some media comment suggested that the civilian deaths were the result of an overreliance on satellite and signals intelligence. Rick Atkinson (1994, p. 276) suggests that this hi-tech intelligence was less than conclusive in the minds of Allied target planners, but that there was also human intelligence from Baghdad which tipped the balance in favour of hitting the installation. This source is said to have informed American intelligence that the building had become the new home of Iraqi intelligence after their Baghdad headquarters had been destroyed. No other evidence has yet emerged to suggest that this was the case. Of course, one of the best ways of avoiding being targeted by aerial attack would be to be constantly mobile. Such a strategy could have meant that buildings might have been used for a time for military or intelligence operations which then moved to another location. Clearly an intelligence mistake led to a successful military mission which hit its target accurately without any collateral damage. The result of this mission, however, was a human tragedy, fully reported by the world's media. Whether it became a propaganda coup for the Iraqis depended not so much on how the event was reported as on how the Pentagon responded to such reports. To this day British flags are displayed in shop windows in the Iraqi town of Falujjah, the result of the admission by the Royal Air Force that they had missed their intended target (with laser-guided bombs) and regrettably killed civilians in the market place. Such candour defused a potential propaganda bombshell. Should the Pentagon have taken a similar line on al-Amariya?

The al-Amariya bombing was a significant breaking story in time of war, reported from an enemy capital under fire: a story where the issues go beyond the simple reporting of events. Propaganda and censorship and indeed self-censorship revolving around questions of taste and decency were all involved, and underlying the whole story was the issue of the role of the electronic media in democratic societies at a time of war. Unique in this case, television reported the event from the same physical point of view as the enemy being bombed. While no broadcasting organisation could be said to have played into the hands of Iraqi propaganda, the pictures that were sent from Baghdad, apparently free of Iraqi restrictions, were of an uncomfortable truth that balanced the message of the 'smart bomb' footage, of the weapons which until then had seemed to do their work clinically and without human victims. Reporters in Baghdad reported what was apparent to them: a building used as a shelter had been hit and many people were killed. They repeatedly asserted that there were no signs to indicate that the building was being used as a military bunker. Their reports seemed to contradict the Allied military assertion that the building was indeed a command and control centre. In this respect television took a part in the dynamics of the war it was covering. For this reason the developing variorum text of the television reporting of the event is crucial both as an index of comparative standards of location-based crisis reporting and as an insight into wider issues.

The event, and the way it was reported, showed that the military control of information was not total, that events will be reported from other physical points of view. Reporters in such situations, however scrupulously objective from every standard, do therefore give literally another point of view. It is then up to the contemporary viewer (MacGregor and Morrison, 1995) and eventually to history to provide the balance between the authorised version and that from ground zero.

The totally unique, and indeed historic, events that transpired in Baghdad on 13 February 1991 were reported in detail by an international press corps working in circumstances unlike any other in the history of the news media. The situation was made possible because, for their own reasons, the Iraqis chose to give them access. Without this there would have been no reporting. Once admitted, the damaged Iraqi infrastructure made it necessary for television to be technologically self-sufficient if reporters were to file their stories without sending them by taxi in the time-honoured Middle Eastern tradition. The fact that television was able to report live was crucial but it was not the whole story, for, once back at base, the uncomfortable images had to be dealt with by staff with other concerns, by managers susceptible to other very real pressures. State-of-the-art technologies made reporting the story possible, but they were only part of a wider picture.

|6|

The technology of newsgathering and production

'Captives of technology'

With the possible exception of the military there is probably no other industry that relies as much on technology as broadcasting does. Its defining technology gives it, in the first instance, an enormous advantage over the print media, but this is a double-edged sword, as greater resources are required simply to do the job at its most basic level. Journalists have always been competitive and the television sub-species are no exception. Getting the story first, a 'beat', the much prized scoop, is a function of two factors: finding the story and then getting it back to base. Whether in the competitive world of the news agencies, newspapers, radio or television, communication technologies are central to the newsgathering process. Nowhere is this more evident than in location-based crisis reporting. In the 30 years from the end of the Second World War to the fall of Saigon, the technology of television news had evolved slowly as the form itself emerged. Television naturally has its own demands, and television reporters, more so than their print and radio colleagues, are 'captives of technology' (Schlesinger, 1987, p. 270). A telephone line is not good enough to get material back to base, and just creating the story has famously been compared by Fred Friendly to writing a story with a two-ton pencil (Mayer, 1987, p. 202). Television reporting is harder to do, more time-consuming and expensive simply because of these technical factors, which need to be examined if one is to understand the form itself and why it has become the way it is.

Film cameras

Cinema newsreels were 'shot silent' by cameramen, with music, sound effects and commentary added later. Location news reporting was done on film, using cumbersome 35 mm cameras. These ranged from three-quarter-ton Biograph monsters used to film the Boer War to hand-held boxes such as the Newman Sinclair. Standard newsreel cameras were large and heavy, typically mounted on the roofs of cars. Such equipment had nevertheless captured such dramatic events as the Hindenburg crash. Although developed before the war, 16 mm film was a long time in arriving as the standard technology of television newsgathering. When television news filming began, NBC used 35 mm, while CBS used 16 mm, which was considered 'not quite professional' (Barnouw, 1970, p. 42). Eyemo (35 mm) hand-held clockwork cameras could record 1 minute 10 seconds of mute footage. One enterprising NBC stringer rigged six such cameras on a pole, controlled them with a single switch and sold his footage to the five newsreels and the network (Frank, 1991, p. 34). Bell and Howell and Auricon 16 mm cameras, originally developed for amateurs, were used in Korea (Frank, 1991, p. 38). The Auricon Cine-Voice could record sound, with the sound recordist needing to be connected to the camera by a thick cable (Cox, 1995, pp. 14, 21 and 66). German Arriflex cameras developed before the war were used for mute work. In spite of these advances, heavy blimped cameras physically linked to tape recorders were still used as late as the Vietnam era (Culbert, 1988, p. 256).

By 1958 BBC and ITN were using magnetic striped 16 mm to record synchronous sound and picture on film (Cox, 1995, p. 138), but by the 1960s documentary film-makers in the USA had developed a 16 mm synchronous sound system which didn't require a wired link between camera and sound, which was recorded separately. This way of working required a two-person crew and the use of a clapperboard to enable synchronisation in editing, but there was no longer an umbilical cord between camera and sound.

Reporters had been used in small numbers in newsreels, simply as interviewers, gathering what later came to be called *vox pops* or 'streeters', a practice which was extended into the early days of television (Cox, 1995, p. 117). Crews would return from location and newsroom sub-editors would write the voice-over commentary from agency copy. The reporter was not seen as a newsgatherer or as the author of the piece. Stand-ups, pieces to camera, were a late arrival as sound recording on location was problematic. Cox attributes their origin in Britain to current affairs programmes such as *Panorama* (pp. 129–130). The *News at Ten* pioneered the British television use of correspondents' commentaries recorded on location. As Nigel Ryan, then Editor of ITN, explains:

In 1969, we made a seemingly minor alteration to our editing procedure which brought about a sea change, particularly to foreign coverage. Under the old system, film shot on location was edited to a given length dictated by its pictorial value; a writer then prepared a script broadly based on the notes from the reporter on the spot and spoken by a studio voice selected for euphony rather than journalistic merit. The innovation involved reversing this pattern: the reporter sent back his commentary, recorded in the field, so his voice was heard over the film which was then edited to match it. . . . The effect on the screen was electric. Viewers had the taste of being on-the-spot with the action rather than attending an illustrated lecture from a voice out of nowhere; and the reporter was clearly placed in charge of his own report (Ryan, 1995, p. 13).

It is hard to imagine that this now universal practice was once considered revolutionary. Its implications are clear, however. Visual imperatives were taking second place to the reporter's script, which was balanced, however, by the extra immediacy of a commentary literally coming from the same place as the pictures.

In domestic newsgathering, crews would have to return to base to have their film processed. Putting this film through 'the bath' would have taken anything from 20 minutes to an hour and a half depending on the film stock being used. The script would generally have been written while the film was being processed. This would then have been recorded, quite often without the reporter or other scriptwriter ever having seen the pictures. This voice-over was then given to a film editor who would insert the pictures over the top of the soundtrack. Journalists, in the early days of television news, came either from radio or from newspaper backgrounds and tended as a consequence to write their reports as self-sufficient pieces with the pictures merely 'wallpaper' inserted over the top of the wordy commentary. Radio was unquestionably the dominant parent of the infant medium in spite of the arrival of certain newsreel figures such as cameraman Ronnie Noble and commentator Leslie Mitchell, who both joined the BBC, and Ray Perrin, who became ITN's chief film-editor. Practice, at NBC, as noted above, was more picture led:

> Our system was to have cameramen film news events, to edit their film into a narrative, then, as a last step, to write a script that included the description of the event and its news relevance. We did not use reporters on the scene, who would speak a script to which pictures would be matched – risking the danger of throwing away the best pictures because they had not been scripted for. So although we had some good reporters, we used them very little, far less than CBS did and perhaps less than we should have (Frank, 1991, p. 118).

Newsreel cameramen working abroad would airfreight their film back to base with 'dope sheets' describing what had been shot. These would be used to edit and script the report. When they began to go abroad, television reporters would despatch a soundtrack together with pictures for processing and editing back at base. They would write and record a script to the standard length of a one-, two-, or three-minute news item, not having seen the pictures, although they were usually present when they were filmed. This of course led to a certain unspecific manner both of filming and writing. The

unprocessed film, voicetrack and a suggested cutting order would be packaged up and sent to the airport for freighting, with a delay of perhaps two
or three days before the material was transmitted. A senior ITN correspondent tells of such an experience when working in Vietnam. During the Tet
offensive, Sandy Gall and his cameraman witnessed and filmed the deliberate burning, by the South Vietnamese themselves, of a Saigon building occupied by Vietcong guerrillas. Gall returned from the field to write his script
and asked the cameraman what he had actually shot. They were unable to
see the pictures and could not, given the tumultuous circumstances, be 100
per cent certain of what exactly had been recorded. All that location journalists in such situations could do was write a general script in the hope that
the story would be coherently assembled in London. This despatch of a kit
of parts was basically the mode of foreign news operation throughout the
1960s and 1970s. Whether at home or abroad, the film still had to travel
back to base and sometimes this was the slowest part of the operation.
Whether they took any glee in it, *The Times* reported the following incident
in 1964 under the headline, 'Railway film of Duke delayed by railway':

> Associated Television today asked for a British Railways inquiry into
> the delay of a delivery of a news film showing the Duke of Edinburgh
> opening the £1,250,000 railways engineering research labs in Derby
> yesterday. The film was handed to the parcels office at Derby station,
> with a five shilling tip, but it did not arrive in Birmingham until today.
> ATV borrowed a BBC film which went by road (*The Times*, 16 May
> 1964, p. 10).

The only thing that had changed since Richard Dimbleby despatched his
discs of the Fenland floods in 1937 was the efficiency of the national parcel
service.

Satellite transmissions

Lightweight cameras using 16 mm film and the arrival of easily recorded
synchronous location sound advanced the situation somewhat in the 1960s,
but the first great breakthrough in newsgathering came with the advent of
telecommunications satellites able to transmit television material instanta-
neously around the world. Prior to the satellite revolution pictures could be
moved by airfreight or over landlines. Transatlantic telephone cable could
transmit film but only at the rate of one minute a day (Mayer, 1987, p. 202).
The first commercial telecommunications satellite, Telstar I, was launched
in 1962 enabling television pictures to be transmitted instantly across the
Atlantic. ITN Editor Geoffrey Cox saw the potential for the news and
booked the first available slot, finding the stories to report afterwards
(1995, p. 163). The BBC too made early use of the transatlantic link. As the
war in Vietnam ended, the actual newsgathering itself was still conducted

on film, but material could be sent by airfreight to Tokyo, where, after processing, it could be satellited to New York and eventually to London where it would have been edited. Pictures would still have been broadcast some time after the event was filmed and well after radio, newspapers and indeed television itself (without pictures) had reported the same story using the telephone and telex to transmit written copy. The technology was very expensive for routine use, with a 1965 price of £3000 an hour. Stuart Hood, writing in 1967, commented on the new technology: 'satellites have so far proved disappointing – partly because of the very high costs of transmission, partly because they depend on ground stations for transmission and reception, and there is as yet no system of stations spanning the globe' (1967, pp. 116–17). Even as late as 1980, during the Falklands conflict, it was said that the event was in the wrong hemisphere for satellite links independent of the military. Prior to 1972, ITN still sent film material back to London by airfreight, adding any updates to the commentary later by telephone. Events in the Watergate case were too fast moving for this, and Michael Brunson used the Atlantic satellite sometimes twice nightly to file reports (Potter, 1990, p. 118). However, this was still far from routine for reasons of cost. In 1976, a 10 minute unilateral US to UK feed cost $1760 (Schlesinger, 1987, p. 69).

Videotape

The recording of television images was achieved by John Logie Baird before the arrival of broadcast television. Using vinyl discs to record at a decidedly very low resolution, this material is on display today at Britain's National Museum of Photography, Film and Television in Bradford. Film recording, effectively the result of pointing a film camera at a television, was always possible, but this method incurred the cost of the film stock which then needed time consuming processing.

The ability to record television pictures onto a reuseable magnetic medium was not practical until Ampex developed the first videotape machine in 1956. The need to record and replay pictures cheaply and easily arose primarily in the United States, where the networks had the problem of transmitting material across five time zones with different peak viewing periods. Like their domestic equivalents some 20 years later, the first broadcast videotape machines were seen as primarily time-shift devices, recording live programmes for subsequent replay. It was thought that there would need to be three such machines in America and a few more in Europe. Like similar predictions made in the late 1940s about the number of computers the world would need, such predictions were to prove spectacularly wrong.

The huge amount of electronic information which constitute television pictures made magnetic tape recording a substantially greater problem than had been the case with sound. The huge bandwidth could only be recorded onto a substantially sized tape moving at very high speed. Early attempts were unsuccessful as the fast moving tape often broke. The problem was solved by using a rotating head system so that the relative speed between tape and recording head was high but the tape could travel at a mechanically manageable speed. These first machines used two inch wide tape, and the design remained virtually the same from 1958 until 1983, roughly a quarter of a century. This pioneering format was replaced by 'C' format, which used one inch tape and which became an industry standard from the late 1970s until it in turn was replaced in the early 1990s by the first digital formats employing cassette tapes of various widths. The BBC and many commercial broadcasters chose Panasonic's composite digital D-3 machines as the broadcast standard, while 1994 saw the release of the D-5 digital component format, reputedly offering the best quality to date. Channel 4 installed 60 D-5 machines in its new premises and uses them as its standard broadcast machine.

Two inch and one inch were studio tape formats requiring large static machines most often operated by graduate electronic engineers. Various attempts were made at portability but location based video newsgathering was not widespread until the 1970s when Sony's U-matic cassette format was developed for shooting single camera location work. This was the *de facto* industry standard for ENG until it was replaced by another Sony format, Betacam, which in its turn has been superseded by a digital version.

The rate of technological advancement in broadcasting can be witnessed simply by videotape technology. The first format (two inch) was in wide use for 25 years, while its successor, one inch, was a standard for roughly a decade. The Betacam format for ENG was introduced by Sony in 1987, but by 1995 this was well on the way to being replaced by a digital version. Broadcast equipment manufacturers naturally encourage a healthy turnover of technology, as does the inevitable urge on the part of broadcasters to try and stay one crucial step ahead of the competition.

At the 1995 News World Convention in Berlin, a compact new tape format from Panasonic, DVC Pro, was demonstrated to news professionals. The lightweight, broadcast-standard, camera was predicted to revolutionise newsgathering. It was so impressive and so compact that it was stolen. The DVC (digital video cassette) tape (and a Sony competitor) is about the same size as an ordinary audio cassette and should be the last digital tape format before various tapeless recording systems become both feasible and widespread. The first disc recording systems developed by AVID\Ikegami have already been launched, as have Nagra solid-state audio recorders.

Electronic newsgathering

The U-matic videotape format, developed in the early 1970s by Sony, was capable of recording broadcast quality pictures onto three-quarter inch magnetic tape using a portable video cassette recorder. Recordists carried a suitcase-size box linked by an electronic umbilical cord to the camera operator who held a reasonably bulky camera. In operational terms the new technology was a step backward from 16 mm film of the day, requiring the physical linking of sound and vision and the use of a heavier, less robust, camera.

These disadvantages for the crew, however, were far outweighed by the key advantage that there was no longer any need to process the film. Journalistically it was possible therefore to speed up the newsgathering, while logistically crews were no longer tied to the film lab. Journalists had instant playback: they could theoretically shoot a sequence, then stop and look at it immediately played back through the viewfinder of the camera, although in practice they rarely had time to do so. Instead of writing and recording a voice-over blind, reporters could return to base and instantly begin editing. Scriptwriting was now done interactively, leading to a much more complementary relationship between words and pictures. Also, a new generation of younger reporters had grown up, many of whom had worked only in television, developing more organic scriptwriting methods, integrating words and picture, leading to less 'wallpapering'.

The delivery of unedited material from abroad by satellite also changed with the arrival of ENG. Instead of having to process the film and put it into a telecine machine before material could be satellited back to base, the location-recorded tape was instantly transmittable. Already in electronic form, tape could be taken to a 'feedpoint' where it could be played straight out of the machine it was recorded on and sent back to base by satellite. This material was still unedited, however, and the disadvantages of filing material in unassembled pieces were still as great as in the days of film. Dope sheets and precisely written cutting orders which had been traditionally physically despatched with the film had now to be delivered orally on the telephone or, in time, faxed.

In 1975, Alan Protheroe, then a senior BBC News manager and later Assistant Director General, saw the new technology in America, which he described 'like stepping out of a Tiger Moth and on to a Concorde' (*Daily Telegraph*, 1979, p. 16). At a special event in 1976, ITN had flown a prototype RCA TK 76 over from New York to demonstrate the technology which would complete the revolution begun by the satellite (Potter, 1990, p. 128). The take-up of ENG technology was not instantaneous. Nearly two years later, Dick Francis, then the BBC's Director of News and Current Affairs, told *The Times* 'you will never get rid of film, even in news production and certainly not in documentary' (*The Times*, 1978a, p. 3). After trials, trade union resistance delayed implementation and a senior BBC manager lamented that 'it was becoming difficult to work on film in the United States because virtually all television stations had converted to ENG' (*The Times*, 1978b, p. 4). ITN first used the technology to cover the 1979 visit of the Pope to Poland (ITN, 1995, p. 32) while the BBC covered the

Commonwealth Conference in Lusaka in the same year, prudently and characteristically using both 16 mm film and ENG.

Camcorders

ENG technology continued to develop after videotape replaced film as the main medium for news picture acquisition. Continued miniaturisation enabled the development of a broadcast-quality camcorder: an all-in-one unit nowhere near as cumbersome as U-matic videotape with its separate camera and recorder unit. RCA developed the camcorder as early as 1977, but it was Sony with the Betacam system that provided the next *de facto* world broadcast ENG standard in 1982. Ironically, the technology was still a generation behind film in terms of handling and actual ease of use, but as is often the case with technology such an issue was not the crucial factor in determining take-up.

Further developments in electronics have already led to additional tape formats which are more compact and still easier to use. Super-VHS (S-VHS) is the electronically enhanced big brother of the domestic format VHS. It has been used by reporters such as Sue Lloyd-Roberts, posing as an ordinary tourist, to work for ITN behind the Iron Curtain.

Hi-8 is yet a further development, another Sony tape format (using 8 mm wide tape) which was used in the Gulf War both by journalists and by the military. The 'smart bomb' footage from combat jets was in fact recorded on this kind of tape.

These developments in picture-acquisition technology bring with them the promise (some journalists would say the threat) of single-person newsgathering based on the idea of multiskilled crewing. The reporter's, camera operator's, sound recordist's and editor's tasks may soon all be performed by one person. This of course has been the norm for radio journalism for some considerable period of time.

'Newshounds' and home movies on air

The VHS videotape format was originally developed for recording in the home and in time became the domestic standard around the world. Cameras and recorders were quickly developed and eventually these were followed by an all-in-one camcorder aimed at the home movie market. The result was a tremendous expansion in the number of units capable of producing television pictures. When 16 mm film was the norm for newsgathering only the staff of large news organisations and their stringers could record pictures for on-air use owing to the cost of the equipment and the film stock. In very special circumstances, such as the Zapruder film of President Kennedy's assassination, 8 mm home movies could be used, but these were hardly a regular source of news pictures. The spread of VHS, and more recently of Hi-8 camcorders, has offered the possiblity of a potentially vast number of newsgatherers around the world.

This vast army of eyes is not without its problems. Aside from the person who happens to be passing by the spectacular highway crash or who records an earthquake or some other hard news event which television then uses and acknowledges, there are other problems. News editors are fairly suspicious of the provenance of such material even though sometimes it offers a record of historic events not otherwise captured. Inexpensive, lightweight, camcorders create the possibility that non-professionals could deliberately go about newsgathering. A notable instance of this was during the troubles in the Baltics in January 1991 when Western newsgathering organisations were not allowed to travel to Riga and Vilnius. Soviet citizens, many from the Baltic states themselves, were recording pictures which they were then bringing back to Moscow and selling to Western news organisations. The activities of these 'newshounds' of course raised a number of questions because these people were filming with the sole purpose of showing the horrors of what was going on. They were befriended by the victim peoples and given access, with the result that their material was shot from a certain point of view. Nevertheless they were getting pictures that would not otherwise be available and broadcasters generally acknowledged their provenance. I spoke to a man who went into Kashmir from the Indian side, posing as a tourist. Taking a Hi-8 camcorder, he filmed literally a suitcase full of material with Kashmiris about the atrocities allegedly perpetrated by the Indian army. No one would buy his material, though a major broadcaster did look at it.

Editing in the field

It had always been possible to edit film abroad provided the requisite processing lab was available and editing equipment and skilled staff could be hired locally or flown out. These demands made it rare in British television for editing to be done on location, a situation which changed with the widespread use of video. Unlike film, ENG videotape editing equipment was relatively portable. Hi-band U-matic edit machines could be put in flight cases and taken abroad, leading to the arrival of the edit suite in the hotel room. No longer was the unassembled kit of parts sent from abroad, and there was accordingly less reliance on local facilities. Rather than send back large amounts of unedited video material, news organisations now only needed to book 15 minutes of satellite time to send back a complete cut story. The reporter and crew could now shoot on location, look at the material, edit it virtually *in situ* and despatch a finished package which could be broadcast within minutes of completion. The 1954 prediction, quoted in Chapter 4 (p. 122), 'Ultimately films may be obtainable from across the world almost as swiftly as telegrams can be received' (*The Listener*, 1954, p. 8) had been realised.

Flyaways and satphones

Satellite feeds back to base were originally from a land station, usually an orthodox television station or a telecommunications installation. By 1985 portable land stations had been developed which were capable of being carried by commercial airlines as excess baggage. These 'flyaway' satellite uplinks, weighing as little as 70 pounds, could be put in flight cases and taken abroad. The American network NBC scooped their rivals with such equipment, covering the TWA hijacking live. It was now possible to report live from anywhere in the world, given the requisite equipment. This had to include the old-fashioned telephone for it is not possible to beam material unilaterally up to a satellite. It is necessary first to telephone and book facilities as damage can be done to transponders on the 'bird' by such unannounced uplinks. Therefore, in addition to the 'flyaway' and a generator to power it, there is also the need for telephone communication. This can be provided by a very small umbrella-like satellite dish connected to a telephone which can fit into a briefcase. The satphone connects into the INMARSAT system of maritime communications satellites and makes it possible for reporters to contact base by telephone from virtually anywhere. A fax machine can be connected to a satphone to receive and send hard copy, while a modem linked to a laptop computer means text in digital form can be transmitted. Richard Dowden of *The Independent* (1994) writes of roaming Africa with hand-held technology which enables him to despatch copy to London instantly by the simple expedient of plugging into the cigarette lighter of a car and beaming into the INMARSAT system. A dramatic high-profile use of satellite technology for television was Sandy Gall's live links from inside Afghanistan as the Russians withdrew (1995, p. 180).

By 1986 the IBA, ITN and Michael Electronics had developed a satellite newsgathering (SNG) unit called Newshawk which used a system of 1.2 metre dishes (ITN, 1995, p. 32) to uplink television pictures. No longer did tape have to be taken to a television station or telecoms facility, and large telephone company dishes were no longer required in the field. These small trucks have become increasingly common. Starbird Satellite Services, a partnership of the WTN news picture agency and British Aerospace, offers broadcasters not only such uplinks but a dedicated satellite transponder, available 24 hours a day. Until the arrival of such unilateral services, satellite time had to be booked with a series of 'matching orders' faxed between the requesting broadcasters, the national telephone companies at both ends of the link and the international satellite organisation. At a minimum this process took half an hour. Understandably, broadcasters objected to this bureaucracy and as a result a consortium, the European News Exchange

(ENEX) was formed between CBS and a number of other commercial stations which leased the exclusive use of a transponder (Hurt, 1996, pp. 24–7). Similarly, in March 1994 ITN signed a deal with British Telecom giving them 24-hour access to a Europewide transponder and therefore no limits on satellite feeds and two-ways (ITN, 1995, p. 34).

These two-way communications systems are of course not just for filing stories but can be used for receiving advice and information. It is common working practice in American network television news for reporters to write scripts on location using laptop computers before sending them back to base via modem for approval, with New York often suggesting changes. This is not necessarily a bad thing, though all the British journalists spoken to in this sample cringed at the prospect of what they saw as a transatlantic aberration arriving as standard working practice with their organisations. Certainly the increased logistical demands of the new technologies and the relative ease of communication have led to reporters at times spending more time on the telephone to base in London or New York than doing journalism. These greater organisational requirements in turn have led to the arrival of location producers, referred to disparagingly by some journalists as 'fixers'. Thus a full crew can now consist of reporter, camera operator, sound recordist, editor, satellite technician, producer and several first-class tickets worth of excess baggage.

Palm-tree journalism

Satellite links give journalists the ability to report from almost anywhere in the world. Of contemporary news services, CNN particularly makes a fetish of live reporting. They even go so far as to choose their bureau locations strategically to provide rooftop offices with panoramic views. Thus viewers got live pictures of a T-72 tank backfiring in the streets of Moscow in August of 1991, an event which was then duly replayed and discussed. CNN had five reporters in Moscow for the storming of the White House, including one inside the Kremlin, and viewers could watch events unfold live. Reporting of this type is inevitably accompanied by an extensive rhetoric constantly reminding the viewer that they are indeed eyewitnesses viewing history being made; 24-hour services such as CNN constantly stress their ability to 'go live' for as long as necessary to cover a story. This difference between them and the traditional fixed-point bulletins of terrestrial broadcasters has become a unique selling point in a fierce journalistic and commercial competition.

There are serious issues at question according to a former ITN diplomatic editor, himself now a rolling news anchor: 'Live is very dangerous, because in live television, particularly if you have to transmit 24 hours a day, you make mistakes'. He sees these not just as mistakes of fact or emphasis, but serious cases of creating misleading impressions with wider international political consequences:

The Soviet coup was a good example of how television is distorting something, having television on the spot live was distorting. Western Governments, including certainly Mitterand and Major, were making very rapid assumptions based on a fixed camera on the CNN office overlooking Kutuzovsky Prospekt where you saw the APCs and the T62s and 72s lined up, that the coup had succeeded, Gorbachev was out and so on. Television is very dangerous.

All momentous events, of course, do not always conveniently occur within range of rooftop cameras. One result is what I call palm-tree journalism. Reporters must remain with their hi-tech installation by the hotel pool to be fed live into the near continuous news system. A BBC foreign correspondent tells of unexpectedly meeting an American counterpart away from the hotel, up-country, in Nicaragua. 'What are you doing here?' he inquired. 'I'm on my day off', came the reply. No longer chained to the satellite dish, the reporter could actually go and attempt to see something of the events he had been reporting on 'live' for the previous week. Even on a mainstream general programming channel, as opposed to a 24-hour news network, there are now so many fixed-point bulletins that reporters often have multiple deadlines, needing to file so often that they have restricted time in the field.

Live two-ways and hotel stand-ups

The state-of-the-art technology that makes live satellite broadcasting possible can of course be used to file pre-recorded video material. It is possible to combine the two basic modes of television newsgathering. Edited location recorded pieces, the descendent of the filmed newsreel, can be filed minutes before transmission and the location reporter can be 'injected' live into a programme. Increasingly, one sees the transmission of an edited location report followed immediately by a 'live two-way' with the location reporter. Such interviews by the studio anchor about the 'latest developments' are often redundant. If the reporter has done their job properly there should, in most cases, be nothing more to say. This situation is exacerbated by the fact that the anchor usually will not have seen the ENG piece, as in many cases it will not have arrived until after transmission has begun. As one veteran correspondent remarks,

> in order to give the impression that you're watching news as it's happening they're now doing these two-ways of reporters. The reporters have nothing to add. They've given you their report and very few of them . . . are capable of actually dealing with a live two-way. Its a difficult thing, not just nerves, but technically its different. This is seen to be live TV – its happened there, let's go to our man there, show the viewers how clever we are . . . recently when I was in Sarajevo I'd sent

over a report, quite a long one, and the newscaster came and said 'What's the latest?' I said 'you've just seen the latest, I've just said it to you, I've got nothing to add to that'. There was a kind of a long pause. I won't put up with that crap, if these guys can't sit down for a few minutes and figure out what they're going to say to me, then they can go and jump. But television is going to be hoist by its own petard because of this business of live television. CNN is doing enormous damage.

This reservation about the cult of the live two-way is shared by a senior CNN correspondent who has remarked: 'It's great if you have a Berlin Wall falling, but that doesn't happen very often. Most of the time you've got a parked car'. This same reporter has issued a standing threat to answer the on-air question 'what's happening Richard?' with the reply 'I have no idea what's happening because I've been standing on this hotel balcony for two hours waiting for you to ask me that question' (Rosenblum, 1993, p. 168). A senior BBC journalist with extensive experience of both sides of the two-way condemns it simply as 'a cosmetic contrivance'.

The two-way communications offered by the satellite link can be used to provide the field reporter with information. At its most basic this can consist of the simple reading of wire service copy over the phone to the reporter, who can then repeat it later on-air (Thomson, 1992, p. 140). The tyranny of the two-way is lamented by many of the journalists who are regularly required to perform them. In this view, such 'live shots' 'originated with some kind of TV witchdoctor in Iowa' (Bell, 1995, p. 67) and can degenerate into a situation little short of the farcical, where reporters are read material which they hear in their earpiece and which they then duly repeat verbatim on air. This scene from the Hollywood film *Broadcast News* is regularly broadcast in the news and has been described by one reluctant participant 'like a sort of news bypass operation, in which only the ear and mouth were actively engaged – not journalism, or even show business, but puppetry' (Bell, 1995, p. 209).

While there is no doubt that something can be added by an appropriate two-way, there is an undoubted tendency to overuse them. During its rolling coverage of the August 1996 TWA crash, CNN went live to their reporter on a Long Island beach. Miles from the crash scene offshore, he could only report that the scheduled press conference was now 41 minutes late. He had nothing more to add and, short of actually saying that on-air, gave every indication that that was the case. Earpieces buzzed and he and the Atlanta anchor had no choice but to fill out the time until the top of the hour. The nearly 20 minutes of dialogue that followed was an impressive testament to the calm professionalism of the two broadcasters concerned but added very little to the story which was to be a mystery for some time.

Expensive newsgathering

There have been undoubted positive effects as a result of the deployment of the new technologies. Editing abroad has led to the creation of completed ENG pieces with a better integration of pictures and words. It is no longer the norm to send scrambled kits of unassembled parts back to base for transmission three days after the event. The advantages of the new ways of working are clear, enabling reporters to fully author their own work, producing a script in conjunction with pictures they can see. Indeed, for the first time foreign news reporters are themselves able to view their pieces as finished products. While location-recorded material now inevitably reaches screens sooner and more coherently than it did before, such practices also have their disadvantages. ENG comes to mean 'expensive newsgathering' when 'excess baggage charges can even account for the major part of the cost of overseas news' (Hawker, 1993, p. 30). A senior BBC news editor has given a figure of £17 500 a week for the maintenance of a fully equipped team with its own satellite uplink (Wallis and Baran, 1990, p. 223), and BBC Foreign Affairs Editor John Simpson describes a trip to Angola with a crew of six (without a dish) costing £50 000 (source: Simpson, 1993). Once this costly commitment has been made to send staff – reporter, camera operator, sound recordist, editor, producer and all the kit – the expense incurred often dictates that the material will be used. Similarly, if a satellite feed is pre-booked there is a tendency to use it and, once the reporter has sent their piece, why not use the remaining satellite time to 'get the latest'? To a certain extent logistical, not journalistic, considerations dictate what gets covered and how. One veteran reporter talked of how, when he began his career on film, logistics were 20 per cent of his job and journalism 80 per cent, while now, with the new technologies, those ratios have been reversed.

Television's main advantage over the print media has been its ability to report the news instantly, and this unique selling point has been stressed by the 24-hour dedicated news services such as CNN. The ability to broadcast live from anywhere results from technological factors. Competitive managers in news organisations have always unquestioningly acquired new technologies in an attempt to get an edge on their rivals; purchases which in turn raise the cost of newsgathering. What develops then is a complex competitive dynamic in which technology is a major, but not the only, factor. In the constant search for a competitive journalistic advantage, technology is acquired which in turn changes the nature of the newsgathering and reporting process.

Dupes

Editing tape on location means that instead of having only the unique original film that was sent back to base for processing, video footage can be copied or 'duped'. Such dupes, duplication pictures from a sister news organisation, might arrive in the edit suite, with a reporter not having been present when the pictures were shot and hence knowing nothing of their provenance. They might be inclined to use them because they are powerful and because of the everpresent competitive factor. This could lead to the use of material from unknown sources. The myth of the eyewitness reporter suffers somewhat if he or she uses pictures kindly provided by somebody in the same hotel. An experienced former foreign correspondent, now anchoring, issues a caution:

> If you look at the development of television journalism in its strongest moments, it's about one camera person, one camera crew and a reporter looking at something, filming it from every position that they can manage, but no more, condensing it into their eyewitness account and sending it home. Whatever the story is. That is now a thing of the past. Because somebody else got a better shot of the second element or somebody else got a fifth element that you hadn't thought of . . . it was cut in. As a result of course, it becomes less one person's eyewitness report, than merely a sausage machine production of images that you may have seen already on another bulletin on another channel . . . I think you'd be very hard put to find a bulletin today that was shot and reported by one person. I think that almost everything that you see has had the input of perhaps five or six teams all doing different elements.

Cost-cutting has led, particularly in the American networks, to fewer and fewer permanently based foreign correspondents. Equally, 'firemen' are despatched abroad less often than was once the case. The result of these finance-led decisions is that more and more reports consist of agency or third-party tape from abroad, voiced at base. This practice of 'packaging' is fraught with difficulties.

During the Gulf War newsrooms received extraordinary footage from inside occupied Kuwait of resistance fighters in action dropping molotov cocktails from a highway flyover onto an Iraqi military vehicle. The material, shot on domestic VHS, looked authentic and was used. After the war it emerged that over a million dollars were paid by the Kuwaiti government to an American public relations firm to produce 24 video news releases (VNRs) which were sent to news organisations around the world (MacArthur, 1992, p. 50). No technology can guarantee the authenticity of such material and the explosion in the amount of footage now available makes verification even more difficult.

Even on location there is a worrying tendency to do things by remote control, as one veteran war correspondent reveals:

> Now so much of television is done from feedpoint, the reporters never leave the building . . . In Sarajevo it was all pool, everyone was

pooling, so if you didn't want to leave the building you didn't have to ... I know a bureau correspondent, and he never leaves his bureau. Never, he's too lazy, he never leaves. His cameraman and producer go out and do all the stories ... They go out and they bring it back ... and the producer writes a rough script and he rewrites it in his words and broadcasts it, and they say well done fella, great story today.

The obvious question that needs to be asked is have the new technologies and, just as importantly, the working practices that come with them, led to better reporting and a better informed viewing public? For Martin Kalb, a former American television correspondent, the answer is simple: 'as technology has grown more sophisticated, the end product has grown more skimpy' (quoted in Vanden Heuvel, 1993, p. 15). Is this view shared by those currently using the new technologies?

The possibilities offered for newsgathering in the satellite age cannot help but excite even the most sceptical journalist:

When the shuttle blew up the first thing I did was pick up the phone and book the satellite for the next 24 hours to secure a line out. Then I realised we could sub-let it after that. The shuttle blew up at 5 o'clock London time, and we had a three and a half minute piece on the air at 5.45. And we'd done a newsflash at about 5.15 with pictures. This was absolutely unheard of.

However, amongst experienced reporters (including the one quoted above) there are undoubted feelings of nostalgia tempered with an air of resignation. The main drawback, to many who grew up with film, is the loss of the 20 or so minutes thinking time while the film was being processed. Instead of a quiet period to make phone calls to base and collect one's thoughts before writing a script, there was now a need to hit the ground running and begin editing instantly. However, younger reporters who had never had this relative luxury did not see the problem. They pointed out that they composed their thoughts as they went along and always began editing with a clear idea of how they were going to craft their piece.

Journalists have always worked to short deadlines. A 'Reuters snap' consisting of the four words 'Ghandi shot, worst expected' flashed around the around world in 1947 within minutes of the event. Print reporters covering President Kennedy's press conferences in the early 1960s tell of running out of the room to open phones to dictate pieces that were composed as they spoke. Foreign correspondents shipping unprocessed film by airfreight always had the deadline of the next flight even if their material might be days in arriving on the screen. Nevertheless, some say there is a case to be made for deliberately putting a delay into the system:

Years ago, when the first landline was put between the White House and New York as soon as a press conference was over, reporters came rushing out straight to the live camera and said 'the president has just said this'. . . . The first guy to get to the camera was on-air first, but the correspondents were getting it so wrong so often because they hadn't got time to sit down and say 'now he said that . . . what did he mean by that?'. . . . The networks and the correspondents were seen to be wrong so often, that all three nets then agreed that there would be a built-in delay, I think it was a 10 minute delay. They all agreed to that so that guys could sit down, reflect and write a proper piece. . . . I'd like to see that happening with us.

Picture explosions

The move from film to video has had other effects than shortening dead-lines. Videotape costs a fraction of what film did and with ENG there is the danger of shooting too much:

> People are actually terribly ill-disciplined with video now, they just turn it on, shooting three hours on a story which in the old days you shot 10 minutes on. Consequently you end up with hours of material, some of which is never seen by anybody. . . . I think it has actually diluted the process of retrieving information and making it consum-able to the viewer. Very often the constraints are not journalistic but mathematical and practical, which is crazy. But in the old days it was just a limit to what you could actually find out. Now, added to that is a limit to how much you can actually trawl through on the video screen before your time is up.

This overkill in the field creates enormous problems as proportionally more material comes in to all news organisations. The result is very worrying, claims one experienced hand:

> because of our wanton abuse of the technology all discipline has bro-ken down. People are spraying at anything, recording for hours. They're sitting across all these satellite feeds that are coming in from the outside world and stuff is being thrown onto the air with very little individual research as to what it actually is really about. It's a third-hand account of what it's really about, often sent in on a dope sheet, by some party who had nothing to do with the shooting of the film in the first place. For example, Visnews or WTN will pick up from some freelance or some local television station. They will have had no conversation with the person who actually shot it. They'll have a con-versation with the person who is selling it to them who may never have had a conversation with the person who shot it. There is then maybe another account from Reuters or AP and all this stuff is married up and you end up with a fairly threadbare contact with the original exe-cution of the material. Whereas in the old days, although there was

less of it, most of it was generated by someone who had seen it, shipped it and sent the information with it.

Changing circumstances

One reporter spoken to for this work called himself one of the luckiest people in the profession as he had only one deadline a day, working as he did for an evening programme only: 'it is wonderful and it is old-fashioned and is civilised'. Unlike some journalists who may have to report to both radio and television or to multiple deadlines either in rolling or fixed-point news, he had the better part of the day to prepare his considered piece. Others of his colleagues are not so fortunate:

> We can now edit on-site, we have little vans with all the machinery in, so you don't have to come back to base with your material, so that means you can get it on more bulletins. In theory you can get on all the bulletins, changing it for each one by editing on site. You have to work much quicker, you must know when to go back and start editing, just because of the deadline and not push your luck. When I first joined ITN the news editor sent me out on a story saying don't bother too much about getting it back for News at One, just aim for the 5.45. And nowadays the first instruction is can you get it back for the 5-to-11 summary and then change it for the One? So everything's moved on in terms of speed and demand on location.

Life is not much easier back at base. Where once film had to be processed, edited and assembled into a transmission roll in the telecine machine, videotape can now arrive when the programme is on-air:

> In the mid-1970s the news was wrapped up before you went on-air. The film had been cut and loaded in the machine ready to roll and you might have one live interview but very rarely. . . . Whereas today stuff comes into the programme constantly that I haven't seen because it's been injected live from wherever it comes from. You are writing and editing introductions to the stories when you haven't seen the pictures yet, so you've got to be much more on the ball. I think all news journalists are far more involved now than they ever used to be by the nature of what they are doing.

In what some would regard as a worst-case scenario, bi-media reporting with its almost constant stream of deadlines can lead to a specialist correspondent remaining at base filing for radio and television (using library footage) while, if he is lucky, a producer is free to go out and shoot fresh location footage (Gallagher, 1996, p. 13). Equally, logistical pressures mean it is easier to have interviewees come to the facilities rather than have crews go to them. Keen-eyed viewers will no doubt have noted the number of

interviews that take place in video edit suites and, clearly, the atrium of
ITN's magnificent London headquarters is a regular backdrop to talking
heads of all kinds. The substantive content of such interviews is of course
not changed with the location, fuel costs are saved and fewer silver cases are
humped up and down stairs. The danger may be in a long-term loss of contact with the outside world. Viewers may have lost nothing in no longer seeing academic experts stereotypically speaking in front of a row of books but
there may be an undue reliance on speakers who can quickly leg it to headquarters or a remote studio. One academic at the London School of
Economics told me that his frequent media appearances were not so much a
function of the quality of his comment as of his proximity to the central
London studios of the various television news organisations. These studios
themselves have undergone radical recent change and newsgathering technology is only half of the story, for, once 'gathered', news must be transmitted; intake must be transformed into output.

The traditional newsroom

The traditional broadcast newsroom was a communication system employing an intriguing mixture of high and low technology. State-of-the-art electronic equipment has always been required for television and radio
programmes simply to be broadcast. However, the journalistic product that
was set before the cameras or read into the radio microphones was traditionally produced using basic technologies such as the typewriter, the telephone, the ballpoint pen and carbon paper. A newsroom has always been a
complex information-flow system where input of various kinds is ultimately
transformed into electronic broadcast output. Input takes various forms,
whether from 'wholesale' (i.e. not available to the general public) sources
such as news agency copy arriving on teleprinters or press releases arriving
in the post. There are 'retail' sources of information as well, with newspapers and other electronic media being avidly consumed in any newsroom.
In addition, the employees of every news organisation generate diverse input
into the system.

   Not all input is moved directly to output. In all newsrooms there is a considerable amount of forward planning, with certain staff being given
responsibility for 'diary' production. Press releases arrive in newsrooms a
considerable time before the event announced and a certain percentage of
news production concerns such diary stories. The announcement of trade
figures or the publication of a major report do not come as surprises and a
substantial part of the input to newsrooms concerns future events which
must be noted and planned for. Press releases and other announcements of
such events are entered into a diary, and prospect sheets are produced for
use in planning meetings. The BBC has a central Future Events Unit which
acts as a clearing house, receiving press releases and other announcements

which are then circulated to output departments with notice of coming events. Agencies equally produce such forward-planning information.

System output

The output of the news system is the programme broadcast on the screen, consisting of the newsreader reading text to camera and introducing location recorded reports. ENG reports are recorded on location with the material being returned to base for assembly into a transmittable package. In addition to these self-generated visual materials, newsrooms receive 'feeds' of still and moving pictures from various external sources which they may use in bulletin creation. The transmitted programme is produced using a script which is written communally over the preparation period prior to the bulletin going on-air. Traditionally, this was by using typewriters and carbon paper. For example, a news agency report would be torn off the teleprinter. A sub-editor would then rewrite the story at a typewriter using a 'four-way' to produce multiple carbon copies. These would be shown to editors and presenters for comment and change. Eventually a script for the whole bulletin would emerge, which was then retyped by typists and reproduced by copying methods such as roneo or mimeograph. In addition, a sheet listing the programme running order and timings would be prepared and printed. Originally, television news presenters read from the paper copy with great skill, looking up periodically to make eye contact with the audience. Prompting devices were later developed enabling anchors to read the script off a screen mounted at first beside then eventually on the front of the camera they were speaking into. This required the retyping of the presenter's script onto a paper roll in large type. This roll simply had a small television camera pointed at it and the output came up on a screen to be read.

Once the paper produced script had been dealt with by journalists it was passed to the programme director who would 'mark it up', indicating which camera was used for which part of the programme. Timings of item and programme length were arrived at by physically counting the words. Normal broadcast speech is reckoned to be delivered at the speed of three words a second. Scripts were often written with only three words in a line, both to facilitate ease of reading and to make counting the words, and hence the script length, easier.

Digitising the news

This whole paper-based script production chain has been replaced by computer-based electronic newsroom systems (ENSs). Such ENSs are a widespread phenomenon in the media industries. One service provider (Bay Area Systems (BASYS)) alone has 450 systems installed worldwide

(*Broadcast* 1995, p. 9). These systems, which first appeared as direct-input systems in newspaper production, are now fairly common tools in radio and television newsrooms around the world. BASYS was originally developed by independent software developers in the United States who designed a computer newsroom system for KRON-TV in San Francisco. In 1982 ITN chose the system for the news service it was to provide for Britain's new Channel 4. At the time this was the largest installation of the system in the world. Subsequently ITN were to purchase the company, but, unable to undertake the investment required to keep the product up to date, sold BASYS to DEC, who manufactured the hardware the system ran on. Ownership eventually transferred to AVID, a leading provider of digitally-based editing systems to broadcasters. Originally designed to run on a VAX minicomputer, BASYS has been ported to the Windows PC environment but most current systems in Britain are still text-based, running on VAX.

An ENS basically consists of a minicomputer with a series of terminals or a network of personal computers linked to a central server into which various forms of 'input' are entered. This input, either from direct entry by journalists or from external sources such as news agency 'wires', is then edited and printed as the script of the radio or television newsroom. It is something of a commonplace that such systems have radically changed the way in which broadcast journalists work, but there has been very little analysis either by the industry itself or by academic observers of the way in which these systems are used and how they have changed working practices. Two recent newsroom studies (Blumler and Gurevitch, 1995, p. 177; Cottle, 1993, p. 43) make note of the arrival of computer newsroom systems but don't make an extensive study of their use or effect. This particular technology is one that is new as the vast majority of the academic production studies were conducted in the 1970s and 1980s.

ENS comes and sits on top of the traditional paper-based information flow, not offering a new paradigm but digitising and automating certain parts of that process. Most contemporary ENS systems consist basically of a text-processing and related communications system. Wire copy comes in on-line from news agencies, which can be edited, new text added and then altered by a succession of personnel. At its most basic an ENS is a large, communally accessed word processor whose product is the script. It processes the text of the script, counts the words and therefore gives timings. The programme running order, once displayed on an office white board, is now manipulated on-screen and the system has simple communications and database functions. It can interface with other technology in the system and download text to graphics and the teleprompter. Most current ENS systems (BASYS, Newstar, Newsmaker) interface with videotape library management systems to control the playing of tapes for transmission.

Originally, computer newsroom systems did not deal with the actual audio-visual output of the programme. Picture editing, graphics and the live studio cameras were a production chain almost totally independent of the script system. A television script is a set of printed instructions written in a special language which skilled staff then use to realise a complex time-based audio-visual construct. The use of an ENS is computer-aided design (CAD) but not computer-aided manufacture (CAM), producing a blueprint in the form of a script but not the actual product.

The library management systems, which control the play-in of video-tapes, enable running orders to be rearranged instantly, with the changes appearing seamlessly on the teleprompter and in tape play-out. I have observed operations where short regional sub-bulletins, edited by one person, are transmitted by that journalist, a specially trained secretary and the newsreader. There are no technicians or other operating personnel involved. A half-hour live bulletin transmitted twice daily to stations from Australia to California equally exploits such newsroom technology and does so with a remarkably small technical and journalistic team.

At the very least, the effect of the text-only newsroom systems has been to speed up the process. Script production requires less menial manual work, with cleaner and better written scripts being produced. Running orders are more flexible and programmes more responsive as scripts can be changed at the last minute, although some journalists do not see this as a blessing. One newscaster was of the opinion that they were now at 'the limits of how fast you can get'. In terms of content one editor downplayed the effect on substance: 'I don't think journalistically it's changed the way we do things at all, but it's made it easier to find out information and exchange information'.

Newer, more integrated, digital systems are arriving which will more closely link script and actual programme production. Digital video servers will enable newsroom personnel to manipulate visual material as well as text in the same desktop system. Journalists working at their workstation will receive a variety of inputs, all of which they will be able to edit. These developments are signalled by institutional change, with AVID, a leading supplier of digital editing software, purchasing BASYS, while Sony, a traditional provider of videotape editing equipment, has joined forces with the software company Oracle to produce a rival integrated newsroom system. This has been adopted for trials by ITN, while the BBC is developing its own electronic news production system (ENPS) in conjunction with Associated Press.

Editing pictures

When newsreel material was shot on location, the film from the camera was developed and an editing or cutting copy produced from the negative. This cutting copy was physically cut using a small guillotine-like device and pasted together with sticky tape or film cement. This edited copy could be viewed, but final exhibition was from prints made by cutting the original negative, using the cutting copy as a guide. In television news production, several methods were used to speed up the process. A method was developed for transmitting negatives before eventually colour-reversal film was used. With this technology, the film that went through the camera was itself edited and eventually transmitted.

Early video editing

In the early days of videotape it was possible to edit a programme by physically cutting the tape and splicing it back together again, as had been the case with film and with audiotape. However, this type of editing required a great deal of skill. Unlike film, there were no sprocket holes or visible pictures on the tape, so it was very difficult to know exactly where each frame of the pictures began and ended. To solve this problem, the tape was sprayed with an iron oxide solution which made it possible to view the magnetic impulses using a microscope. This allowed the editor to determine the beginning and end of one picture and to cut accordingly. As sound was recorded slightly differently, it had to be laid off onto audiotape to be edited and laid back again. Suffice it to say this was an extremely awkward method of editing but it was used by television sports right up until the late 1970s. Changes in videotape technology, however, eventually made much more sophisticated editing possible. Nowadays recorded video material is edited by copying or dubbing material from one tape to another. A minimum of two machines are required, a recorder and a player synchronised by a computerised edit controller. Such dub editing has come to be known as linear editing because the material is copied from the original tape onto the edited tape in a linear fashion, with shot A following shot B, followed by shot C, with every edit copied in real time. With film, a two minute sequence and a 30 second shot can be edited together simply by joining the two pieces of film, whereas with video the full two and a half minutes would be needed for the copying. With film a single shot could be removed from the middle of a piece, whereas with videotape such a thing would be impossible without having to re-edit the whole programme. Any change anywhere within a finished videotape means a complete re-edit from the point of change onwards. In terms of editing flexibility, the use of videotape was a step backwards from film. Film had always been frame accurate, in terms of both sound and picture. Film was always random access in that any shot could be put quickly into any location and the length and order of a programme could be changed relatively quickly. To begin with, the cutting of videotape was such a complex process that it could only be done by a qualified engineer inside a broadcasting organisation and was never even considered for newsgathering. The arrival of portable videotape recorders in the 1970s and edit controllers advanced videotape editing but still brought it nowhere near the flexibility that already existed with film. The linear dubbing process, which lay at the heart of video editing, meant that any change in the length or order of a programme required a complete re-edit. In 1981, when the Israelis invaded southern Lebanon, *Newsnight* were the only major daily news programme still working on film. Their crews and editors actually had advantages over their competitors who were using more advanced electronic technology. Although *Newsnight* had to send their film into Tel Aviv for processing before they could begin editing, they were nevertheless always the first team to show their completed product to the Israeli censor. When the military authorities required the removal of any material, the *Newsnight* film editor was able to perform that task quickly, while competing videotape editors, when required to make even minor alterations, often had to start all over again and completely re-edit their piece. They may have been able to insert an alternate shot effectively covering over the forbidden material but this was not possible in every case. The result was that the team shooting and editing on film were inevitably the first to transmit the material from the feedpoint back to London. The choice of videotape over film as a newsgathering medium was taken both because it was cheaper than film but also because it was not always possible to find a fast and efficient laboratory to develop film.

The relatively inflexible linear editing process of videotape is still very much used for newsgathering. Advances in computer technology have led to disc-based picture editing which has come to be known as non-linear editing because, unlike videotape editing, material can be assembled and re-assembled in virtually any order. In effect, this is a return to the way of working known in the days of film, except that shots do not have to be physically accessed from trim bins but can be manipulated as images on a computer screen. The development of editing systems such as AVID, Lightworks and others has been a revolution in television post-production. These machines which began arriving in the early 1990s were originally used only for off-line editing. Material shot on videotape or film was brought into a non-linear edit facility, the rushes were selected by viewing the tape and the material required was digitised and loaded into the hard discs of the edit station. It could then be manipulated in digital form producing not a final product but an edit decision list which was a set of computer instructions on a floppy disc. This was then taken into an on-line video edit suite and auto-conformed, producing a final finished product on videotape. This off-line digital process could also produce an edit decision list which would be a guide for negative cutters so that both film and videotape could be edited off-line using non-linear digital equipment. The tremendous demands in terms of time in news production have always meant that news production, whether film or video, has always been on-line where the actual edited material was that which was transmitted. The first generation of random access non-linear digital editing equipment did not produce pictures of a sufficiently high quality to be broadcast 'on-line'. However, improvements in hardware and software have led to the development of machines such as the Heavyworks and the AVID Newscutter and the Quantel Clip Box, which actually produce broadcast quality pictures which can be transmitted straight off the hard disc of the computer. This method of working has yet to gain universal acceptance, for a number of reasons. As most videotape shot is still analogue, the material recorded on location still has to be digitised. It is brought into an edit suite, reviewed, played through in real time, digitised and saved onto a hard disc array before editing can begin. This is effectively a return to the days when the film might spend between 20 and 40 minutes in the lab being developed. The digitising time actually slows down the newsgathering process. When all material is recorded either on digital videotape or eventually onto hard disc in the camera, this will become simply a copying process and will increase in speed. In news operations which have tried to work entirely in a digital domain there have been problems. Channel One in London which records on analogue videotape has AVID Newscutters to enable it to edit its news material digitally but has in fact continued to use two-machine Betacam edit suites to edit the material on analogue tape. Some of the new disc-based systems, operating in America and in other parts of the world, have proved to be less reliable than was originally hoped. The second generation of digital non-linear editing systems in fact are hybrid systems which enable the editing to be done either on disc or on tape in recognition of some of the problems that have arisen.

The roles played by personnel in the editing process are important. The mechanical and technical skills required to edit the film were such that, although it required training, there was no specific qualification, and film editors were often arts-school graduates who learned quickly the physical, mechanical, skills and the more important creative skills needed to edit complex time-based audio-visual constructs. When videotape first arrived, the operator of a videotape recording machine had to be a graduate electronic engineer simply to make the machine operate. The complex procedure of cutting videotape equally required sophisticated technical skills. Later generations of videotape equipment, i.e. one-inch machines, were equally operated by electronically trained engineers. The arrival of the U-matic tape format in the 1970s created a situation where, although some knowledge of the way in which pictures were recorded onto tape was required, the operator simply did not have to be an electronic engineer to edit. Film editors were able to make the transition to become tape editors. These 'picture editors' became the norm in news production. The relative simplicity of technical operation meant that it was theoretically possible to train arts and social science graduates to become videotape editors and, indeed, this was a policy followed by the BBC. The next logical step was, of course, that people from a journalistic background could be trained to do these tasks, enabling what is called 'multiskilled operation'. But this and some of the other implications of digital technology are not being greeted with enthusiasm by journalists.

Conclusions

The radical changes in the institutional settings of all television news organisations on both sides of the Atlantic are well documented. Books with attention-grabbing titles such as *Who killed CBS?* (Boyer, 1988), *The battle for the BBC* (Barnett and Curry, 1994) and *Who stole the news?* (Rosenblum, 1993) have told the story of how television and the news have changed. Eager informants have queued up to tell the story and it is no doubt easy to find horror stories and vitriol from disgruntled journalists, but beneath this comment what are the long-term implications of the new technologies and working practices they dictate? Some journalists admitted to having a Luddite streak and worried about the headlong rush into the newer and the faster, with one senior correspondent, now anchoring, quite prepared to talk about 'our wanton abuse of the technology'. Many journalists insisted that just as important as the need to be first was the need to be right, not sacrificing accuracy in the rush to be on-air first. This same journalist spoke of the need to continue to provide more than just quick breaking news, explaining, rather than being seduced by the CNN approach:

> I think the problem really is that everybody has got sucked towards what CNN is doing because it's so exciting. But it is superficial and it is in fact simply giving people initial information. What you need in tandem with that is somebody explaining the material.

Why, given this evident caution and indeed scepticism on the part of such senior journalists, has news gone down the path it patently has?

> I think one of the real problems is the people who manage television are absolutely, they're completely in love with the 'toys' as they describe them and the toys are lightweight dishes and everything is about technology, nothing is about content. There is no debate about content. The debate is about the technology. It is about 'how can we do this?', you know, they are already thinking 'what are we going to do about Gorbachev here? Well we could have a link here and a satellite dish there, and we could use a lightweight satellite dish there'. These are the editorial meetings. This is about the how rather than the what. These are the things which drive people in television news, not the content.

Interestingly, 'the people who manage television' are not, and have never been, location reporters and hence do not understand first-hand the problems involved. As one former foreign correspondent remarked, 'it's like having an air force where the pilots are barred from command'. Editors are responding to perceived competition from CNN and similar services. The first night of the Gulf War put the letters 'CNN' on the front pages and on the lips of millions who could not see the service. This seeming success has propagated the notion of a live, hi-tech, wired world where viewers can see history being made 24 hours a day. This may be true on certain rare occasions but there are still other considerations. Slow down, says one relatively young old-hand, offering an interesting alternative:

> there is almost a case really for returning to the old newsreel thing and set the whole thing to music. I'm suggesting not even a commentary. If you don't know what the hell's going on and you've got instant pictures. You just say that these are the scenes in Moscow, make of them as you will. You're seeing them as we are seeing them. Tune in again in about an hour and we'll start to make some sense of them, or more likely in twelve hour's time. We respect your right to see them. This could be the great relationship between terrestrial and satellite television. Satellite could do the instant job and we could do the real analysis. But you see in fact what's happening is the idiots are trying to pursue the satellite operation at their own game, and they are going to be beaten; badly beaten. People are going to say, well why the hell should I pay for this when I've got it coming out on the Sky and I saw it at five o'clock this morning?

We may have been able to see tanks rolling live in the streets of Moscow and been told of the liberation of Kuwait City by a reporter with a flyaway, but traditional journalistic considerations still apply. Access is still needed and judgement is still paramount. Media response teams formed during the Gulf War had the satphones and flyaways but what did viewers see as a result? Did we see live war? No, nor were we likely to because the Allied military controlled access. And, one must ask, what would it have added to our understanding if we had? Rooftop shots of tanks in a Moscow street cannot tell us the will of the Russian military. In Bosnia there is no point in having all the kit if you can't get to Goražde and all you can offer the world is hotel stand-ups and shots of a radio receiving messages reputedly from the besieged city but which cannot be verified. Satellite communications, digital technologies and 24-hour global broadcasting didn't stop CNN coming within 20 seconds of announcing that George Bush had died in Tokyo, the victim of a hoax carried out by a disgruntled competitor (Rosenblum, 1993, p. 181). The consequences of such inadvertent news-making hardly bear thinking about, but then of course 'the marketing people can boast that it was live' (p. 168). Margins of error are slimmer than ever and no technology has yet been found to improve human judgement. The competitive, management-driven, and often unthinking deployment of technical resources has changed location-based news reporting utterly. In the eyes of those actually doing the reporting, this change has been a mixed blessing and there is a perceived danger that by making the live and the exclusive into primary news values, accuracy and understanding will be lost. While Luddite anti-technology sentiments were muttered by some, these were qualified as soon as they were spoken. There was a near universal plea to use the new technologies properly and not to get seduced by the all too easily measured criterion of being first, being live or having something no competitor has. Equally, by constantly chasing the audience, there is a perceived risk that they might actually be lost, impatient with change for change's sake. As one veteran correspondent laments:

It's this lust that news editors have for taking news one step forward or one step sideways or one step further. I think the old formulae were the best. It's a saleable thing, it's like cornflakes, it's like washing powder, you've got to find a new improved formula. . . . It's the new improved news. That irritates me, there's nothing new in television, because there is nothing new in the world situation. Wars look the same, earthquakes look the same, but they're all trying to find new ways of doing it better, covering it better, or in a newer fashion than the guy next door, and I think they're damaging themselves. The viewers aren't impressed by it.

|7|

Multiskilling or deskilling?
Visions of the future and
realities of today

The Birtian reforms at the BBC, the commercial pressures on ITN, the changing ownership of the American networks, the development of specialist news channels, the globalisation of broadcasting and new digital technologies have all changed the face of television news, but this change is far from over, for the future promises certain developments which are perforce difficult to discuss but which must nevertheless be investigated. As is so often said in such predictive circumstances, imagine the following.

The future?

The future

A twenty first century, wired, journotech receives input on a breaking story in her patch. Remote visual sensors, the descendants of today's surveillance cameras, have recorded a newsworthy real world event onto a vast visual data bank. The journalist's Knowbot, an expert news 'agent' consisting of specially trained expert systems software, recognises the importance of the story and draws her attention to it. Instantly the hack can re-view the event and, if dramatic enough, she can code it for instant transmission on *Newswatch*, the 24-hour surveillance camera channel. A camcopter may be diverted if the story is judged likely to develop significantly and, if it is really big news, a piloted helicopter will be despatched. Otherwise multimedia background information on the story is downloaded to her Personal Information Assistant as the reporter fights her way through the low-tech traffic jam in search of the ever-elusive exclusive. If she is truly multiskilled she will be motorbike-capable and have an advantage over her four-wheel competitors. Arriving at the scene she proceeds to record additional elements of the story, 'filming' using solid state digital recording equipment, effectively the equivalent of wearing glasses and a Walkman. If the story is big enough, she can inject live into a global, national or local news network. Her kit has both its own IP number (Internet address) and an on-board GPS (global positioning system) which identifies, locates it and routes its output transparently using the appropriate combination of microwave, satellite and landlines. If the story is not thought worthy of instant live transmission, the twenty first century hack shoots the pictures and assembles the story using her Intelligent recorder and the news templates she has developed over the years. Using these aids there should be very little need for editing as such, but should any post-production be required the same video goggles which recorded the images become the head up display screens of her virtual edit suite, controlled by the hand-held picture pack. The journalist recomposes the visuals and records the voice-overs for presentation in various forms. Thus 'edited' the package need not be sent back to base but can be transmitted straight from the reporter's kit onto a dedicated rolling news service, while a longer premium version is filed on a pay-per-view news-on-demand video server. Marked with her unique digital signature, the story is automatically downloaded to the home servers of all her subscribers who are informed that her story is there. A limited version is available on-line for those possessing only antiquated technologies such as the World Wide Web, and the story will also be available in printed form the next morning on reusable polymer news-sheets. There is even a version as ink on dead trees. This genuinely exclusive, premium service, is available only to those elites lucky enough to be above being merely wired; those who can afford the real value-added service of having someone else edit out the news from the incessant information flow and present it to them.

Hype and superhype

Any vaguely aware member of the media-consuming classes today cannot help but have been aware of a flood of digital hype flowing inexorably from the supposedly soon to be obsolete, but surprisingly hyperactive, printing presses of the planet. A subset of the revolutionary claims being made for the new digital technologies are the changes that are prophesied for newsgathering and consumption. The scenario outlined above is perhaps a wild exaggeration; a foray into the very risky business of predicting the future. Such visions create either techno-wonder, sceptical amusement or instant dismissal amongst disinterested readers, but the subject is of great concern, and not only to those who pontificate about the digital revolution. It is a matter of professional life and death to those journalists immediately affected for whom it is not just talk of some vague future but today's reality where television reporters are about to become something else.

VJs and BJs

Lightweight camcorders now make it possible for video journalists, or VJs, to operate as one person newsgathering units, unencumbered by the baggage of 'the crew'. Instead of reporter, camera operator, sound recorder and possibly a fixer/producer, it is now possible to despatch one person who, having shot the story, can then return to base and edit the material into a transmittable package. This mode of working which started with TV 3 in Bergen in 1988 has been adopted by two cable news operations in New York and London. Both called Channel One, these 24-hour rolling local news stations are funded by newspaper industry backers and employ specially trained multiskilled VJs instead of specialist reporters, camera operators, sound recordists and videotape editors. Michael Rosenblum, an American consultant who advised both Channel One operations, describes the new camcorders as being 'the video equivalent of the Leica', a liberating lightweight technology which replaces the labouring beast of the crew with the flexible single-person newsgatherer, doing for television news what the 35 mm stills camera did for photojournalism. He sees the new technologies as giving television news certain advantages that print journalism already has. Roaming unobtrusively, armed only with a notebook computer and mobile phone, the newspaper reporter doesn't have the logistical limitations that restrict the lumbering television crew. Such a reporter can research, write and file a story unassisted. Soon, with new technologies, television journalists will be able to do the equivalent with equal ease.

There are other advantages, says Rosenblum, demanding that television news should 'introduce the spike'. All too often the commitment of scarce technical resources means broadcasters have to use the material produced by a reporter and crew whether or not it is up to scratch. There should be no need to air substandard video material just to fill the screen, as suddenly news organisations can have 30 or 40 crews where they once might have had 10, and, given this increased input, it is possible to be much more discerning. New technologies and the working methods that they make possible will give television the same advantages as print in terms of news-gathering flexibility, and they will give television news a greater ability to take risks.

There is a certain inevitability about such developments, not because of simple technological determinism, as if the technology somehow foisted itself on the profession, but because of management led economic decisions. 'Make no mistake, this is cost driven', says Ted Taylor, Director of Technology at ITN, who speaks of 'journotechs' capable of writing copy and editing pictures with equal ease. In his estimation, seven functions in the production process would be removed by such multiskilling. Chris Cramer, then Head of BBC Television Newsgathering, told assembled hacks at an international conference simply: 'Video journalism will hit you whether you like it or not'. Already, BBC *World* and CBC *Newsworld* are employing specially equipped and trained VJs or BJs (broadcast journalists) and the BBC recently bought its regional correspondents Hi-8 camcorders, while CNN executives openly talk of 'job compression'. Management, many of whom have never done the jobs in question and who often come from an engineering background, make cost led decisions about equipment provision which inevitably result in working practices changing radically. What effect such changes have on journalistic output appears to be rarely considered.

In the United States the revolution is already happening by default. Hard-pressed stations running local news operations on a shoestring are paying poverty wages to recent communications and journalism school graduates who slave using all too old technology to file two or three stories a day, reporting, shooting and editing alone in the vain hope that such Herculean labour will one day raise them into the realm of such high earners as Peter Jennings, Dan Rather and Christiane Amanpour. The mere mention of such working practices becoming the norm is enough, however, to send many of today's established journalists into apoplectic sound bite. Martin Bell, whose reporting for the BBC from Bosnia has attracted universal professional acclaim, says with characteristic brevity that he hopes he'll be underground when it arrives as common practice, and his colleague Michael Buerk expresses a concern that 'journalism will suffer'. Jon Snow is equally sceptical:

> The trend towards multi-skilling is limited. One person cannot do the job of five and I am worried that information loses out to delivery. . . . There has to be a recognition that people who can write and report have different skills from those who operate cameras (1996, p. 23).

One-man bands

There is in fact nothing new about single-person newsgathering. The BBC's *Television Newsreel* coverage of the Korean War was conducted first by cameraman Cyril Page and then by Ronnie Noble, both of them working for the most part alone. They used lightweight 35 mm cameras and were able to record some actuality sound, including interviews with soldiers conducted by a newspaper reporter named Alan Whicker who would of course make his own unique contribution to the development of British television.

Clockwork Simplex and small Arriflexes film cameras, which were literally hand-held, unlike the shoulder-mounted beasts of today, have been around for decades. Such cameras recorded mute film only, and with the demand for synchronous location-recorded sound, equipment necessarily became heavier. Nevertheless, news agency staff and many stringers regularly worked alone, capable of recording broadcast quality sound and pictures on 16 mm film.

Nik Downing, a former SAS soldier, filmed the war in Rhodesia alone, and later, with heavier U-matic video equipment, worked without a crew in Afghanistan. Arthur Kent covered the same story as a freelance one man band and has subsequently made a 16 mm documentary film about Bosnia. Sue Lloyd-Roberts, working first for ITN and now for the BBC, has been a one woman band recording first on S-VHS, and now Hi-8. She started such work behind the Iron Curtain when there was such a thing, and moved on, recently travelling around China with dissident Harry Wu, filming secret forced labour camps. Often questions of access force such working practices on journalists who can hardly film undercover with a full crew. Lloyd-Roberts describes her work as 'enormous fun' and doesn't understand why more people don't do it. Such notable exceptions certainly prove that it is possible, although, to be fair, Lloyd-Roberts herself doesn't think the practice should be universal and points out that she never travels alone and that all the material is edited by dedicated editors on her return.

Outside of the hurly-burly of news, other areas of programming have employed new video technologies, even going so far as to give the public the equipment. The BBC's *Video Diaries*, recorded on Hi-8 videotape, have extended the envelope of what is technically and editorially possible. This example has been followed by others, including *Undercover Britain,* investigative documentaries filmed with hidden cameras, and travel programmes. There has always been a traditional broadcast standard of technically acceptable picture quality. In the days of film, 16 mm was above this threshold, but 'amateur' 8 mm cine-film was not. When videotape arrived as the newsgathering standard, Hi-band U-matic was acceptable whereas technically inferior Lo-band was not. Similarly, Super-VHS has been a minimum acceptable standard used by stringers, but domestic VHS has been declared beyond the pale. Cynics suggest that these broadcast standards are merely artificial barriers designed to stem the tide of material streaming into television organisations, and to some extent this is true, but of course anything really unique and vital gets used regardless of the picture quality, witness the 8 mm film of JFK's assassination and the camcorder footage of Israeli Premier Rabin's murder which went for £50 000 for UK television rights alone. Countless examples of VHS camcorder footage now appear on everything, from the news to light entertainment programming. One senior newsgathering executive even goes so far as to suggest that his organisation should hand out cheap camcorders to travellers at Heathrow and other airports, claiming that such an exercise would result in 150 useable stories a year. Cynics might remark that video holiday snaps and poolside nudity would be the likely result rather than a stream of world exclusives.

When an orthodox crew is sent abroad they very often take a spare camera 'channel' to guard against what would be very expensive equipment failure. This second camcorder very often gets deployed in the hands of the recordist, providing the team with more 'camera power' and, as the team's reporter can clearly only be in one place, this second unit very often becomes a one man band. During the admittedly special circumstances of the Gulf War, ITN cameraman Jim Dutton filmed alone inside Iraq and was then interviewed from London about what he had seen and filmed. *Newsnight* correspondent Mark Urban and Producer Steve Anderson covered the same conflict from the Saudi side, working at times without what they called 'a proper crew'. After this experience Urban says:

> I don't think one should be under any doubt though, that obviously the pro cameraman is going to make a better job of it . . . there's a loss of quality. You have to be able to justify in terms either of the old thing of being too intrusive, four people with a proper camera on a tripod and all the rest of it, or some other need to get into some bizarre inaccessible place.

Another foreign correspondent said he could not see any reason whatsoever why he shouldn't be able to edit. He suggested that in some cases you didn't necessarily need journalists and suggested the way forward, in some instances, was to send camera operators out and then interview them about what they had seen and recorded. Indeed, this way of working has existed in certain variations since the days of the newsreels. It is certainly more common than people might think for crews to work independent of reporters and producers, for whatever reason.

Will it work?

Clearly, the supposed revolution is to some extent already under way, but what it will mean for the nature of television news is not quite clear. Radio has depended on single person newsgathering and editing for years, using reel-to-reel tape recorders, low-tech razor blades and cellotape. Little comment is made about this technologically enabled revolution and it would be hard to point to any perceptible decrease in the quality of radio journalism that is attributable to single-person working.

Television news stringers sent to shoot pictures and natural sound only nevertheless often conduct basic interviews with, say, a fire officer or policeman at the scene of an event. Yorkshire Television's local news magazine programme, *Calendar,* has for some years employed a woman stringer, who was originally a journalist, working with S-VHS equipment. When I asked her about the shortcomings of such working methods she replied simply that there was no one else to share the driving.

In extreme circumstances, such as Bosnia, overriding security and safety considerations tend to lead to the smallest crew possible, usually two-person teams of reporter and camera operator plus a locally hired interpreter/fixer. With a team any smaller, there is not enough support, and with a crew any larger the risks increase. Tony Birtley, working for ITN and ABC, filmed alone in Bosnia, winning awards for his exclusive despatches. From a purely pragmatic point of view, it is simply a case of horses for courses.

Teamwork often increases efficiency, with two heads or three being better than one. A second pair of eyes can often be crucial, it being all too easy for a camera operator to become so engrossed in filming that they simply do not notice something of importance happening just out of shot. In my own experience working as a director, I very often noticed things that the camera operator, with an eye to the viewfinder, did not. Equally, personal experience from the other end of the equation, doing camera work in educational programme-making, has confirmed this, with it clearly being very easy to become so engrossed in filming that one simply does not notice something of importance happening just out of shot.

Working in a team makes it possible to arrive at a location and split up, with the reporter talking to people and getting a feel for the story before doing any interviews, while the camera operator shoots general views. Once interviews start each member of the team can concentrate on their own role, for an interview of any length is hard enough to conduct properly without worrying about the size of shot and the sound levels.

Once the material is shot and the crew return to base the picture editor is effectively the first member of the audience, quite ready to question and to dismiss footage regardless of the time and trouble taken to obtain it. While the editor and reporter put the story together, the camera crew are redundant. Oddly enough they rarely look at their own material and there is a case to be made that they should in fact edit it. Sheer pressure of time works against the multiskilling ethic. If a job takes two person-hours to complete, the single person newsgatherer will need two hours, no doubt missing a deadline, while a team of two will do the same job in one hour.

Technically speaking, multiskilled operation is not a problem. In my experience undergraduate students can learn to shoot and edit easily enough, but they have notable trouble doing the difficult job of creating structure in a time-based visual medium. The human skills needed for the task should not be underestimated. Whatever the technology there is still a need to have a 'nose for news', to go to the right place in the first place and negotiate the access needed, a delicate balancing act that no technology will aid, to ask the right people the right questions, and to possess the background knowledge needed to set the event in context. As input turns to output, as newsgathering becomes broadcasting, the multiskilled journotech must be able to write concise copy that complements pictures, have a good broadcasting voice to record those words, possess an appropriate on-screen manner that 'comes through the glass', not to mention the steady nerves and technical skill required to broadcast live to half the globe while a producer back at base is screaming in your earpiece telling you what to say and some demented zealot is unloading his AK 47 in your general direction.

Great skill in using words and pictures together is not always apparent on our screens today. Few reporters are good film-makers and in my experience they certainly don't think of themselves that way. Writing is still the most valued of a reporter's skills. Will this change with new technologies putting the reporter behind the camera? In terms of professional culture change it is very early days yet and the enabling technologies are likewise in their infancy, regardless of what their proponents claim. Broadcast journalism is constantly evolving. In 1936, when BBC television first went on the air, it would have been a foolish person who would have predicted 24-hour a day global television news networks or indeed even predicted 'the news'.

Revolution or evolution?

Actual investigation on the ground reveals that the revolution is not quite so advanced as some would have you believe. Channel One, London, actually employ fairly standard middleweight technology, and, although their VJs shoot their own stories, the stories are almost all edited by dedicated technicians. Moving totally to multiskilling was seen as 'a step too much' by news editor Peter Wallace. The organisation has small lightweight Hi-8 camcorders, but given the choice almost all newsgathering is done on the same Beta SP camcorders that more orthodox broadcasters use. The professional credibility that comes with professional kit is important. Equally, non-linear digital editing exists at Channel One, London, in the form of state-of-the-art AVID Newscutters, but any time-critical news story is still edited using videotape, simply because it is faster. When asked what was at the top of his technology wish list Channel One's Head of News replied that he would be happy with a simple two-machine video edit suite in a van.

Their revolution, if it is indeed a revolution, is that they have tried to use newer working methods. Channel One in New York use ordinary taxicabs to get around, and Channel One in London has its own cab. Channel One originally had a chauffeured motorbike to take VJs through the London traffic, but the motorbike driver has now become the capital's most mobile cameraman. The station 'runs on the enthusiasm of the VJs' according to a Press Officer. It is one thing, however, to be the first to have a camera at the scene of a fire to get an exclusive shot of the outside of a blackened building and quite another to have the journalistic skills required to report the Scott Inquiry or interview a doe-eyed Princess orchestrating her marriage break-up in public.

What BBC *World* anchor Nik Gowing has described as the 'robo hack' of the future, will need to be Robert Fiske, Maggie O'Kane, Martin Bell, Christiane Amanpour, Eammon McCabe and Don McCullin rolled into one multiskilled miracle worker whose work we encounter as we surf through the 500 digital channels. But in the uniskilled world of today, Robert Fiske and Martin Bell are exceptions rather than the rule. Technology may make certain mechanical tasks easier, but it does not necessarily make the journalism better; it offers opportunities, but they must be realised. Technical developments and institutional change made possible the journalism of Ed Murrow and Richard Dimbleby, but those opportunities had to be taken by enterprising and talented broadcasters who defined a form with their own unique work. Multiskilling may lead to work that is a pale imitation of the real thing, but, equally likely, somewhere a young man or woman, looking through a viewfinder, will go on to define a new form of visual journalism that in time will make television news look like the cinema newsreel. The huge unionised crews of the 1970s and early 1980s didn't automatically lead to good television journalism. Often the most important considerations were parking and catering. A friend who worked on *Thames at Six* as a free-lancer, literally making up the union-required numbers, said that airborne pigs were more likely to arise from such a situation than either good film-making or good journalism.

Perhaps the most efficient and socially agreeable solution would be a two-person operation of journalistically competent producer and reporter both of whom could perform the technical tasks of camera, sound and editing. Background research and logistics could be conducted by either, and one would present the piece while the other effectively directed it, conducting the filming with the visual very much in mind. This would be something very like the current affairs way of working (minus the crew) and could result in a more visually dynamic, medium-appropriate style.

Television will change, offering a wider range of diverse services from raw footage to the polished documentary. This diversity of product will result from an equally diverse range of working methods. The world of the journotech of the future, with which we began, is clearly some way off, but if this twenty-first-century descendent of Kate Adie is to do her job properly she will need more than simply the enabling technology. She will need education and training, experience in a supported environment and institutions that care about her, the story and the viewers and who are not just obsessed with trying to keep the cost numbers down and the audience numbers up.

Packaging

Back at base, in the newsroom of the not too distant future, young journalists sit at their electronic news production system (ENPS) digital work-station. Input, in the form of the news agency wires and picture feeds, is now integrated into one endless flow of digital data arriving on the young hack's screen. As is the case today, there is something of a picture flood, with images often arriving unaccompanied by descriptive copy or a shotlist. Many of the agency pictures are little more than wallpaper, formal settings, full of shots of people getting out of cars outside negotiations. Some less well resourced organisations are totally dependent on this third-party input and there is even a tendency for major networks to rely on this material for foreign coverage instead of sending expensive teams themselves: 'when *Nightly* [News, NBC] needs breaking foreign news footage, they'll just dip into the "video river" and script it from the wire services' (Kent, 1996, p. 158). Ironically, as technology has arrived that makes foreign news gathering easier and quicker, such reporting is in danger of disappearing from some services:

CBS is putting on very little foreign news. Reporting and writing skills, knowledge of background, history, language, economics are no longer considered vital for the new broadcasters. Information, even pre-written scripts can be provided in the field through a laptop computer. Pictures? Why send our own crew when you can lift what you need off the airways? One satellite dish up, two or three bureaus [*sic*] down (quoted in Kimball, 1994, p. 142).

Journotechs on the desk edit these pictures at their workstation and, using the wires as source, write voice-overs which they record using lip-mics. It is certainly possible now to 'package' Parliament without going near the place, indeed without getting out of your chair. Increasingly there is a separation of input and output, newsgathering and broadcasting. Whereas these functions had always previously been clearly delineated inside news services, they are now often done by different organisations. The Reuters–Sky News relationship is a prime example of this, with Reuters supplying the material from which the news is packaged. The newsroom is where the real, digitally enabled, changes will take place. News is gathered only once but can be packaged many ways (or so we are told). The disk-based video server is creating a new multiskilled, desk-based journalist, very like a battery hen.

Robo hack and the battery hen

The future, then, presents two roles for the journalist: the robo hack on location and the battery hen at base. In the field the harassed and harried hack is linked all too well into the system, with too many jobs to do while the desk-based journalist never leaves the building, swamped by the enormous input of material which needs to be 'packaged'. The standards set over the years by the BBC, ITN and the American networks may be lost, or dynamic new forms may emerge. Too much is at stake just to leave it to chance or the accountants.

Suggestions of the future of television news

There is a case to be made for more applied research whereby television professionals and researchers acquainted with the practices of television news actually investigate the process of newsgathering and production. The aim of such work would be to improve the quality of the output and to integrate the new technologies effectively. In the day-to-day rush of ordinary programme production it is very difficult even to get a programme on-air without there being much scope for self-analysis. Nevertheless, such reflexive, applied research can in the end produce an improvement in the production process. Most television production organisations limit their use of research to audience issues, with such work conducted by third-party commercial researchers or by in-house research departments. Generally speaking, programme-makers neither understand this research nor trust it.

Production-orientated, reflective, applied research would certainly be possible to do. The practical problems of such an approach should not be underestimated. Television professionals and process researchers are two occupations which are distinct, calling for different skills and aptitudes. American-style news consultants were not set up for this kind of activity and inevitably have economies of scale in mind, with the results of their research being sold to a large number of diverse organisations. Their recommendations about the 'look and feel' of a programme are often very similar, resulting in an identifiable style of programme which arises in different local markets, with knowledgeable observers actually being able to tell which news consultant has been employed by which American local TV station. Reflexive applied research conducted by suitable trained practitioners, working in conjunction with researchers from other backgrounds, could potentially create a dynamic of information, knowledge and understanding to feed back into the actual production process itself. News has just arrived as a form through years of organic development. It could be different, says one senior figure:

> I don't actually think that anybody knows what television news is to be honest. I think the people who work in it have never really found out, and I bet you they would just tell you 'oh we cover everything that moves'. That's all the way it is. 'If it's happening, we're there, we've got it'. And what do I think it is? Well I think to some extent it is a serious attempt to address what's going on day to day, but it's also a con, because a lot of what is portrayed as being new information is in fact old information regurgitated. And the viewer knows it too. And I actually think that news bulletins have become blander and more interchangeable. I think you could shut your eyes and open them again and you would not be certain of what you were watching whereas at least if you were reading *The Independent* you could tell if somebody's replaced page 10 with page 10 of *The Guardian*. I think it's incredible that we've got four channels here and in essence they're all doing exactly the same thing. I think *Channel 4 News* and *Newsnight* are the kind of nodding gesture towards needing to do something more profound. But at the end of the day people take their information off the 9 o'clock and the 10 o'clock or the 5.40 or the 6 o'clock. And they, I think, are doing exactly the same things. Possibly ITN slightly more downmarket, but in essence the same. I can't believe that the day is not much more variegated than that. You really could come up with something absolutely distinctly different.

Most news professionals would be horrified at the thought of news doctors, management consultants and academic researchers joining them in the search for new forms. Such a proposal evokes the old adage that a camel is a horse designed by a committee, which maligns camels and committees alike. Certainly, there is a case for cross-fertilisation and for applied research and development. Ironically it will probably not be done by existing organisations and experienced professionals but by adventurous youngsters exploring the creative and journalistic possibilities in the territory between traditional television and the Internet.

Information flow

A general observation that has arisen from some of the newsroom visits undertaken for this study has been the way in which such environments, although highly attuned to information retrieval and news production, do not often have certain parts of the system sufficiently equipped for the task. Film libraries and newspaper cuttings provide journalists with recycled information from their own world. This is supplemented by the activities of individual journalists ranging from personal document libraries to the simple reading of the day's newspapers. Many newsrooms have a small, and inevitably tattered and decimated, collection, with *Who's who* and other reference books gathering dust. Some television organisations maintain reasonably stocked reference libraries, although the proximity of these to the newsroom is often less than ideal. These professionally equipped libraries can be extremely useful, but in many cases they service other parts of a larger organisation.

On-line databases supplement the existing news sources and are seen for the most part to be underused by television professionals and, although these are certainly no panacea, greater use of these might be made. Nowadays most librarians are trained in information science, with a detailed knowledge of databases and how to use them, but this type of information professional is underused by journalism organisations. There is the case to be made for having a kind of hybrid, information retrieval training in traditional journalism education. There is a potential for research here to discover what would be required by way of improving the information available to journalists working on a desktop, either by means of information reference support and on-line information, continually bearing in mind that the most important newsgathering technology will always be the telephone and nothing will replace plain old-fashioned digging, provided there is time to do some before the next two-way.

Whither television news?

Morale is not good in any of the traditional news organisations. All three American networks' news divisions and ITN have had substantial job cuts and the commercial pressures on all broadcasters have led to downmarket, increasingly tabloid, agendas with less foreign news. The Birtian reforms at the BBC have had little good said about them by most BBC staff. Such re-organisations are inevitably unpopular, especially among people losing their livelihood and with professionals being told how to do their job. There are frequent complaints that journalism is changing for the worse, with fewer resources, more pressure, more bi-media deadlines and the perceived threat of multiskilling, devaluing traditional excellence.

The shotgun wedding of news and current affairs is not seen as a happy one. Making 50-minute *Panorama* films and 'the breathless one minute 40 seconds' of television news are very different skills, and few journalists can move from one form to the other easily. Not long after the birth of radio news, a commentator in the *Radio Times* remarked that bulletins were arbitrary and fragmented and concluded that 'the general import of unadorned news without explanation, illustration or commentary was hard to grasp' (Scannell and Cardiff, 1991, p. 117). The danger that broadcast news can become a ceaseless flow of discrete dramatic events without any pattern is perhaps endemic to the form. The institutional separation of news and current affairs was one solution to the problem, allowing each discipline to concentrate on its strengths. Radio talks and television newsreels historically provided a balance to the hard news of the main bulletins. This variety could be said to serve the audience better, but only if it takes advantage of such diversity.

Pictures, the great advantage television has over the print media, are in one sense also a problem, one which the Birt–Jay thesis did not address directly. Although they attacked 'the documentary film ethos' (Birt and Jay, 1975a, p. 12) and the effect it had on journalism, they never explained what their mission would look like. Like it or not, in television there has to be something on the screen and it was not clear that Birt or Jay fully appreciated the visual imperatives. Too often pictures appear with relatively little connection to the words and it is not unknown for correspondents to script stories, the visuals of which are entirely from the library. It has been suggested (Gallagher, 1996) that the implementation of the mission to explain has led to a visually impoverished television news which stands in contrast to ITN which still maintains its traditional picture and news values.

Has the 'mission to explain' succeeded? 'I think that we do abandon the viewers very often to a sort of jumble of facts which we throw at them without a framework', one senior newscaster told me in 1992, well into the Birtian revolution. Perhaps television is not a medium for explanation. This is the view of one correspondent:

> it is not about analysis at the end of the day, it's about perception and we are in the business of putting over perception and it is the most powerful way of putting over perception, but it is not the most powerful way of putting over analysis. I know John Birt would kind

of hang me at dawn for saying that, but I do firmly believe it to be the case.

Ask 100 viewers to tell you the difference between a Serb and a Croat and only two or three per cent will know, even after years of detailed television news coverage, current affairs analysis and broadsheet journalism. The same ignorance, sadly, could be found regarding Northern Ireland, after more than two decades of reporting.

Together with radical institutional change, increased commercial pressure and new working methods there seems to be a move downmarket in all television news. Often this is described as Americanisation and is far from popular among professionals:

American news programmes are like an ashtray of world television. They are absolutely awful and yet there are a lot of people who kind of want to push, a lot of people; a lot of executives who want to push British television news in that sort of direction. I just want to sink people like that in concrete. I just do not begin to understand it.

The changes in American network news are well documented and certainly point to a certain recognisable transformation. With diversity now much more possible, ironically everything starts to look the same:

There is an inhibiting, discouraging sameness to TV news. The journalism schools, consultants, researchers, timid corporate executives, and narrowly targeted audiences have had the impact of reducing TV news to a spongy blur existing in a narrow framework of creativity. . . . It is as though each city out there had three or five or seven newspapers, and each had the same format, the same target audience, the same editorial attitude, the same photographs (quoted in Kimball, 1994, p. 17).

This comment comes not from a disgruntled junior reporter frustrated in his rise to stardom, or a left-wing sociologist raging against the media, but from a former President of CBS News, and he is far from alone in holding such views. Audiences are falling, both for fixed-point and for rolling news, and, as ratings drop, viewers are chased more actively. Changes are made in order to hold audiences which may in fact have the opposite effect. Indeed, this blind search for audience becomes a form of bias.

And thus we end with the headline with which we began, with the vexed notion of bias. Much of television news is biased precisely because it is live and direct, giving a different slant on the world, possibly exciting, possibly accurate, possibly boring and possibly misleading, for not everything important happens in range of the rooftop camera or the helicopter. Some things need explaining; some do not. Some events television can explain; some it cannot; some it can merely relay. We need to see television news both for what it is and for what it is not. We need to understand its inherent biases and weaknesses and its undoubted strengths. It is good at pictures and bad at words. It can illustrate what we have read about in our morning papers or scoop them by hours.

As we move into the much hyped, digitally enabled, multichannel future many things will happen. Step changes now underway will mean tri-media 24-hour rolling news with reporters filing for radio, television and for on-line services. All manner of personalised services are possible, with the Chomsky Channel, Tebbit Television and the Newt Network just some of the 500 or more digital services available. News will continue to grow and diversify. In 1979, a television executive, giving a public lecture, warned his peers:

> If television fails to adopt a more pluralist approach, it will continue to have no clear line behind which to stand, and no call to which to rally. It will become more and more vulnerable to a lack of confidence within and to an attack from without. If we don't reform ourselves others may do it for us; and we won't like the result (Birt, 1979, p. 71).

He went on to hold up a slim optical fibre and to explain that

> we now have the technology to create a television publishing market as open as the print publishing market is. Anyone with a camera and video recorder would be free to publish a programme at any time, and to charge the price they wanted for it. The viewer's set would be metered and the producer re-imbursed (1979, p. 71).

John Birt's vision of the future has not yet arrived. Technology has not yet moved us from the broadcast model of mass communications to the on-demand publishing model, and in the mean time we must try and make sense of the news we have, watching it in all its increasingly varied forms. We must watch it with a certain degree of knowingness, perhaps with copy of *Bad news* to hand, treating each with equal scepticism, each as a valuable source in the formation of one's own knowledge and opinions. It is an abdication of personal responsibility to expect the television news (or any other media source) to provide us with a complete view without any effort on our part. To some extent we get the news we deserve, and whether that is just 24 hours of the 'white noise of the news' (Katz, 1996, p. 2) or something more profound depends on what active role we play in assembling our own jigsaw of truth. Whatever map we have, we still have to navigate ourselves.

References and further reading

Abramson, A. 1995: The invention of television. In Smith, A. (ed.), *Television: an international history*. Oxford: Oxford University Press, 13–34.

Allen, T., Berry, F. and Polmar, N. 1991: *CNN: War in the gulf*. New York: Maxwell-Macmillan.

Alter, J. 1991: When CNN hit its target. *Newsweek* 28 January, 41.

Anderson, S. 1990: Who calls the shots? *The Listener* 22 November, 14–15.

Annan 1977: *Report of the Committee on the Future of Broadcasting*. Chairman: Lord Annan. London: HMSO.

Arnett, P. 1994: *Live from the battlefield*. London: Bloomsbury.

Atkinson, R. 1994: *Crusade: the untold story of the Gulf War*. New York: Harper Collins.

Auletta, K. 1991: *Three blind mice*. New York: Random House.

Banks-Smith, N. 1994: Cameras roll, it's intervention. *The Guardian* 20 September, G2, 24.

Barnett, S. and Curry, A. 1994: *The battle for the BBC*. London: Aurum Press.

Barnouw, E. 1968: *The golden web; a history of broadcasting in the United States, 1933–53*. New York: Oxford University Press.

Barnouw, E. 1970: *The image empire: a history of broadcasting in the United States from 1953*. New York: Oxford University Press.

BBC 1992: *BBC English dictionary*. London: Harper Collins.

Bell, M. 1995: *In harm's way: reflections of a war zone thug*. London: Hamish Hamilton.

Birt, J. 1975: Can television news break the understanding-barrier. *The Times* 28 February, 14.

Birt, J. 1979: Freedom and the broadcaster. Clive Goodwin Lecture 1979. Rpt. In *Television and the real world*. Edinburgh Television Festival programme, 1980.

Birt, J. and Jay, P. 1975a: Television journalism: the child of an unhappy marriage between newspapers and film. *The Times* 30 September, 12.

Birt, J. and Jay, P. 1975b: The radical changes needed to remedy TV's bias against understanding. *The Times* 1 October, 14.

Birt, J. and Jay, P. 1976a: How television news can hold the mass audience. *The Times* 2 September, 12.

Birt, J. and Jay, P. 1976b: Why television news is in danger of becoming an anti-social force. *The Times* 3 September, 6.

Blumler, J. and Gurevitch, M. 1995: *The crisis of public communication.* London: Routledge.

Boden, D. 1991: Reinventing the global village. Paper presented to European University Institute, Florence.

Bolton, R. 1990: *Death on the rock and other stories.* London: W. H. Allen.

Bolton, R. 1995: Agenda benders. *New Statesman and Society* (24 March), 4–6.

Boyer, P. 1988: *Who killed CBS?: the undoing of America's number one news network.* New York: Random House.

Breed, W. 1955: Social control in the newsroom. *Social forces* 33, 326–35.

Briggs, A. 1961: *The birth of broadcasting: the history of broadcasting in the United Kingdom Volume 1.* London: Oxford University Press.

Briggs, A. 1965: *The golden age of wireless: the history of broadcasting in the United Kingdom Volume 2.* London: Oxford University Press.

Briggs, A. 1970: *The war of words: the history of broadcasting in the United Kingdom Volume 3.* London: Oxford University Press.

Briggs, A. 1979: *Governing the BBC.* London: BBC Publications.

Briggs, A. 1985: *The BBC; the first fifty years.* Oxford: Oxford University Press.

Briggs, A. 1995: *Competition: the history of broadcasting in the United Kingdom Volume 5.* London: Oxford University Press.

Broadcast 1995: In-production supplement, 9 June, 9.

Burns, T. 1977: *The BBC: public institution and private world.* London: Macmillan.

Chambers 1992: *Chambers English dictionary.* 7th edn. Edinburgh: W & R Chambers.

Collins, R. 1990: Walling Germany with brass: theoretical paradigms in British studies of television news. In *Television: policy and culture.* London: Unwin Hyman, 225–54.

Corner, J. 1995a: Media studies and the 'knowledge problem'. *Screen* 36, 147–55.

Corner, J. 1995b: *Television form and public address.* London: Arnold.

Cottle, S. 1993: *TV news, urban conflict and the inner city.* Leicester: Leicester University Press.

Cox, G. 1995: *Pioneering television news.* London: John Libbey.

CNN 1995: Press release, Atlanta.

Culbert, D. 1988: Television's Vietnam and historical revisionism in the United States. *Historical Journal of Film, Radio and Television* 8, no. 3, 253–68.

Culf, A. 1993: CNN wins the media war with its continuous live coverage. *The Guardian* 5 October, 3.

Culf, A. 1995a: A bigger bash. *The Guardian* 6 March, G2, 14.

Culf, A. 1995b: Greenpeace used us broadcasters admit. *The Guardian* 28 August, 5.

Culf, A. 1995c: BBC changes tack on Greenpeace. *The Guardian* 11 November, 3.

Culf, A. 1996: The global news frenzy. *The Guardian* 6 March, G2, 16–17.

Daily Telegraph 1979: Electronics and British trade unionism: how compatible? 6 July, 16.

Day, R. 1990: *Grand inquisitor*. London: Pan.

Deacon, D. and Golding, P. 1994: *Taxation and representation: the media, political communication and the poll tax.* London: John Libbey.

Dennis, E. 1989: *Reshaping the media: mass communication in an information age.* Newbury Park: Sage.

Dexter, L. and White, D. (eds) 1964: *People, society, and mass communications.* New York: Free Press.

Donovan, R. and Scherer, R. 1992: *Unsilent revolution: television news and American public life, 1948–1991.* Cambridge: Cambridge University Press.

Dowden, R. 1994: Satellite dishes amid the Iron Age spears. *The Independent* 13 April, 9.

Dugdale, J. 1995: Seeing and believing. *The Guardian* 4 September, G2, 12.

Duncan, A. 1987: Power behind the screen. *The Observer Magazine* 22 January, 29–37.

Duncan, A. 1996: Mixing with the media. *Despatches: The Journal of the Territorial Army Pool of Public Information Officers* no. 6, 13–32.

Economist, The 1992: Armchair generalship. 2 May, 78.

Engel, M. 1996: Waves of unrest. *The Guardian* 20 June, G2, 3.

Epstein, E. 1973: *News from nowhere.* New York: Random House.

Ericson, R., Baranek, P. and Chan, J. 1987: *Visualizing deviance: a study of news organization.* Milton Keynes: Open University Press.

Ericson, R., Baranek, P. and Chan, J. 1989: *Negotiating control: a study of news sources.* Milton Keynes: Open University Press.

Ericson, R., Baranek, P. and Chan, J. 1991: *Representing order: crime, law and justice in the news media.* Milton Keynes: Open University Press.

Fairhall, D. 1996: How they played those Patriot games. *The Guardian* 15 January, 42.

Feingold, D. 1996: Television news – where things are going. Paper presented to the International Newsfilm Conference. British Film Institute, 2 October.

Fiddick, P. 1993: BBC and CNN go to war. *The Times* 6 January, 30.

Fiddick, P. 1995: Here is the news. *Journal of the Royal Television Society* 32, no. 10 (November/December) 10.

Fielding, R. 1972: *The American newsreel*. Norman: University of Oklahoma Press.

Flournoy, D. 1992: *CNN World Report: Ted Turner's international news coup*. London: John Libbey.

Frank, A. 1992: A third-world war: a political economy of the Persian Gulf War and the new world order. In Mowlana, H., Gerbner, G. and Schiller, H. (eds), *Triumph of the image: the media's war in the Persian gulf*. Boulder: Westview Press, 3–21.

Frank, R. 1991: *Out of thin air: the brief wonderful life of network news*. New York: Simon & Schuster.

Franklin, B. 1994: *Packaging politics: political communications in Britain's media democracy*. London: Arnold.

Gall, S. 1995: *News from the front: the life of a television reporter*. London: Mandarin.

Gallagher, T. 1996: Out of focus: the move away from picture culture in BBC Television news under John Birt. Bachelor of Broadcasting dissertation, Institute of Communications Studies, University of Leeds, Leeds.

Geertz, C. 1993: *The interpretation of cultures*. Reprint of 1973 edn. London: Fontana Press.

Gieber, W. 1956: Across the desk: a study of 16 telegraph editors. *Journalism Quarterly* 33, 423–32.

Gieber, W. 1960: How the 'gatekeepers' view local civil liberties news. *Journalism Quarterly* 37, 199–205.

Gieber, W. 1964: News is what newspapermen make it. In Dexter, L. and White, D. M. (eds) *People, society, and mass communications*. New York: Free Press, 173–82.

Glaister, D. 1996: War report. *The Guardian* 28 March, 17.

Goldie, G. 1977: *Facing the nations: television and politics 1936–76*. London: Bodley Head.

Golding, P. and Elliott, P. 1979: *Making the news*. London: Longman.

Gow, J., Paterson, R. and Preston, A. (eds) 1996: *Bosnia by television*. London: BFI.

Gowing, N. 1996: Confessions of a news gatherer. *Broadcast* 26 January, 13.

Greenberg, B. and Gantz, W. (eds) 1993: *Desert storm and the mass media*. Cresskill, NJ: Hampton Press.

Greene, H. 1969: *The third floor front: a view of broadcasting in the sixties*. London: Bodley Head.

Guardian, The 1991: 'Lord Haw-Haw' protest. 30 January, 2.

Guardian, The 1993: Where is the news? 1 May, 26.

GUMG 1976: *Bad news*. Glasgow University Media Group. London: Routledge and Kegan Paul.

GUMG 1980: *More bad news*. Glasgow University Media Group. London: Routledge and Kegan Paul.

GUMG 1982: *Really bad news*. Glasgow University Media Group. London: Writers & Readers.

GUMG 1985: *War and peace news*. Glasgow University Media Group. Milton Keynes: Open University Press.

GUMG 1993: *Getting the message: news truth and power*. Glasgow University Media Group. London: Routledge.

GUMG 1995: *Glasgow media group reader volume 1: news content, language and visuals*. Glasgow University Media Group. London: Routledge.

GUMG 1995: *Glasgow media group reader volume 2: industry, economy, war and politics*. Glasgow University Media Group. London: Routledge.

Gunter, B. 1987: *Poor reception*. Hillsdale, NJ: Lawrence Erlbaum.

Gurevitch, M. 1991: The globalization of electronic journalism. In Curran, J. and Gurevitch, M. (eds), *Mass media and society*. London: Edward Arnold, 178–93.

Halberstam, D. 1979: *The powers that be*. New York: Knopf.

Hall, S. 1973: The determination of news photographs. In Cohen, S. and Young, J. (eds) *The manufacture of news*. Beverly Hills: Sage, 176–90.

Hall, T. 1992: More news from the BBC. *The Independent* 23 September, 15.

Hallin, D. 1986: *The 'Uncensored War': the media and Vietnam*. New York: Oxford University Press.

Harris, R. 1983: *Gotcha: the media, the government and the Falklands crisis*. London: Faber.

Harrison, M. 1985: *TV news: whose bias?* Hermitage, Berks: Policy Journals.

Hartley, J. 1982: *Understanding news*. London: Methuen.

Hawker, P. 1993: ENG: expensive news gathering? *Television: The Journal of the Royal Television Society* 30 no. 1, 30–1.

Henry, W. 1992: History as it happens. *Time* 6 January, 1–21.

Hetherington, A. 1985: *News, newspapers and television*. London: Macmillan.

Hole, T. 1955: News. *The Times* National Radio Show supplement, 19 August, xii.

Hood, S. 1967: *A Survey of television*. London: Heinemann.

Hood, S. 1980: *On television*. London: Pluto Press.

Hopkinson, N. 1995: *The impact of new technology on the international media and foreign policy*. Norwich: HMSO.

Hurt, M. 1996: TXP 45: The European News Exchange. Bachelor of Broadcasting dissertation, Institute of Communications Studies, University of Leeds, Leeds.

Independent, The 1992: Blast proves wisdom of reinforcing no 10. 31 October, 2.

International Broadcasting 1995: That Simpson trial in full. November, 19.

International Broadcasting 1996: Major's plan to rival CNN. January, 9.

ITN 1995: *ITN – the first 40 years.*

Katz, I. 1996: Into thin air. *The Guardian* 21 August, G2, 2.

Keating, R. 1993: Yugoslavia: when reporters go over the top. *The Guardian* 18 January, 15.

Keegan, J. 1991: A plague on the BBC. *The Spectator* 2 March, 11–12.

Kellner, D. 1992: *The Persian Gulf TV war.* Boulder: Westview Press.

Kent, A. 1996: *Risk and redemption: surviving the network news wars.* New York: Viking Press.

Kimball, P. 1994: *Down-sizing the news: network cutbacks in the nation's capital.* Washington, DC: Woodrow Wilson Centre Press.

Knightley, P. 1975: *The first casualty: the war correspondent as hero, propagandist and myth maker from the Crimea to Vietnam.* London: Andre Deutsch.

Koch, T. 1990: *The news as myth: fact and context in journalism.* Westport, CT: Greenwood Press.

Koch, T. 1991: *Journalism in the 21st century: online information, electronic databases and the news.* Twickenham: Adamantine Press.

Lang, K. and Lang, G. 1953: The unique perspective of television and its effect: a pilot study. Reprinted in Corner, J. and Hawthorn, J. (eds) 1993: *Communications studies: an introductory reader.* 4th edn. London: Arnold, 185–97.

Lazarsfeld, P. 1948: The role of criticism in the management of mass media. *Journalism Quarterly* 25, 115–26.

Lichter, R., Rothman, S. and Lichter, L. 1986: *The media elite.* Bethesda, MD: Adler & Adler.

Listener, The 1954: Here is the news. 1 July, 8.

MacArthur, B. 1990: Mouth of the world. *The Guardian* 3 September, 21.

MacArthur, J. 1992: *Second front: censorship and propaganda in the Gulf War.* Berkeley: University of California Press.

MacGregor, B. 1993: 'Peter Arnett, CNN Reporting Live from Baghdad' *Film & History* 22, 26–33.

MacGregor, B. 1994: International television coverage of the bombing of the Baghdad 'Bunker' February 13, 1991. *Historical Journal of Film, Radio and Television* 14, no. 3, 241–68.

MacGregor, B. 1995: 'Our wanton abuse of the technology': television newsgathering in the age of the satellite. *Convergence* 1, no. 1, 80–93.

MacGregor, B. and Morrison, D. 1995: From focus groups to edit groups: a new method of reception analysis. *Media Culture and Society* 17, 141–50.

McManus, J. 1994: *Market-driven journalism: let the citizen beware.* Thousand Oaks: Sage.

McNair, B. 1994: *News and journalism in the UK.* London: Routledge.

McQuail, D. 1994: *Mass communication theory.* 3rd edn. London: Sage.

Mayer, M. 1987: *Making news.* Reprinted 1993. Boston: Harvard Business School Press.

Miall, L. 1994: *Inside the BBC: British broadcasting characters*. London: Weidenfeld and Nicolson.

Miller, M. 1988: TV's anti-liberal bias. *New York Times* 17 November.

Milne, A. 1988: *DG: the memoirs of a British broadcaster*. London: Hodder and Stoughton. 1989: Paperback edn. London: Coronet.

Morrison, D. 1992: *Television and the Gulf War*. London: John Libbey.

Morrison, D. and Tumber, H. 1988: *Journalists at war*. London: Sage.

Mowlana, H., Gerbner, G. and Schiller, H. (eds) 1992: *Triumph of the image; the media's war in the Persian Gulf*. Boulder: Westview Press.

Naughton, J. 1991: Hacked off with TV brigade. *The Observer* 3 March, 76.

Naughton, J. 1995: Fantasies of fact and fiction. *The Observer* Review 23 April, 25.

O'Kane, M. 1996: *How to tell lies and win wars*. Channel 4. 3 January.

Paulu, B. 1961: *British broadcasting in transition*. London: Macmillan.

Pavlik, J. and Thalhimer, M. 1991: The charge of the e-mail brigade: news technology comes of age. In LaMay, C., Fitzsimon, M. and Sahadi, J. (eds) *The media at war: the press and the Persian Gulf conflict*. New York: Gannett Foundation Media Center.

Perry, T. 1992: Forces for social change. *IEEE Spectrum* October, 30–2.

Philo, G. 1990: *Seeing and believing: the influence of television*. London: Routledge.

Pilger, J. 1991: Video nasties. *New Statesman and Society* 25 January, 7.

Pilger, J. 1992: *Distant voices*. London: Vintage Books.

Pilkington, E. 1993: Shots that shook the world. *The Guardian* 11 October, G2, 20.

Potter, J. 1990: *Independent television in Britain, volume 4; companies and programmes 1968–80*. Basingstoke: Macmillan.

Pound, R. 1954: Critic on the hearth: television broadcasting. *The Listener* 29 July, 186.

Preston, A. 1991: The impact of technology on current British television news bulletins. Unpublished MA thesis, Institute of Communications, University of Leeds, Leeds.

Preston, A. 1996: Television news and the Bosnian conflict. In Gow, J., Paterson, R., Preston, A. (eds), *Bosnia by television*. London: BFI, 112–15.

Pringle, P. 1993: Horror comes home. *The Independent* 13 October, 2–21.

Robinson, J. and Levy, M. 1986: *The main source: learning from television news*. Beverly Hills, CA: Sage.

Rojo, A. 1991: *Bagdad hotel*. Paris: Gallimard.

Rosenblum, M. 1993: *Who stole the news?* New York: John Wiley.

Ryan, N. 1995: Calling the shots. *The Guardian* 4 September, G2, 13.

Scannell, P. and Cardiff, D. 1991: *A social history of British broadcasting. Volume 1 1922–1939*. Oxford: Basil Blackwell.

Schlesinger, P. 1978: *Putting 'reality' together: BBC news*. London: Methuen. (Rpt. 1987, 1992.)

Schramm, W. 1965: Communications in crisis. In Greenberg, R. and Parker, E. (eds), *The Kennedy assassination and the American public: social communication in crisis*. Stanford: Stanford University Press.

Schudson, M. 1991: The sociology of news production revisited. In Curran, J. and Gurevitch, M. (eds), *Mass media and society*. London: Arnold, 141–59.

Shawcross, W. 1995: Satellite television: reaching for the sky. *New Statesman and Society* 24 March, 12.

Shevardnadze, E: 1991: How we beat the coup. *The Observer* 1 September, 21.

Shoemaker, P. and Reese, S. 1991: *Mediating the message*. New York: Longman.

Short, K. 1989: A note on BBC Television News and the Munich crisis 1938. *Historical Journal of Film, Radio and Television* 9, no. 2, 165–79.

Shrock, K. 1994: Twists and turns in Sarajevo's 1000–day siege, Reuters Newswire 29 December 1994. Available on-line Reuters Textline.

Simpson, J. 1991: *From the house of war*. London: Arrow Books.

Smith, A. 1973: *The shadow in the cave*. London: Allen and Unwin.

Smith, A. 1978: *The politics of information*. London: Macmillan.

Smith, A. (ed.) 1995: *Television: an international history*. Oxford: Oxford University Press.

Smith, H. 1988: The BBC Television Newsreel and the Korean War. *Historical Journal of Film and Television* 8, no. 3, 227–52.

Smith, P. 1991: *How CNN fought the war*. New York: Birch Lane Books.

Smith, S. 1990: *In all his glory*. New York: Simon & Schuster.

Snoddy, R. 1993a: Birt launches counter-attack on BBC 'snipers'. *Financial Times* 15 July, 9.

Snoddy, R. 1993b: BBC staff criticises bureaucracy. *Financial Times* 17 July, 7.

Snow, J. 1996: Test card. *Spectrum* issue 20 (Winter) 1996.

Stephenson, H. 1987: Our narrow window on the world. *The Guardian* 16 March, 15.

Svennevig, M. 1991: Public opinion on the media coverage of the Gulf War. Institute of Communications Studies University of Leeds, Leeds.

Taylor, P. 1992: *War and the media: propaganda and persuasion in the Gulf War*. Manchester: Manchester University Press.

Thomson, A. 1992: *Smokescreen: the media, the censors, the gulf*. Tunbridge Wells: Laburnham Books.

Thynne, J. 1991: Media battle of the bunker. *The Daily Telegraph* 28 February, 6.

Times, The 1955: Personality in news. 21 September, 4.

Times, The 1956: Changing television programmes. 22 August, RTS supplement, iii.

Times, The 1957: Seven decisive years for sound and vision. 28 August, RTS supplement, iii.

Times, The 1964: Railway film of Duke delayed by railway. 16 May, 10.

Times, The 1978a: Electronic news-gatherer looks ahead. 18 July, 3.

Times, The 1978b: Union bar forces BBC to store equipment. 9 October, 4.

Times, The 1992: Can Major take the strain? 21 October, 17.

Tracey, M. 1995: Non-fiction television. In Smith, A. (ed.), *Television: an international history*. Oxford: Oxford University Press, 118–47.

Tuchman, G. 1972: Objectivity as strategic ritual: an examination of newsmen's notion of objectivity. *American Journal of Sociology* 77(4), 660–70.

Tuchman, G. 1973: Making news by doing work: routinizing the unexpected. *American Journal of Sociology* 79(1), 110–31.

Tuchman, G. 1978: *Making the news: a study in the construction of reality.* New York: Free Press.

Tuchman, G. 1991: Qualitative methods in the study of news. In Jensen, K. and Jankowski, N. (eds), *A handbook of qualitative methodologies for mass communication research*. London: Routledge.

Turner, E. 1991: The power and the glory. In *The role of the media in international conflict*. Working paper 38. Canadian Institute for International Peace and Security, Ottawa, 40–50.

Vanden Heuvel, J. 1993: For the media, a brave (and scary) new world. *Media Studies Journal* 7 (Fall), 11–20.

Vincent, R. 1992: CNN: elites talking to elites. In Mowlana, H., Gerbner, G. and Schiller, H. (eds), *Triumph of the image: the media's war in the Persian Gulf*. Boulder: Westview Press, 181–201.

Vulliamy, E. 1994: *Seasons in hell: understanding Bosnia's war*. London: Simon & Schuster.

Vulliamy, E. 1996: Hard truths swept under red carpets. *The Guardian* 22 June, 16.

Wallis, R. and Baran, S. 1990: *The known world of broadcast news*. London: Routledge.

Washington Post 1991: 16 February.

Washington Post Weekly 1991: Senator Simpson and Peter Arnett. 18–24 February, 28.

Wiener, R. 1992: *Live from ground zero*. New York: Doubleday.

Weispfenning, J. 1993: The routinization of news production. In Greenberg, B. and Gantz, W. (eds), *Desert Storm and the mass media*. Cresskill, NJ: Hampton Press, 48–57.

White, D. 1950: The 'gatekeeper': a case study in the selection of news. *Journalism Quarterly* 27(4), 383–90. Reprinted 1964: In Dexter, L. A. and White, D. M. (eds) *People, society, and mass communications*. New York: Free Press, 160–72.

Williams, G. 1993: Murdochvision. *Free Press: Journal of the Campaign for Press and Broadcasting Freedom* no. 76 (September/October), 1.

Winston, B. 1993: The *CBS Evening News,* 7 April 1949: creating an ineffable television form. In Eldridge, J. (ed.), *Getting the message: news truth and power.* London: Routledge, 179–209.

Zelizer, B. 1992: CNN, the Gulf War, and journalistic practice. *Journal of Communication* 42, 66–81.

Sources

Inside TV: making the news 1986: 30 October, BBC Schools.

ITN – the first 40 years 1995: 17 December, ITV. Produced by ITN.

Larry King Live 1991: 23 January, CNN.

Larry King Live 1996: 16 January, CNN.

O'Kane, M. 1996: *How to tell lies and win wars*, Channel 4.

Pearson, A. 1995: *J'accuse: the news*. 28 March, Channel 4.

Simpson, J. 1993: *Making the news.* Huw Weldon Lecture to the 1993 Royal Television Society, 22 September, BBC2.

Tales from Sarajevo 1993: *Late Show* special, 21 January, BBC2.

The death of Yugoslavia 1995: Four-part television series, September, BBC2. Produced by Brian Lapping Associates.

The Gulf War 1996: Three-part television series, January, BBC2. Produced by Fine Art Productions.

The Tycoon 1995: 23 March, Channel 4. Produced by Oxford Television Company.

Vietnam stories: the camera at work 1995: 27 March, BBC2.

Index

ABC television, 6, 25, 34, 35, 101, 102, 105, 121, 167, 168
access, 36, 40, 53, 83, 85, 94, 105, 107–8, 156, 171, 173, 182, 200
Adams, Eddie, 131
Adie, Kate, 164, 210
Afghanistan, 183
Agnew, Spiro, 133
air freight, 176, 178, 189
al Asad, Mohammed Ali, 156
al-Amariya, Baghdad. Air raid shelter, 147–9, 151–4, 156, 158, 165, 170, 172
Al-Rashid hotel, Baghdad, 6, 149, 151, 153, 156
Alexandra Palace studios, 117, 121, 122, 126, 127, 128, 141
Alpert, Jon, 84
Amanpour, Christiane, 205, 206
Anderson, Steve, 206
Andrews, Jo, 98
Annan Committee on Broadcasting, 136, 138–40
Antennae 2, 153
Arens, Moshe, 9
Armitage, Michael, 134
Armstrong, Fiona, 159
Arnett, Peter, 6, 17, 35, 50, 83–4, 123, 147–53, 155, 157, 158, 161, 166
Ashdown, Paddy, 66
Aspell, Tom, 6
Associated Press news agency (AP), 94, 112, 131, 190, 195
Atkinson, Rick, 172
ATV, 177

AVID, non-linear digital picture editing, 194, 195, 197, 198, 209

Bad news, 79, 135–6, 139. See Glagow University Media Group (GUMG)
Baghdad, 6, 10–12, 15, 16, 17, 56, 67, 83, 84, 115, 143, 145, 147–173
Baird, John Logie, 178
Baker, Kenneth, 103
Barron, Brian, 3, 132
BASYS news room computer system, 193–4, 195
BBC, 6, 8, 9, 10, 12, 13, 14, 17, 19, 23, 24, 31, 33, 37, 38, 41, 42, 54, 55, 57, 62, 63, 67, 68–9, 70, 74, 76–7, 79, 81, 86, 89, 91, 92, 93, 94, 95, 96, 97, 99, 100–7, 110–11, 113, 115, 116, 117, 121, 123, 124, 125, 126–8, 129, 130, 133, 134, 136, 137, 138, 139, 140, 141–3, 144, 145, 148, 151, 152, 153, 154, 155, 156, 158, 159, 160, 161, 163, 164, 166, 167, 168, 171, 175, 176, 177, 179, 180, 186, 187, 192, 195, 198, 199, 201
BBC Nine O'Clock News, 104, 161
BBC Six O'Clock News, 42, 82, 104, 168
BBC World Service Television, 2, 3–4, 17, 23, 35, 145, 209
Beaver, Paul, 86, 102
Beirut, 34, 39
Bell, Martin, 64, 66, 70, 127, 142, 181, 186, 205, 209
Berlin Wall, fall of, 5, 17, 39, 186, 190
Bestic, Richard, 88

Betacam video tape format, 179, 181, 198
Bhutto, Benazir, 42
bi-media working, 74, 142, 191
bias, 1, 2, 19, 25, 26, 47, 48, 59, 67, 113, 120, 135, 137, 139, 141, 142, 215
Big news, the, 130
Birt, John, 1, 67, 68, 69, 77, 137, 138, 139, 140, 141, 142, 214, 216
Birtley, Tony, 207
Blackwell, James, 158
Blakemore, Bill, 167
Blitzer, Wolf, 7
Bloomberg Information Television, 24, 25, 46
Blumler, Jay, 55, 68, 77, 81, 194
Boghossian, Paul, 157, 158, 160, 161, 162, 167, 168, 169
Bond, Jennie, 97, 104
Bosnia, 17, 35–7, 66, 70, 74, 200, 202
Boulton, Adam, 88
Bowen, Jeremy, 148, 152, 153, 157, 158, 160, 161, 162, 167, 168
Boyer, Jean Francois, 130, 169
BR3, 170, 171
Brent Spar, 40
Brereton, Charlie, 94, 97, 100, 102
Brightstar satellite feed, 39
British Telecom, 184, 189
Brokaw, Tom, 39
Brunson, Michael, 93, 98, 178, 184
Buchanan, Pat, 133
Buckley, Nick, 100, 102
Buerk, Michael, 157, 162, 166, 205
Burnett, Alastair, 128, 163
Bush, George, 4, 6, 9, 14, 15, 34, 161, 200, 202
Bye, Phil, 148, 156

Cabell, Brian, 90, 94, 95, 106
Calendar, Yorkshire Television news magazine, 207
camcorder, 34, 181–2
Camel News Caravan, 118
Camel Newsreel Theatre, 118
Carpenter, Sue, 88, 93, 96
CBC *Newsworld,* 2, 23, 204
CBC, 2, 23, 37, 42
CBS News with Douglas Edwards, 118
CBS, 9, 11, 12, 25, 34, 36, 41, 42, 46, 47, 101, 105, 112, 113, 114, 117, 118, 119, 120, 121, 124, 125, 128, 130, 132, 167, 175, 176, 184, 199

CD-ROM, 18
cellphone, use in newsgathering 88, 90, 102, 107, 109
Challenger space shuttle, 12, 144, 189
Chamberlain, Neville, 113
Channel 4 News, 63, 71, 75, 81, 105, 140, 161, 163, 194
television, UK, 24, 139, 194
Channel 4, Oklahoma City, 39
Channel One, 204, 209
Checkland, Michael, 68, 140
chemical weapons, 8
Cheney, Dick, 15, 16, 169
Clinton, Bill, 4, 34
CNN, 2, 4, 6, 7–17, 19, 23, 24, 25, 26, 34, 37, 38, 39, 40, 41, 42, 61, 74, 83–4, 85, 86, 88, 91, 92, 93, 94, 95, 98, 102, 105–6, 107, 109, 114, 115, 143–6, 148, 149–53, 155, 156, 157, 158, 159, 161, 170, 171, 184–6, 187, 199–200
Cole, John, 100, 104
Collins, Reid, 158
Collins, Richard, 133
computers in news production, 2, 73, 94, 104, 183, 193, 194–5, 197–8, 202–3, 210, 213. *See* BASYS
Cookson, John, 165
Coombs, Katherine, 105, 107
Coronation of Elizabeth II, 1953, 120
Cottle, Simon, 75, 76, 77
Cotton, Paul, 90
Cox, Geoffrey, 124–5, 128, 130, 177, 209
Cramer, Chris, 204
Crawley, Aidan, 124, 127
Cronkite, Walter, 83, 118, 119, 130, 132
Crosby, Bing, 113
cruise missiles, 36
Culf, Andrew, 145
Curran, Charles, 138
Cutforth, Rene, 122

Davis, Neil, 132
Deacon, David, 69
deadlines, 185, 189, 190, 191, 208
Dewar, Mike, 155
diary production, 111, 192,
Dimbleby, David, 68, 134
Dimbleby, Richard, 111, 114, 115–6, 127, 164, 177, 209
dominant ideology, 1, 78, 84
Donohue, Gus, 109
Doonesbury, 11

Dowle, Martin, 97
Downing, Nik, 205
Dresden, bombing of, 164, 170
Dugan, Michael, 9
Dugdale, John, 42
Dunsmore, Barry, 101
Dutton, Jim, 148, 156, 206
DVC Pro video tape format, 179. *See*
　　video tape

e-mail, 14
Electronic News Production System
　　(ENPS), 195
Elliott, Philip, 67, 69
ENG (electronic newsgathering), 21,
　　33, 143, 179–82, 185, 187, 190
ENS, electronic news room systems,
　　194–5
Epstein, Edward Jay, 59–63, 67
Euronews, 2, 17, 23, 24, 37
European News Exchange (ENEX),
　　184
excess baggage, cost of, 184, 187

Falklands conflict, 12, 81, 132, 134,
　　140, 178
Falujjah, Iraq, 172
fax machines, 2, 14, 16, 183
film cameras, 174–5, 181
film editing, 197
film, 16 millimetre, 175–7, 180, 181
Fiske, Robert, 209
Fitzwater, Marlin, 162, 169
'fly-away' satellite dishes, 11, 183,
　　200
Flynn, Paul, 94
Ford, Anna, 33, 103
Foreign Office, British, 70, 74, 87, 92,
　　97, 99, 106, 108
Francis, Dick, 180
Frank, Reuven, 118, 119, 129
Friendly, Fred, 119, 121, 127, 144,
　　174
Frier, Anglea, 148, 156

Gall, Sandy, 132, 177, 183
'gas-mask journalism', 7, 9
'Gates', Mr, 48–51, 58, 73, 146
Gates, Bill, 146
gender factors in news production,
　　57–8
General Strike, 1926, 111, 133
Ghandi, 189
Gieber, W., 50–1

Glasgow University Media Group
　　(GUMG), 18, 71, 79, 135–7, 138,
　　140
Gleny, Misha, 35
global village, the, 8, 16, 42
GMTV, Good Morning Television, 24
Goldie, Grace Wyndham, 117, 127
Golding, Peter, 67–72
Goodwin, Stewart, 98, 99, 102
Gorazde, 70, 200
Gorbachev, Mikhail, 14,
Gowing, Nik, 209
Grade, Michael, 68
Graves, Keith, 40
Greene, Hugh, 123, 126, 141
Greenpeace, 40
Grenada, 133
Griffiths, Trevor, 4
Guardian, The, 41, 43, 81, 69, 148
Gulf War, 4, 6, 8, 9, 11, 12, 13, 15,
　　16, 17, 18, 19, 37, 39, 50, 56, 66,
　　69, 85, 86, 89, 108
Gurevitch, Michael, 55, 68, 77, 81,
　　194,

Haiti, 34
Haley, William, 117
Hall, Robert, 93, 98, 155
Hall, Stuart, 53
Hanrahan, Brian, 33
Harris, Robert, 134
Harrod, Dominick, 142
Hart, Louis, 143
Hastings, Max, 10, 12
Hear it now, 120
helicopter newsgathering, 4, 11, 37,
　　38, 87, 88, 89, 90, 91, 93, 95, 96,
　　97, 98, 101, 104, 106, 109
Hi-8 video tape format, 204, 206, 209.
　　See video tape
Hindenburg crash, 112, 175
Hole, Tahu, 123, 126, 127, 141
Holliman, John, 6
Hood, Stuart, 126, 127, 129, 178,
Horse Guards Parade, 87, 88, 89, 91,
　　100, 104, 106, 108
Houghton, Neil, 97, 98, 99
Huntley-Brinkley Report, 129
Hurd, Douglas, 70, 101
Husing, Ted, 112
Hussein, Saddam, 15

IBA, 69, 183, 188
Indonesia, 17

INMARSAT system of maritime communications satellites, 183
Internet, 14, 16, 24, 25, 39, 46, 144, 202, 213
IRA, 85, 89, 90, 99, 100, 101, 104, 108, 140
Iraq, 16
Irving, Niall, 155, 159
Issacs, Jeremy, 68
ITN, (Independent Television News), 7, 13, 24, 25, 36, 38, 39, 40, 41, 43, 46, 65, 77, 86, 87, 88, 89, 90, 91, 92, 93, 94, 95, 96, 97, 98, 99, 100, 102, 103, 104, 105, 106, 107, 109, 124, 125, 126, 127, 128, 129, 130, 132, 135, 136, 139, 140, 142, 145, 148, 151, 152, 155, 156, 157, 159, 160, 161, 163, 164, 166, 171, 177–8, 180, 181, 183, 184, 191, 194, 195

Jay, Peter, 1, 137
Jennings, Peter, 167, 205
Johnson, Lyndon, 131, 132

Kashmir, 182
Kasmire, Robert, 60
Kent, Arthur, 38, 205
King, Tom, 154
Koljevic, Nikola, 36
Korean war, 119, 122
Kosovo, 33, 64, 66
Kurds, 16
Kuwait City, 11, 12, 200

Lang and Lang, 45, 120
Larry King Live, 11, 15, 39
Late Show, The, 145
Lawley, Sue, 79
Lewis, Martyn, 19, 81, 99, 100
Library Management Systems, 194, 195
Lithgow, Lynnette, 94
Little, Alan, 148, 151, 153, 154
live links, 1, 4, 5, 6, 7, 8, 9, 10, 11, 12, 13, 17, 19, 33, 34, 35, 36, 37, 38, 39, 40, 41, 53, 63, 66, 83, 87, 88, 89, 90, 91, 92, 93, 94, 95, 96, 97, 98, 99, 100, 101, 102, 103, 104, 105, 106, 107, 109 111, 112, 113, 115, 116, 117, 118, 120, 121, 122, 130, 143, 144, 147, 149, 150, 151, 152, 153, 155, 157, 158, 159, 161, 164, 173, 183–7, 191, 194, 195, 200, 201, 202, 203

Live TV, 23–4
Lloyd-Roberts, Sue, 181, 205, 206
Loan, Nguyen, 131
logistical demands of newsgathering, 10, 11, 38, 47, 59, 60, 61, 63, 67, 80, 167, 171, 184, 187
Longbridge dispute, 1956, 125, 135

MacArthur, General Douglas, 47, 48
Macmillan, Michael, 7
Madrid, Arab–Israeli peace talks, 16
Major, John, 14, 108, 109, 145, 185
manufacture of consent, 84
mapping reality, 62, 74, 82, 83, 216
market driven journalism, 75–6
Marshall, Penny, 36
McEwan, Bob, 11
McManus, John, 75–6
McNair, Brian, 79
Mellor, David, 103, 104, 105, 107, 109
Michael Electronics, 183
Milne, Alasdair, 123, 126, 140
Milosevic, Slobodan, 35
Ministry of Defence, Whitehall, 87, 88, 89, 90, 93, 94, 95, 96, 108
Mitchell, Clarence, 36, 95, 100
Mogadishu, 35
Morrison, Herbert, 112
MSNBC, Microsoft–NBC, 23, 146
Mubarak, Hosni, 15
Muggs, J. Fred, 119
multi-skilling, 181, 198, 202, 204–10, 211
Munich Crisis, 113, 114
Munro, David, 69, 73
Murdoch, Rupert, 4, 5, 145, 146
Murrow, Ed, 113, 114, 115, 119, 120, 121, 127, 144, 164, 209

National Museum of Photography, Film and Television, Bradford, 178
Nationwide, 141
Naughton, John, 43
NBC television, 6, 8, 24, 25, 35, 39, 41, 45, 46, 47, 60, 84, 101, 102, 105, 112, 113, 118, 119, 121, 129, 130, 131, 132, 143, 146, 154, 167, 168, 175, 176, 183
NBC *Today*, 102, 119, 154
Neal, Richard, 157, 158, 166, 169
Neely, Bill, 38
Neil, Ron, 79

Netanhayu, Benjamin, 15
News at Ten, 104, 128, 139, 163, 166,
    175. See ITN
News Bunny, 24
news items on bunnies, 43
Newsday, 36
'newshounds', 182
Newsnight, 63, 81, 105, 109, 134,
    139, 141, 161, 165, 166, 197
newspaper cuttings, 12, 64, 65, 141,
    213
newsreels, 46, 117, 118, 119, 121,
    124, 127, 175
Newsround, 159
NHK, 160, 165
Nicholson, Michael, 132
Noble, Ronnie, 122, 176, 205
non-linear editing, 197. See film and
    video tape editing

O'Kane, Maggie, 69, 209
Oklahoma City bombing, 39, 43
Omarska camps, former Yugoslavia,
    36
on-line research sources, 65
Ozal, Turgut, 4

packaging of news agency material,
    171, 188, 210–11
Page, Cyril, 122, 205
Paley, William, 113
'Palm tree journalism', 184–5
Panama, 133
Panorama, 71, 75, 127, 140, 141, 175,
Panorama, 75
Patriot missiles, 4, 9
Paxman, Jeremy, 134, 165, 166
Pearl Harbour, television coverage of,
    117
Peck, Rory, 153
Pentagon, US Dept. of Defence, 6, 7,
    16, 132, 134, 144, 157, 158, 167,
    172
Perrin, Ray, 176
Pettitt, Tom, 130
picture clusters, 152, 154, 172
picture editors, 57, 73, 74
pieces to camera (standups), 175
Pilger, John, 19, 20, 69, 134, 161
Pilkington Committee, 1962, 127
Plantin, Marcus, 69
President Kennedy, 130
Press Association news agency, 87,
    101, 110

Protheroe, Alan, 180
Purvis, Stewart, 163

Rabin, Yitzhak, 40
RAI Uno, 170, 171
Randall, Gene, 158
Rather, Dan, 119, 130, 167, 205
Reagan, Ronald, 76, 144
Rees, Merlyn, 103
Rees, Norman, 104
Register, Larry, 7
Reith, John, 111
Reuters news agency, 25, 34, 40, 46,
    54, 86, 92, 94, 110, 123, 130, 189,
    190,
Reynolds, Rob, 89
Rojo, Alfonso, 148
Romanian revolution, 5
Rosenblum, Michael, 204
Royal Air Force, 155, 172
Rwanda, 17, 35
Ryan, Nigel, 175

Sadler, Brent, 148, 155, 156, 159, 161,
    163, 164, 171
Saeed, Abs As-Salem Muhammad, 166
Sarajevo, 35, 36, 37, 64, 185, 188
satellites, 2, 3, 4, 6, 7, 9, 11, 13, 14,
    17, 19, 24, 33, 35, 36, 38, 39, 40,
    50, 54, 60, 83, 84, 85, 96, 108,
    110, 128, 129, 131, 133, 143, 144,
    145, 149, 150, 152, 153, 161, 164,
    172, 177–8, 180, 182–7, 189, 190
satphone (satellite phone), 17, 183
Saudi Arabia, 6, 158
Schabowski, Gunter, 5
Schecter. A.A., 112
Schlesinger, Philip, 63, 71
Schofield, Carrie, 13, 33
Schramm, Wilbur, 58, 74, 131
Schudson, Michael, 59, 79
Schwarzkopf, Norman, 47
Scud missiles, 4, 8, 9, 10, 15
Second World War, 70, 74, 117
See it now, 120, 121
self censorship, 162, 166, 167, 172
Sergeant, John, 99
Sharpeville, 64
Shaw, Bernard, 6
Shepherd, Gary, 6
Shevardnadze, Eduard, 14
Shirer, William, 113, 119
Shukman, David, 33, 94, 100, 103,
    104

Simpson, John, 33, 55, 148, 187
Simpson, O.J., 37–39
Sissons, Peter, 82, 160
Six Day war, 129
Sixsmith, Martin, 33
Sky News, 2, 14, 17, 23, 24, 39, 40, 41,
    85, 86, 89, 90, 95, 106, 109, 145,
    150, 154, 157, 159, 164, 165, 169,
    171
smart bomb, 158, 173
smart bombs, 19–20, 29, 84, 147, 148,
    149, 155, 158, 165, 166, 168, 172,
    173, 181
SNG, satellite newsgathering, 183
Snoddy, Ray, 142
Snow, Jon, 13, 161, 205
Snow, Peter, 134
social construction of reality, 52, 59,
    78, 79, 81, 137
Somalia, 34
Somerville, Julia, 163
sound recording, 115, 116
Soviet coup attempt, Moscow August
    1991, 13, 14, 15, 17, 33, 185
squirrel, dangerous, 42
stand up, 175, 185, 200. *See* pieces to
    camera
Star Television, 4, 145–6
Starbird Satellite Services, 183
State Department, 36, 134
steel tape, 116
Steel, David, 86
streeters, 175 *see* vox pops
Suchet, John, 97, 155
Suez, 129, 133
Swann, Michael, 138

Taylor, Ted, 204
Tebbit, Norman, 133
telediplomacy, 5, 16, 146
television, the birth of, 116
TF1, 169
Thames at Six, 210
theory, 18, 74, 59, 69, 75, 78, 82, 84,
    137, 138
Tiananmen Square, 5, 16, 17, 39
time in television news, 63, 65
Toynbee, Polly, 100
Tripoli, bombing of, 140, 164,
Tuchman, Gaye, 21, 52, 59, 77, 80
Tully, Mark, 142
Tunnell, Doug, 167, 168
Turner, Ted, 4, 5, 12, 83, 143, 144,
    145, 146

Tuzla, 36
TV 3, Bergen, 204
TWA Long Island crash, 61, 186

Urban, Mark, 206

Vanderbilt University Television News
    Archives, 65
video tape editing, 196–8
video editing suite, 2, 182, 188, 198
'video game' footage in the Gulf war,
    19, 20
video servers, 195
videotape, 60, 73, 95, 178–9, 181, 187
Viet Cong, 83, 131, 177
Vietnam war, 11, 36, 83, 121, 131,
    132, 133, 134, 147, 175, 177, 181,
    183
Vilnius, Lithuania, 67, 182
Visnews television picture agency, 129,
    190
VJs (video journalists), 203–4
VNRs (video news releases), 149, 154,
    188
Voice of America, 14, 130
vox pops (streeters), 175
Vulliamy, Ed, 35–6, 65

Waco, 39
Wallace, Peter, 209
Watergate, 133, 178
Wenham, Brian, 68
Whicker, Alan, 205
Whittaker, Bill, 101
Wiener, Robert, 148
Winston, Brian, 117, 118
Witchell, Nicholas, 42
World in action, 71
World Wide Web, 203
WTN, television news agency, 156,
    162, 183, 190

Yarmuk Hospital, Baghdad, 149, 150,
    151, 153, 155, 157, 159, 160, 165,
    169
Yeltsin, Boris, 14
Yom Kippur war, 55
Yugoslavia, former, 35, 36, 64, 66, 69,
    70, 74

Zapruder film of President Kennedy's
    assassination, 181
Zelnick, Bob, 167